Flames of Love

1 John 1:5

Flames of Love

Hell and Universal Salvation

Heath Bradley

WIPF & STOCK · Eugene, Oregon

FLAMES OF LOVE
Hell and Universal Salvation

Wipf & Stock
An Imprint of Wipf and Stock Publishers
199 W. 8th Ave., Suite 3
Eugene, OR 97401
www.wipfandstock.com

ISBN 13: 978-1-62032-048-8
Manufactured in the U.S.A.

Unless otherwise stated, scripture quotations are from the New Revised Standard Version. Please use standard language for this Bible translation.

For Andrea,
who gives me daily glimpses of Divine Love.

Contents

Preface

THIS BOOK IS ABOUT the Christian view of hell and the Christian hope in universal salvation. More specifically, it is about thinking through how both of these can be integrated into the Christian faith in a coherent way that is faithful to the scriptures and the spirit of Jesus. It is, of course, up to you to decide if the view proposed and defended in this book displays this kind of coherence and fidelity. My own view has emerged slowly over the past fifteen years as I have studied, prayerfully reflected, and changed my mind multiple times. I started wrestling with this issue as soon as I began reading the Bible when I was a freshman in college. Through my reading of the Bible I felt my heart captivated by Christ (and I still do), but I had a hard time just accepting that an eternity of punishment awaits anyone who doesn't trust in Christ the way I do.

My biggest problem all along has been Jesus. I believe Jesus is Lord, and I stumble around trying to make him be at the center of my life. What I most want out of life is to discover the riches of following Christ whole-heartedly. I want my life to make Jesus proud. The story of God's reconciling mission in Christ shapes my life more than any other story. So here is my problem: It is Jesus who reveals to us an unfathomably loving God, and yet Jesus is also the one in the Bible who talks about hell the most. Jesus has been both the source of my belief in hell, and the source of my discontent with how hell is often conceived and conveyed from the pulpit.

In several ways, this book is the fruit of wrestling with the spirit of the risen Jesus and refusing to let go until I received a blessing. I believe I have received the blessing for which I have been wrestling for a long time, and that it has come in the form of a *distinctively Christian vision of universal salvation* that still has an integral and biblically-faithful role for the reality of hell.[1] I don't mean to imply that I think I have it all figured

---

1. Far and away the most influential author in my thinking on these matters is Thomas Talbott, a contemporary philosopher of religion. I owe a huge debt of gratitude to him, not only for his own writings, but also through his work I was pointed towards

out now, or that this belief has been specially revealed to me in some sort of mystical or supernatural way. Although I am bold enough to believe the Holy Spirit lives in me and guides me into truth (John 16:13), I am realistic enough to know that my grasp of God's truth is always limited in many ways (1 Cor 13:12). But discovering the Bible-honoring, Christ-centered, and God-fearing vision of universal salvation that has been present in the church from the beginning has brought me a great deal of joyful confidence, even though not absolute certainty. Although I am sure I still have some loose ends in my theological outlook, the way of thinking about the end of all things that I will struggle to articulate in this book strikes me as the most coherent and compelling way of making sense of how God's story of redemption through Christ will turn out.

Here is one of the questions you may be wondering up front: Do I *believe* that all will be saved or do I just *hope* that all will be saved? This seems to be a very important question for most people when it comes to this issue. Hope is permitted by most, but if you cross over to belief, you risk being branded a heretic.[2] In my own attempt to understand and live out the Christian faith, this distinction doesn't really mean a whole lot, because while I do believe that all will ultimately be saved through Christ, it is hope that constitutes the very nature of my belief in God and the power of God's holy love to destroy all sin and save all sinners. I certainly don't believe in God in the same way that I believe that $2 + 2 = 4$. I am not certain that God exists, and I often find it hard to believe that love is really the most ultimate reality in the universe. Sometimes it seems blindingly obvious to me, and at other times it seems highly unlikely. But I have put my trust in Jesus to show me God and God's purposes for my life. My belief in the God that Jesus reveals is most fundamentally a hope. It is not just a mere wish, because I do think that my belief in the God that Jesus reveals can be intellectually supported. A wish, you see, is something that you want to be true but don't have any good reasons for thinking it is. A hope, on the other hand, is something you think could

---

the writings of George MacDonald, a nineteenth-century Scottish preacher and author, and both have had an enormous impact on my theological imagination.

2. See, for example, Olsen, *Mosaic of Christian Belief*, 276. The primary worries with affirming a belief, as opposed to a hope, in universal salvation seem to be a concern that it diminishes (if not eliminates) human freedom, and that it is presumptuous to declare what God must do. As I will go on to argue, I do not think either of these worries are legitimate for the version of universalism that I hold.

be possibly or probably true, but simply don't know for sure. Hope can come in varying degrees of confidence. I think most days my hope in God can be described as confident and strong, but I must say there are days (that sometimes stretch into weeks, and once or twice have stretched into months) where it seems to me that the Christian faith is either too good to be true or too incoherent to make sense. But most of the time, thankfully, the voices of hope and trust within drown out the whispers of cynicism and skepticism. I deeply hope and am (usually) strongly confident that the theological vision of the ultimate reconciliation of all things in Christ that I try to articulate and defend in this book is true. I can't say for sure that it is. But I have chosen, in faith, to live as if it is. I could turn out to be wrong. God may not exist and this life may be all there is. Or, God may exist and hell may be forever for some people. These are possibilities. But I have chosen to stake my life on the conviction that Jesus is Lord. If Jesus *is* Lord, and our gravest sin has been nailed to a cross and our deepest despair has been left behind in an empty tomb, then I believe these real possibilities have become virtual impossibilities.

As you begin this book, I ask of you to approach this subject, and the arguments offered, with the Golden Rule as your guide. You will likely disagree with some of my arguments, and it may turn out that at some future point I may disagree with some of my arguments! But I hope that you will extend the same kind of attention and openness to the position I argue as you would want someone to give to your position. I have tried to adopt this posture towards the views I criticize in this book. That isn't hard for me, because at one time or another I have personally and strongly held several of the views I now disagree with and argue against, including the dominant view of an everlasting hell for all non-Christians. If I have misrepresented or unfairly characterized any of the views I take to task, then I apologize. It may be that I have perhaps oversimplified some of the views I discuss in the interest of being concise, but I do hope that this hasn't lead to any distortions.

Finally, while I have sought to respond to the main objections that can be raised for a Christian who believes in the reconciliation of all things, I am well aware that these responses are by no means exhaustive or definitive. More questions could be asked, more responses could be given, to which more questions could be asked, and so on. That is just the nature of thinking theologically. While most people would acknowledge this to be true in general about theology, in discussions about universal salvation in particular, this is often forgotten. There is often an assumption that if there is the slightest validity to an argument against universal salvation, then one should not believe in it. I think we would be wise to hear this reminder from the contemporary philosopher of religion, William Hasker:

> The notion that a person must have compelling answers to all of the objections that may be raised against a belief in order to be rationally entitled to believe as he or she does is fundamentally unsound, and if pursued consistently would reduce virtually everyone to a state of perpetual agnosticism. In practice, this requirement is only insisted on when it seems an opportune way to put pressure on a belief system one dislikes; in the meantime, one conveniently forgets or ignores unanswered questions that may be lurking in the vicinity of one's own preferred way of understanding things.[3]

The Christian belief in universal salvation certainly has points of theological tension, difficulty with specific biblical texts, and incongruence with much of church tradition. But this shouldn't disqualify it from a fair hearing. Most things Christians have believed and still believe face these same sorts of issues. If a theological viewpoint has to have perfect coherence, be in clear accord with every relevant biblical text, and mesh with what the majority of Christians hold in order for it to be valid, then I am afraid that many of our cherished beliefs would be disqualified. We certainly need to listen to Jesus's teaching about specks and logs, not only for our moral judgment about others, but in the way we approach theologies different from our own (Matt 7:3).

---

3. Hasker, *Triumph of God over Evil*, 115.

CHAPTER 1

Get the Hell Out of Here?

The Motives and Reasons for Questioning Hell

HELL IS HARD TO talk about. For starters, many Christians cannot even bring themselves to say the word, much less talk about it with any honesty or depth. In numerous conversations I have witnessed people nervously refer to "the place down there" or "the bad place." On one occasion (and I am not joking) I actually heard a pastor substitute the word "heck" for "hell" when she was reading a passage of scripture in worship! But the biggest problem isn't just that the word "hell" seems out of bounds for many Christians, the main problem is that the traditional idea of hell often seems off limits for a serious conversation. Christians have discussions and debates about a lot of things, but "the bad place down there" usually is not one of them.

For some more liberally-minded Christians, hell is simply an antiquated piece of ancient mythology that should be jettisoned from Christianity, and the sooner the better. For other more conservatively-minded Christians, belief in an eternal hell is absolutely foundational to Christianity and to question it is tantamount to rejecting the gospel message altogether. While I can genuinely sympathize with both of these popular responses, I also strongly disagree with them. As you will see, I believe hell is very real, yet I also believe that a God who is love is also real, and that this God gets the last word.

Hell is serious, and it is seriously important for us to think about. But, as I will contend, hell is not the dark side of the gospel message that we should be afraid to discuss. I believe the good news of Jesus is genuinely and deeply "good news of great joy for all the people," in the words of the angels who heralded Jesus's birth (Luke 2:10). I think it is safe to say that most Christians do not really believe this angelic announcement. Most Christians believe that, in fact, Jesus is very bad news to those who have not explicitly confessed their faith in him in this lifetime. Several years ago I read a book entitled *The Other Side of the Good News* that defended the traditional view of hell.[1] Think about that. Is there really *another side* to the good news? If so, is it really *good* news? If the message that Jesus came to bring is that most people will actually spend an eternity experiencing the most horrible torment conceivable, well, to be honest, I can think of much better news than that! That theological vision does not strike me as good news at all. It certainly does not set my heart on fire with a joyous desire to share this news with as many people as I can. In fact, when I thought that this view of things was indispensable for Christianity, it made me feel anxious to think about and embarrassed to talk about. God, it seemed to me, had a dark side underneath the veneer of grace and goodness, contrary to how John summed up the meaning of Jesus's message that "God is light, and in him there is no darkness at all" (1 John 1:5).

There is, however, a theological vision that does strike me as good news, indeed as the best news possible for the world. It is a vision that fills my heart and soul with grateful awe and joyful excitement. It is a vision that I believe is Christ-centered, biblically-grounded, spiritually-compelling, and life-inspiring. In this book, we are concerned with understanding and evaluating a specific Christian vision of God and God's relationship to humanity known as Christian universalism. Although this view will be fleshed out throughout the book, we can define it initially and simply as the belief that *ultimately every person will be saved through Christ.* This vision of salvation stands in sharp contrast, of course, to the dominant Christian vision of hell which we can define as the belief that *all people who are not Christians will spend eternity in conscious torment.*

Often, in discussions about hell, I have discovered that a knee-jerk response is that there must be an everlasting hell for moral monsters such as Hitler. Oftentimes the existence of people like Hitler is seen as a trump card in this discussion. "You don't really think Hitler will be in heaven alongside Mother Teresa do you?" is a frequent response when

1. Dixon, *The Other Side.*

universalism is put on the table. I understand this concern, and will address this question specifically later in the book. There is, in fact, a very important moral intuition underneath the question that is legitimate and needs to be retained. People like Hitler and people like Mother Teresa deserve different fates, and I believe that a proper understanding of Christian universalism not only makes room for this intuition, but actually makes more sense of it than the alternative views. As odd as it might sound, I think Christian universalism actually predicts a more just fate for Hitler than does the traditional view of everlasting hell. But for now, I want to point out something crucially important at this stage in putting our cards on the table. From the outset it should be noted that on the Christian church's traditional view of hell, not only Hitler spends an eternity in hell, but also his victims. Six million Jews suffered horrific torment in this life from Hitler, yet on the dominant Christian view of hell, after they died they entered into a realm of unending torment and punishment at the hands of God because they did not profess Christ as Lord. One has to honestly ask who comes off looking worse, Hitler or God? I bring this point up now just so we can have clear in our minds what we are dealing with when it comes to the traditional view of hell. This is certainly a doctrine that raises lots of theological questions and moral objections that need to be given thoughtful attention.

Probably the best way to begin the discussion is to simply lay out the main objections that one can raise against the doctrine of everlasting torment. However, we should step back and ask a more foundational question about this whole enterprise of critically reevaluating what has come to be for many an indisputable and unquestionable teaching of the Christian faith, namely, "Is it okay to do this?" Asking questions about hell makes people nervous, and understandably so. For one, we may be afraid that it offends God to question the truth of something that seems to be so clearly revealed in the Bible. We may think that questioning the traditional view is tantamount to questioning the authority or inspiration of the Bible, which in turn is tantamount to questioning God, which in turn puts us in danger of going to hell! Indeed, I think one of the reasons why this doctrine has received so little critical attention is because the doctrine itself has built into it a certain kind of immunity from questioning. After all, who wants to ask questions that may end up putting us "down there"? The ancient Christian preacher John Chrysostom saw very well the harsh and troubling implications of the doctrine of everlasting damnation. "But," Chrysostom said in a sermon on 1 Corinthians, "we must teach it, in order that we will not end up in hell."[2]

I don't think these worries are justified, obviously, or I wouldn't be writing this book or encouraging you to think critically about this with me. It is always important to realize that our interpretations of the Bible are not the Bible. They are our interpretations. Anyone who says that they are just telling you what "the Bible says" without any interpretation is either deluded, deceptive, or both. Each of us approaches the Bible with a grid of assumptions that influences what we see and how we see it. I am certainly not immune from this either, which is why you should be willing to question my interpretations as well. I should be very clear that my interest lies not in questioning the inspiration or the authority of the Bible in general, but in specifically questioning the dominant way that Christians have been taught to put together the pieces of the Bible concerning this issue.

Regardless of one's view of the infallibility of the Bible, any honest reader must acknowledge the fallibility of all human interpretations of the Bible. Indeed, even holding to a doctrine of biblical inerrancy, a very conservative view that holds that the Bible is absolutely true in all that it teaches on every subject,[3] does not guarantee that one's interpretation of the Bible is the best one, no matter how deeply entrenched in church tradition. One thing that is abundantly clear from even a brief survey of the beliefs of Christians who hold to an inerrant view of the Bible is that the Bible is in fact not very clear on lots of important theological subjects, because inerrantists themselves disagree on everything imaginable. In a recent critical evaluation of the doctrine of inerrancy and how that belief functions for Christian communities, sociologist Christian Smith points out that "on important matters the Bible apparently is not as clear, consistent, and univocal enough to enable the best-intentioned, most highly skilled, believing readers to come to agreement as to what it teaches. That is an empirical, historical, undeniable, and ever-present reality."[4] This is not to slip into a sort of interpretative relativism where any interpretation is just as good as any other. I will be arguing that some interpretations are, in fact, better than others. But in doing so, I am ever mindful of the

---

2. Quoted in Bonda, *One Purpose of God*, 17.

3. For a more thorough definition and defense, see Geisler, *Inerrancy*.

4. Smith, *Bible Made Impossible*, 25.

complexity and ambiguity involved in the project we are undertaking, and will never assume that those who disagree are somehow intellectually deficient or religiously unfaithful. Interpreting the Bible can be very tough work, and to some degree all of us must make interpretive leaps based on our best understandings at a given time.

All this is to say that if you find yourself agreeing with my interpretations, don't assume traditionalists are thick-headed or hard-hearted for not seeing what we see. On the other hand, if you find yourself disagreeing with my interpretations, don't assume that your viewpoint is unquestionably the "real biblical position." Christians have been reading the same Bible and holding greatly different beliefs for over two thousand years now. Awareness of this historical fact alone should make us quick to listen to others, and slow to assume our position is the *obviously* right one. It should also give us pause before accusing someone of denying biblical authority just because they question the legitimacy of our interpretations. In other words, in questioning hell we are not throwing away the biblical puzzle pieces we do not like, we are simply questioning if the picture on the lid that we have received from the dominant tradition actually gives us the best way to put all the pieces together. Perhaps there is a better picture that can make room for more of the pieces to fit together better. At this point we need to acknowledge that people who disagree with our own biblical interpretations are not necessarily denying the Bible, but simply questioning the lenses through which we currently see the Bible.

The very popular Calvinist preacher and theologian John Piper, in lamenting the current willingness among Christians to question the traditional teaching on an everlasting hell, writes, "Treating the Bible as our authority in matters of faith and practice is being lost in regard to the matter of people's destiny."[5] For Piper, and for many others, questioning the interpretation of the Bible that leads to the affirmation of an everlasting hell is the same as rejecting the Bible as an authority for faith and practice. They see it this way because the teaching of the Bible on this subject is so clear and obvious to them. What such folks fail to consider is that what seems clear and obvious to them doesn't seem clear and obvious to many other Christians. As the Westminster Confession puts it, "All things in Scripture are not alike plain in themselves, nor alike clear unto all."[6] It is for this reason that objections to the effect that I am rejecting

5. Piper, *Jesus*, 9.

6. Center for Reformed Theology, 1.7. This Reformed confession of faith was first

the authority of the Bible in entertaining universalism would simply be an irrelevant distraction in this discussion. If one isn't willing to admit that there is space between the Bible and their reading of the Bible, then this book can be put down at this point.

On that same note, if we are to be intellectually honest believers in God, it is absolutely imperative that we acknowledge that there is always a difference between God and our ideas about God. Although for many of us this may seem to go without saying, this is actually a point not fully understood or embraced by many Christians. Take, for example, another comment made by Piper in a discussion of the nature of God's justice in punishing people forever, where he compares the view of Jonathan Edwards with some other contemporary theologians. He writes, "One key difference between Edwards and our contemporary spokesmen who abandon the historic biblical view of hell is that Edwards was radically committed to deriving his views of God's justice and love *from God*. But more and more, it seems, contemporary evangelicals are submitting to what 'makes sense' to their own moral sentiments."[7] Because Edwards is Piper's favorite theologian, Piper simply assumes that Edwards's views of divine justice and divine love *come straight from God*. This is a highly dangerous and deceptive way of arguing because it masks the human element in any view of God. When arguing about competing conceptions of the divine, it will not do for one person to simply charge the other with relying on human knowledge and understanding, instead of simply accepting divine revelation. Everyone who thinks about God, even those willing to accept divine revelation of some sort, must filter the pure light of that revelation through the prism of their own experience and understanding. When someone claims to be getting their view of God straight from God, there is either a profound ignorance of the inherently partial and provisional nature of all human knowledge about God, or there is willful deception at work.[8] Acknowledging the deeply limited

---

drawn up in 1646 and remains an influential standard of theological authority for several denominations, primarily the Presbyterian churches.

7. Piper, *Jesus*, 51–52 (italics original).

8. It seems to me that in Piper's case that it is the former at work. I should hasten to say that I am not claiming that Piper is profoundly ignorant in general, but only that I think he is missing the boat in this particular assumption. Piper's works are filled with erudite and passionate exposition of scripture, and, although I now disagree with a great deal of his theology, I have benefited greatly from a number of his works, especially earlier on in my Christian journey. Piper's writings display a strong concern to never give

and contextually conditioned nature of all human knowledge, especially theological knowledge, is not a descent into an irresponsible agnosticism or a cowardly compromise to postmodern culture, it is a reverent way of relating to God, and simply an honest admission about the human condition. Only God has "purely" objective and complete knowledge of the truth. It may be worth pointing out that the human desire to attain that sort of God-like knowledge, and not be content with the movement of faith that must accompany our partial and fragmentary understandings, is presented in Genesis 3 as the "original sin" of humanity.

This isn't a matter of slipping into a vague relativism where anything goes in our thinking about God. This is foundational biblical religion. Moses finds this out when he tries to pin down God by getting God's name. God responds by saying, "I am who I am" (Exod 3:13). God refuses to be boxed into the conceptual categories of human thought. God is always more than our thoughts about God. This is why the apostle Paul reminds the Christians at ancient Corinth that all of us have only a partial grasp of the divine mystery, and that our unity here and now comes, not from what we think we know, but in the faith that we are all known and loved by God (1 Cor 13:12).

This is one of the key insights of the broad intellectual shift that goes by the label "postmodernism." Postmodernism, at least in the philosophical realm, does not necessarily imply the relativity of truth ("What's true for you isn't true for me"), but rather highlights the relativity of all human knowledge ("I see things differently than you see them"). There is an objective, absolute, universal truth about who God is, but our knowledge of this truth is never objective, absolute, or universal. To pretend otherwise is a testimony to human pride. Postmodernism, while bringing a mixed bag to contemporary theological discussions, has certainly provided a much needed correction and chastisement to the overconfident certainty that often tempts us religious believers.

Questions, then, are not a sign of a lack of faith. Questions are what help us to preserve a sense of the bigness of God. In questioning our ideas about God, however traditionally grounded they may be, we are actually showing a great deal of reverence for God because in doing so we

---

in to cultural trends, and he shies away from acknowledging interpretive ambiguity, it seems, out of a desire to avoid slipping into theological relativism. I would not, however, take acknowledging the finite and fragmentary nature of human knowing as constituting "cultural compromise" in the way he does. Piper, *Jesus*, 13.

implicitly confess that God is bigger than our ideas about God. God cannot be contained in graven images, whether those are made of wood or ideas. There is a sacredness to asking questions, because the act of questioning is rooted in the deeper conviction that we are only human and all of our knowledge of God is always partial, provisional, and perspectival. This doesn't mean that we can't know anything about God. It just means that our knowledge is never full or complete, it is always open to revision, and it is always coming from a certain angle.

Also, questioning theological traditions in the light of fresh and new understandings of the scriptures is an essential part of the Protestant branch of the Christian faith. Part of our Protestant DNA is the willingness to challenge church teaching in the light of new and better biblical scholarship. The Bible itself is our ultimate guide to faith and belief, or more accurately, a Christ-centered view of the Bible is our ultimate guide to faith and belief, not what the tradition has said about the Bible. Jesus himself said to the religious leaders of his day, "You have a fine way of rejecting the word of God in order to keep your tradition!" (Mark 7:9). Challenging tradition isn't necessarily a sign of rebellion or arrogance; it can be a sign of spiritual fidelity and theological vitality.

Hell in the Christian Tradition

In questioning hell, it may bring some comfort to know that the "traditional view" hasn't always been the only or even the dominant view. Prior to the fifth century there were three alternatives within mainstream Christianity concerning the fate of non-Christians: eternal conscious punishment (non-Christians suffer everlasting torment), annihilationism (non-Christians simply die and that is that for them), and universal salvation (all people will be saved through Christ).[9] This is important to know because oftentimes in this debate people accuse Christian universalists of being "heretics," that is, people who are outside the bounds of legitimate, orthodox Christian faith. For the first four hundred years of the church's existence, this was not the case. There was disagreement among Christians as to how to envision the life to come, but the universalist option was considered to be one of the alternatives within the bounds of ortho-

9. See Daley, *Hope of the Early Church*; Brattston, "Hades, Hell and Purgatory"; Sachs, "Apocatastasis in Patristic Theology."

dox faith, along with the other two named above. Scholars who believe in an everlasting hell are often too quick to project a theological uniformity on the early church that simply wasn't there. Albert Mohler, for example, claims that a belief in universal salvation was clearly a minority belief that rejected the "patristic consensus" on the existence of an eternal hell.[10] But the only way to claim a "consensus" in the early church is by making the biased and unfair prior decision to exclude those theologians who did not clearly believe in an eternal hell and who made a mixture of both cautious and bold affirmations of the salvation of all through Christ. The theologians that fall in this category include folks like Clement of Alexandria, Origen, Macrina, Gregory of Nyssa, Gregory of Nazianzus, Evagrius of Pontus, Cyril of Alexandria, Ambrose of Milan, and the early Jerome. The list reads like an all-star team of early church theologians. These were some of the most significant formers and shapers of the Christian faith, and all of them held forth the possibility, and some the certainty, of a universal reconciliation. Significantly, St. Augustine, writing in the early fifth century as a strong advocate of the belief in eternal conscious torment for non-Christians, does not ever attempt to appeal to a consensus among church leaders on this issue to settle matters. In fact, he makes reference to the "very many" that held the universalist view.[11] So, it is simply historically false to claim that belief in universal salvation was from the beginning a fringe view deemed to be heretical by most church leaders. It was clearly a live option for many Christians in the first four centuries of the church.

Of all the theologians named above, probably the most revered and influential one of them all was Gregory of Nyssa, who was a major player in developing the orthodox doctrine of the Trinity. The universal church respected him so much that he was later named the "Father of fathers," and he was a key player at the Council of Nicea in the fourth century, from which we received the "Nicene Creed." Gregory strongly affirmed the restorative and temporary nature of God's punishments and the eventual salvation of all people, and he was never condemned for this

---

10. Mohler, "Modern Theology," 18. The term "patristic" is often used to refer to theologians of the first few centuries who are seen as "fathers" to the church. I don't like the term because there were some significant "mothers" to the church as well, such as Macrina, the sister of Basil of Caesarea and Gregory of Nyssa, and teacher to them both.

11. Augustine, *Enchiridion*, 473.

position.[12] However, later Christians did try to edit his writings in order to expunge the universalist affirmations, claiming that these were later additions and not Gregory's original writings. This project failed, however, because Gregory's universalism is woven too deeply throughout his writings to simply cut out a paragraph here or there.[13]

It is worth noting that the Nicene Creed, which is the touchstone of orthodoxy for Christianity globally and historically speaking, does not contain any affirmation about the nature or duration of hell. It affirms that Christ will come in judgment and that there will be a resurrection of the body and life everlasting, but it doesn't specify an eternally dualistic outcome of the judgment. It leaves enough conceptual space to make room for any of these three positions. This creed affirms what all Christians hold in common regarding the afterlife (divine judgment and resurrection to life everlasting), but allows for divergent perspectives on what happens to non-Christians or "the wicked." Although much later creeds and formulations of faith would often include an affirmation of everlasting damnation for the wicked,[14] none of the definitive, ecumenical creeds of the first four hundred years include such an affirmation. In a well-circulated and often-quoted essay on the history of universal salvation, the highly respected biblical scholar Richard Bauckham writes, "Eternal punishment was firmly asserted in official creeds and confessions of the churches. It must have seemed as indispensable a part of universal Christian belief as the doctrines of the Trinity and the incarnation."[15] This assertion, however, simply does not fit the historical reality of the theological breadth and doctrinal focus of orthodoxy in the first four centuries. Gregory of Nyssa, again, was one of the primary shapers of the orthodox formulation of the doctrine of the Trinity, and yet he was a universalist. This example, along with several others, shows clearly that beliefs about the Trinity and the incarnation were much more central to defining orthodoxy than were one's views on salvation and punishment in the life to come.

12. See Daley, *Hope of the Early Church*, 69–92; Ludlow, *Universal Salvation*, 21–104.

13. See Trumbower, *Rescue for the Dead*, 124.

14. The first creed to include such a dogmatic affirmation was the so-called "Athanasian Creed," which scholars now believe to have been formulated sometime in the middle of the sixth century.

15. Bauckham, "Universalism," 47. The earliest creed that Bauckham cites is the Athanasian Creed, and the rest are from the post-Reformation period.

We must be careful not to assume that currently dominant views about the afterlife have always been that dominant. The popular Christian author Randy Alcorn, in his foreword to Mark Galli's book *God Wins* (which is a response to Rob Bell's *Love Wins*), makes this mistake when he asserts, "If the orthodox view on salvation and damnation are up for grabs, then surely virtually everything in the Apostles' Creed is also."[16] This statement is misleading on several levels. First, it fallaciously appeals to a "slippery slope" that is intended to scare people away from asking questions out of a fear that if we question *anything,* we will go on to be critical of *everything,* and eventually we will be left with *nothing.* Second, and more importantly, it reveals a deep ignorance of the plurality of views about the afterlife that have existed within the Christian church from the beginning. Although Alcorn considers one's view of punishment in the age to come as just as basic to Christianity as everything else in the Apostles' Creed, the framers of this creed would disagree, since themselves didn't even make belief in an everlasting hell an essential doctrinal item in the creed! I personally believe every line of the Apostles' Creed,[17] and I haven't found that my questions related to the punishment in the age to come have led me in any way to renounce anything essential to the Christian faith. Contrary to Alcorn's assertion, my acceptance of the universalist vision has only served to heighten my gratitude and enhance my conviction of the beauty and truth of the Trinity, the incarnation, Christ's atoning work on the cross, etc. A Christian universalist, Gregory MacDonald argues, can certainly "maintain *all* the central elements of orthodox Christian faith."[18]

It is so important to know that while questioning the infinite duration of hell may seem for many of us modern Christians as tantamount to questioning the triune identity of God revealed as Father, Son, and Spirit,

16. Galli, *God Wins,* x.

17. While some are quick to label Christian universalists as "liberal," I do not think of myself as a theological liberal. Theological liberalism is a wide and diverse movement, to be sure, but at its core is a tendency to try to reinterpret the Christian faith within a naturalistic metaphysic and a rationalistic epistemology. In other words, liberalism seeks to make the Christian faith acceptable to people who see science as the ultimate arbiter of truth. While theological liberalism has produced many insights in biblical studies, and has a laudable emphasis on social action, its attempt at redefining the Christian faith to fit "modern" people strikes me as misguided.

18. Gregory MacDonald, *Evangelical Universalist,* 175. This is a pseudonym for Robin Parry.

it has not always been so. I think the discussion around this issue could become much more constructive if defenders of an everlasting hell would stop uncritically assuming and deceptively asserting that the church has always agreed with them. I have never seen as much "revisionist history" as I have while studying the contemporary defenses of an everlasting hell from conservative Christian authors. While many things that I argue for in this book are controversial and debatable, this isn't one of them. It is a historical fact that there have been orthodox Christian leaders and thinkers from the beginning of the church who have embraced, if not an outright belief in universal salvation through Christ, at least a strong hope in this grand and beautiful ending to the story that God is writing.

Why, then, did the traditional view "win"? How did eternal conscious torment for all non-Christians become the dominant view, while universal salvation has come to be considered heretical? While the answer to this question is no doubt more historically complex than the brief sketch offered here, three main factors can be identified. First, the so-called "Constantinian shift" in the late fourth century affected the church in many ways, sociologically and theologically. When the Christian faith went from being a persecuted minority to a state-sponsored majority in the Roman Empire, this changed the tone of the church's theology and the means by which the church could settle theological disputes. Now church leaders could settle theological disputes not only with philosophical and biblical arguments, but also with political power and military action. So, just because a belief survived as the majority belief doesn't necessarily mean that it is the right belief. It may just mean that the people who believed it had more political power than those who did not.[19]

Along these same lines, it could be argued that when Christianity became the official creed of the Roman Empire under Constantine's successor Theodosius, a belief in the eternal conscious torment of non-Christians became very politically useful for its leaders. After all, what better means of social control is there than this? And if everlasting hell is what awaits all non-Christians, then shouldn't any means necessary to get them to convert to the Christian creed (and, by implication, Roman imperial rule) be used, including force? So, while political context isn't everything for answering this question, it cannot be ignored or minimized.

19. See Jenkins, *Jesus Wars*.

The next major factor would be the inestimable influence of the theology of St. Augustine, a late fourth and early fifth-century African theologian. Augustine strongly and forcefully articulated the view of hell as everlasting torment in a way that no one else up until him had. He held that all people come into the world tainted with "original sin," and by their nature deserve eternal separation from God for the guilt inherited from Adam's sin. While this was a novel view in his day, and was rejected by many, through Augustine's influence as a bishop and voluminous writer, the idea that human beings are born deserving everlasting hell would become firmly established in the Western church (never, though, in the Eastern church), and has cast a long shadow over most Catholic and Protestant thought.

The third factor is that in 553 the church at the Council of Constantinople officially condemned belief in a certain kind of universal salvation. I say "a certain kind of universal salvation" because this ecumenical council condemned the theology of Origen and his followers.[20] His specific type of universalism was inextricably bound up with other philosophical views he held concerning a cyclical view of the universe (perhaps bordering on what some would call reincarnation) and the preexistence of human souls in heaven before coming to earth. In some places Origen also seems to suggest that the devil and demons will be saved as well, although in other places he denies this. So, what was condemned was not Christian universalism as such, but the whole package of Origen's views that went along with this.[21]

But even if the church did pronounce Christian universalism as such to be heretical, does this really settle the issue? It is interesting to me that many Protestant theologians, pastors, and church folk quickly and easily dismiss universalism as heretical because a church council said so. This strikes me as a very arbitrary and selective use of tradition as the trump card in theological debate. Again, questioning tradition is at the heart of the Protestant movement. This doesn't mean that as Protestants we must ignore or throw away tradition as we please. We must wrestle with it deeply, but we must also not be afraid to go beyond where others have gone. After all, where we would be if the Reformers did not do this?

20. It is a matter of historical debate whether the views condemned were actually those of Origen or just those of his followers. See Ludlow, "Universalism in the History," 195.

21. See Crouzel, *Origen*, 257–66.

In short, we need to be very cautious about applying the label "heretic" to others. This charge is often self-serving and shortcuts the tough and necessary work of biblical exegesis and theological reflection. It is fine for us to disagree and to state our reasons why, but to bring out the "h-word" at the beginning is a cheap shot that precludes any useful dialogue and learning.[22]

Calvinism, Arminianism, and Universalism

It is fascinating to me just how quick many Christians are to dismiss the possibility of universal salvation as heresy and not give it a fair trial, especially considering the latitude that Christians often give to one another on other difficult theological matters. Within the Christian church, one of the issues that most Christians have agreed to disagree on is what theologians would call the doctrine of providence, or, in other words, how God relates to the world to accomplish God's purposes. Does God control everything or does creation have a degree of freedom to act in ways that God cannot control? Simply put, there are two main camps in this debate, the Calvinists and the Arminians. Calvinists hold that whatever God desires to happen will in fact happen, and that ultimately God is "behind" all that occurs in the world. No doubt this definition is very basic, but it gets at the heart of this theological position. God is in control, and what happens is what God wants to happen. On the Calvinist view, the inhabitants of hell are there ultimately by God's choice.

On the other hand, Arminians insist that because God has given human beings free will, there are some things that God cannot make happen. Human freedom places certain limits on what God can do and what God cannot do. They would be quick to add that this limitation for God is self-imposed though, and not thrust on God, since it was God's decision to create human beings with genuine freedom. On the Arminian view, the inhabitants of hell are there ultimately by their own choice.

Most Christians will agree that we can be a Calvinist or an Arminian and still be a Christian. This is an area that we can question and ponder and there is a range or continuum of beliefs that are acceptable within the

22. One recent conservative theological work goes so far as to say that universalists have succumbed to a "satanic lie." Miles, *God of Many Understandings?*, 120.

Christian community.[23] Oftentimes, however, this same degree of latitude is not taken with different views on hell. Christians seem much quicker to make the charge of heresy when it comes to questioning or denying the traditional view of hell as everlasting punishment. I simply want to point out that there is no reason why Christian universalism should be treated any differently within the Christian community than Calvinism or Arminianism.[24] At least on the surface, there are biblical passages that seem to support all three theological viewpoints about the fate of non-Christians. This is not to say that all interpretations are equal, but it is to say that universalism is in very much the same boat as the other two options: all three positions have some passages that seem to support them, and they all must find ways to interpret difficult passages that seem to support other views.

This example of the theological latitude that is usually allowed for Calvinists and Arminians is especially pertinent for the issue at hand, because the universalist viewpoint simply takes a major premise of each position and puts them together. Calvinists hold that God can accomplish whatever God wants to accomplish, it's just that on their view God doesn't really want to save all people.[25] Arminians hold that God wants to save all people, but unfortunately God cannot make free human beings choose salvation. Christian universalism simply affirms with Calvinists that God can and will do whatever God desires to do, and with the Arminians that God desires to save all people. Put those premises together, and you get the conclusion that God will save all people.[26]

I am not at the moment arguing for the truth of Christian universalism. That will come later. What I am pointing out here is that there is no good reason why Christians should be any more afraid of embracing Christian universalism than they would of embracing either Calvinism or Arminianism. No doubt many would respond that the difference between Calvinism and Arminianism, on the one hand, and universalism, on the

23. See Basinger et al., *Predestination and Free Will.*

24. On this point I am indebted to Talbott, "Towards a Better Understanding," 11–13, and *Inescapable Love of God,* 43–54.

25. St. Augustine writes, "And, moreover, who will be so foolish and blasphemous as to say God cannot change the evil wills of men, whichever, whenever, and wheresoever He chooses, and direct them to what is good? But when He does this, He does it of mercy; when He does it not, it is of justice that he does it not" (*Enchiridion,* 97–98).

26. See Parry, "Between Calvinism and Arminianism," 157.

other, is that both former viewpoints make room for an everlasting hell, while the latter does not. But this reveals an important bias that needs to be acknowledged. Consider the following three statements, each of which at least on the surface has some degree of biblical support[27]:

1. God loves every human being the same and desires all to be saved.

2. God has the power to accomplish God's redemptive desires.

3. Some people will remain in hell forever.

The three statements, taken together, are contradictory. One of them must be false. Calvinists deny the first one. Arminians deny the second one. Universalists deny the third one. At the beginning of the debate, why assume that the first two are up for discussion, but the third one is untouchable, as Christians so often do? Why assume the priority and clarity of the everlasting hell passages while being willing to reinterpret the passages used in support for the other two claims? At the end of the day, each position has to try to explain why some passages do not mean what they appear to mean.[28] While I think the universalist position does a better job than the other two in making the most sense of the whole of the biblical witness, at this point my hope is that you can see that Christian universalism is a position at least as worthy of consideration as the other two major theological systems. It can be derived from two orthodox premises, and, like Arminianism and Calvinism, it requires careful biblical interpretation that goes beyond the apparent surface meaning of certain texts.

The Big Questions

Now that we've explored some of the reasons why the task we are setting out on is one that is legitimate and even necessary for the reflective Christian, it is time to put out on the table the big questions that one can raise for the traditional view of hell. In this section, our primary concern is simply to bring to the surface the various reasons that many Christians find the traditional view theologically incoherent and spiritually inadequate. These concerns are not simply the product of "modern sensibilities," as some would charge, as there have been Christian universalists throughout the centuries and from the beginnings of the Christian movement

27. See Talbott, "Towards a Better Understanding," 6–11.
28. See Talbott, Inescapable Love of God, 43.

who have raised these concerns.[29] Not everyone will, of course, think that these objections are insurmountable, but hopefully all readers can agree that these concerns make the search for an alternative Christian perspective on the afterlife a reasonable response.

One final note before we get into questioning hell. As a preacher, I can testify to the fact that it's often very hard to say *anything* without feeling like we need to say *everything*. In other words, because everything is ultimately related and interconnected, especially in our theological viewpoints, it is hard to stay here without also going there, and when you go there you discover that you need to talk about this, and when you talk about this you see that you really need to talk about that, and so on and so on. The questions that are raised often overlap and intersect with one another, and each question also raises a handful of other questions. Some of the issues will come up again later in the book and will be addressed further, but some will inevitably get the short end of the stick. I will do my best, however, to articulate the fundamental questions and bolster their strength through an initial response to the primary ways in which traditionalists have responded to them.

How could anyone deserve infinite punishment for finite sins?

This question is probably the strongest objection to the traditional view from a purely rational standpoint. It is extremely hard to understand how even the worst of human crimes could ever deserve *everlasting conscious torment*. (It would be appropriate for the reader to pause and reflect on the gravity of those three words put together.) On this view, non-Christians will experience an unending duration of the worst pain imaginable. Let's say John dies at the age of 23, having rejected the Christian faith. On the traditional view, John is in for 23 trillion years of horrible punishment, and that is only the beginning. Indeed, on this traditional view it doesn't even make sense to talk about the "beginning" of his punishment, since he will always be at the "beginning" of his unfathomably hopeless destiny. The thinking Christian can certainly be excused for doubting that this is a just arrangement. Christian theologians have, of course, been aware of

---

29. This is a consistent charge made throughout Morgan et al., *Hell Under Fire*. Indeed, the subtitle of this work makes this claim: "Modern Scholarship Reinvents Eternal Punishment."

this troublesome question from the beginning, and have offered several responses to it.

Many have said that it is just what the scriptures teach and so we shouldn't question it. The most popular response that attempts to give a reason for this asserts that sin against an infinitely holy God deserves an infinite punishment. Those who respond in this way argue that even the slightest of human sins is worthy of eternal damnation because it transgresses the holy nature of God. Several responses can be made to this line of reasoning. First, it is important to note that nowhere in the Bible is this reasoning used. That doesn't necessarily make it wrong, but it is important to see that not a single biblical writer explicitly endorses this strain of thought. A better response, though, is to question the logic of the statement. This reasoning certainly isn't intuitive to many people. Just what is it about God's holiness that requires such a punishment? What is divine holiness in the first place? Holiness is what makes God different, separate, or "other" from the rest of creation. While many Christians from the traditional view would say that the holiness of God consists primarily in moral purity and revulsion against sinners, the prophet Hosea defines God's holiness in terms of God's unrelenting mercy towards sinners. The Lord says through the prophet, "My heart recoils within me; my compassion grows warm and tender. I will not execute my fierce anger; I will not again destroy Ephraim; for I am God and no mortal, the Holy One in your midst, and I will not come in wrath" (Hos 11:8–9). It is highly significant that the reason God gives for his compassion and refusal to come in wrath is precisely because he is "the Holy One" who is far different from mere mortals. Far from God's holiness requiring that God punish people eternally, Hosea affirms that God's holiness is actually what compels God to refrain from wrath and to have mercy. What makes God holy, or different from human beings, is that God has the capacity to transcend revenge and offer mercy.

Similarly, Jesus defined God's holy perfection, not in terms of vengeful and retributive justice against sinners, but in terms of all-inclusive compassion and love. It is often overlooked that when Jesus tells his followers to be "perfect" as God is perfect, this statement comes right on the heels of Jesus's command for his followers to love enemies because this is what God does:

> You have heard that it was said, "You shall love your neighbor and
> hate your enemy." But I say to you, love your enemies and pray
> for those who persecute you, so that you may be children of your
> Father in heaven; for he makes his sun rise on the evil and on the
> good, and sends rain on the righteous and on the unrighteous. For
> if you love those who love you, what reward do you have? Do not
> even the tax-collectors do the same? And if you greet only your
> brothers and sisters, what more are you doing than others? Do
> not even the Gentiles do the same? Be perfect, therefore, as your
> heavenly Father is perfect. (Matt 5:38–43)

Luke makes it even clearer that Jesus defines God's holy "perfection," not
as vindictive anger towards sinners, but as compassionate love towards
all people: "But love your enemies, do good, and lend, expecting nothing
in return. Your reward will be great, and you will be children of the Most
High; for he is kind to the ungrateful and the wicked. Be compassionate,
just as your Father is compassionate" (Luke 6:35–36). God's perfection is
not in tension with God's compassion. According to Jesus, *God's perfection is defined precisely by God's compassion.* We must be careful to not
import our own ideas of what divine perfection must be into the biblical
text, as has so often it has been done. It is hard to take Jesus seriously and
still come away with the assumption that God's holy perfection requires
the infinite punishment of sinners, especially when Jesus defines this
perfection in the complete opposite direction. Those from the traditional
view have quite a task before them in explaining how God can be said to
be "kind to the wicked," as Jesus affirms, and yet still inflict maximal suffering and torment on them. Those who defend a view of hell as eternal
conscious torment are quick to appeal to the divine attribute of holiness
and to construe that as God's "commitment to punish the guilty" while
accusing universalists of "redefin[ing] holiness and justice as an aspect
of His love."[30] It was Jesus who defined God's holy perfection precisely as
God's compassionate love of enemies. It seems to me that it is the defenders of an everlasting hell that are taking Jesus's definition of divine holiness and redefining it along the lines of how they think God should be.

At this point I can imagine the traditionalist saying (because traditionalists have said this to me many times), "But you are assuming that
God can be judged by human standards. God's ways are different from
our ways. Goodness and kindness from a divine perspective are different

---

30. Miles, *God of Many Understandings?*, 117.

from goodness and kindness from a human perspective." This response may sound spiritually humble and religiously reverent, but it is actually intellectually incoherent and exegetically disastrous. First of all, if from a divine perspective "kindness" can be defined as inflicting maximal pain and unending suffering, then the word is simply emptied of any meaning-ful content at all. Language simply breaks down completely if our human concepts have no relation to God at all. On this view, "good" is simply whatever God does, so to say that "God is good" is simply to say that "God does what God does," which doesn't say very much. Besides being inco-herent, this view actually undermines the very purpose of the teaching of Jesus regarding God's perfect kindness and compassion. Jesus tells his followers that they are to model their lives according to the compassion-ate kindness of God, but if God's character is beyond our understanding altogether, then how could this provide any useful ethical guidance? How can we strive to "imitate God" (Eph 5:1) if ultimately God's goodness can-not be understood by us?

Traditionalists often insist that universalists are simply being "senti-mental" or "emotional" in how they define the love of God. Conservative theologian Millard Erickson writes,

> The Scriptures often refer to God's love. But what is its nature? As Pinnock, Stott, and others depict it, His love seems to be a senti-mentalized version, in which God would not do anything to cause pain, displeasure, or discomfort to anyone. Thus endless suffering would be incompatible with divine love. Is this really the picture of God's love given in Scripture? May it not be that God chooses some actions that cause pain to some persons for the sake of a higher good, namely, the greater joy or welfare of the whole of humanity, or more significantly, the good of the whole of reality, especially, the glory of God Himself?[31]

While Erickson is certainly right that divine love can be compat-ible with causing pain, displeasure, and discomfort, it is a much different claim to say that divine love can be compatible with inflicting an indi-vidual with maximal torment for an unending duration. Exactly how the infliction of such torment can make things better for "the good of the

---

31. Erickson, "Is Hell Forever?" 267. Clark Pinnock and John Stott are defenders of the annihilationist perspective which holds that when the wicked die, they are snuffed out of existence, not tortured forever in hell. Some annihilationists hold that there will be a time of punishment before they are totally destroyed.

whole of reality" (whatever that means) or how it can bring glory to a God who revealed himself fully by letting go of power and selflessly dying for the sake of others (Phil 2:5–11) is something that is beyond me. How can this God get glory by inflicting endless suffering? That is the kind of "glory" sought by an evil tyrant, not by the father of our Lord Jesus Christ. Universalists (and annihilationists, for that matter) are not being sentimental when we claim that divine love and the divine infliction of never-ending maximal torment are incompatible. We're being moral and rational. If love can include inflicting the worst fate possible on someone, then how exactly will that "love" be any different from hate? If divine love can include something this horrible, then how can we ever tell the difference between a divine action and a demonic action? How can we tell the difference between a revelation from God or the Devil?

There is probably no quicker way to turn a morally sensitive believer into an atheist than by telling her that she has to set aside her deepest moral intuitions when thinking about God. Based on my own experience, and on a recent sociological study of what compels a person to become an atheist, people who are told to blindly submit to a harsh and vindictive conception of God that seems completely opposed to everything they know about what is good and just places an enormous psychological burden on them that is too great to bear.[32] Oftentimes the only way people can see to be released from this is to stop believing in a God altogether. While I don't blame them, and even think that atheism can be a much better worldview than bad theism, there is another option.[33] That option is to let go of a certain conception of God, while still being open to envisioning God in a different way. Traditional teaching on hell, and its insistence that God's moral goodness is totally different from human moral goodness, has probably done more to contribute to atheism than anything else. Atheists are traditionally branded as immoral, but many of them reject traditional theism out of deep moral convictions; convictions that say that a God who tortures people forever for sin that they couldn't help avoiding in the first place is not worth worshiping. I think they are on to something, and they are right to challenge a religious response that appeals to divine mystery to justify actions that we would immediately and unequivocally label as evil if attributed to human beings.

32. Zuckerman, *Faith No More*, 33–39.

33. For a thoughtful reflection on how bad religion spawns atheism, see McLaren, "On Atheism."

Christians with a traditional perspective on everlasting punishment often appeal to the "God's ways are higher than our ways" argument, implying that we should just believe the traditional view and not ask questions. But why not apply this argument to the traditional view as well? Traditionalists often assume that their theological viewpoint is knowable, yet when questioned they point to the mystery of God. Why assume that their understanding of God can't be subjected to the higher-ways-of-God argument as well? In other words, this argument is often used in a one-sided way: it applies to *your* reasoning about God, but not *mine*.

I would also point out that God's ways are *higher* than our ways, not *lower* than our ways. I have always heard the higher-ways-of-God argument brought out when some kind of cruel picture of God is being defended. Before looking into it, I just assumed that wherever in the Bible people got this argument must have been in a context where God's vindictive and retributive punishment was being defended. I expected the passage to read something like, "My anger burns forever against the wicked, and my punishment, unlike that which comes from mortals, shall know no end. My ways are higher than your ways, declares the Lord." That isn't in the Bible, but this is:

> Seek the LORD while he may be found, call upon him while he is near; let the wicked forsake their way, and the unrighteous their thoughts; let them return to the LORD, that he may have mercy on them, and to our God, for he will abundantly pardon. For my thoughts are not your thoughts, nor are your ways my ways, says the LORD. For as the heavens are higher than the earth, so are my ways higher than your ways and my thoughts than your thoughts. (Isa 55:6–9)

When Isaiah throws out the higher-ways-of-God argument, it isn't to defend the vengeful punishment of God, it is to defend the abundant mercy of God! To take this text and use it to defend a conception of divine justice and goodness that certainly seems much worse than any human understanding of justice and goodness is to use this text for the opposite purpose than it was originally intended. If we take the context seriously, and we should, the higher-ways-of-God argument can be more appropriately used to defend the universalist position than the traditionalist one. God's ability and desire to pardon is beyond our understanding!

Another major related difficulty with the concept of infinite punishment for the wicked is that everyone ultimately receives the same type and degree of punishment. But how could it be just for Hitler to receive the same punishment as 23-year-old John who just rejected the faith of his upbringing? So, not only does the idea of infinite punishment seem incongruent with finite sins, it also doesn't allow for any significant difference between the wide variety of finite sins that can be committed. Surely stealing bubble gum deserves a different punishment than murder, but on the traditional view there is a one-size-fits-all punishment for all people. Ironically, then, a position that claims to be based on retributive justice ends up violating one of the fundamental principles of retributive justice, namely, the punishment should fit the crime.

There are many Christians who will agree with everything said so far in favor of this objection, but who will still hold to a belief in an everlasting hell because they do not think that God imposes an infinite sentence of punishment on sinners at all. Rather, they think that some people will be eternally separated from God by their own choice. On this more modern interpretation of an everlasting hell, popularized especially by C. S. Lewis, God does not send anyone to hell. Instead, people choose to live in rebellion against God and are free to continue in this rebellion against God forever. Hell is not populated by divine decree, but by human choice. God doesn't send people to hell as a punishment because they freely chose to reject God, as the traditional Arminian position holds. Instead, on this revised Arminian view, some people will freely reject God forever. It is by their eternally-renewing choice that they remain separate from God. While this view avoids the problem of the injustice of an infinite sentence imposed for finite sins, it comes with its own set of unique challenges and problems.

One of the main problems with this response is that it really doesn't get God off the hook completely. Even though on this view God isn't the one imposing an eternal punishment on people, God still is keeping the people in hell in existence. As the contemporary philosophers of religion John Kronen and Eric Reitan put it in their recent highly sophisticated philosophical defense of universalism, "There is something God does that contributes to damnation: *He preserves the damned in being.*"[34] Mainstream Christian theology envisions God as the sustainer of all things, and that without God's choice to hold something in existence it would cease to exist. So, even on this modified defense of an everlasting hell

---

34. Kronen and Reitan, *God's Final Victory*, 18 (italics original).

that relies on the freedom and autonomy of human beings, God is not completely absolved of responsibility for their eternal misery. If they are going to resist God forever, then it would more loving for God to simply let them cease to be. Later when we address the issue of human free will in relation to the divine will that all be saved, we will delve into this perspective much more deeply. For now, though, it provides a nice transition into our next major question to be asked of the traditional view.

How can God be victorious over evil
if some are forever in rebellion against God?

Even though the revised view of everlasting hell that centers on human freedom and not divine justice does have certain advantages over the traditional view, it leaves us with the proposal that evil will be in existence forever. This certainly seems problematic, because the Bible offers us the hope that ultimately God will be victorious over all the forces of rebellion and evil in the world. For example, consider Paul's words to the Christians at Corinth:

> Then comes the end, when he hands over the kingdom to God the Father, after he has destroyed every ruler and every authority and power. For he must reign until he has put all his enemies under his feet. The last enemy to be destroyed is death . . . When all things are subjected to him, then the Son himself will also be subjected to the one who put all things in subjection under him, so that God may be all in all. (1 Cor 15:24–26, 28)

On the revisionist understanding of everlasting hell, it is very hard to see how God can be "all in all" when some remain forever opposed to God. It is also very hard to see how Christ can be said to have destroyed all evil powers when these powers clearly remain "alive and well" in the hearts of all those who are in hell. Jesuit theologian William Dalton writes,

> The destruction of "death," which in Pauline terminology does not mean merely physical death but also spiritual death, seems to imply that, at the end, nowhere in God's creation will there be the discordant note of sin, but that complete peace and harmony will reign. It is hard to see how this picture will be fulfilled if, for all

eternity, there could be a number of human beings who reject God and remain alienated from him.[35]

More will be said about the problems with the "free-will defense" of an everlasting hell later, but here we should be very clear that this view severely compromises, indeed negates, the promise of the fullness and finality of God's victory over evil that is at the heart of the Christian faith.

The contemporary philosopher Jerry Walls attempts to counter this objection by making a distinction between God's love being "defeated" and being "declined."[36] He asserts that even if people decline God's love forever, God is still not defeated because God goes on loving them forever. The only way God's love could be "defeated," on his view, is if people could get God to stop loving them, and that he will never do. While this strikes me as a legitimate distinction when it comes to interpersonal relationships, I do not find it convincingly applicable when thinking about what an ultimate victory of divine love would look like. On Walls view, in principle every human being could decline God's love and eternally resist God, and God could still be said to be "victorious" over evil and sin. This is not only conceptually problematic, but it also cannot be fit within the New Testament vision of all things being made subject to Christ. How can someone be both subject to Christ and eternally resistant to Christ? It seems that if God's love is eternally declined, then it would be perfectly accurate to say that God's loving desire for all to be saved would be defeated.[37]

How can anyone be happy in heaven if there is anyone in hell?

If being in heaven entails being united with God, and if God's essence is love (1 John 4:8), then it follows that to live in heaven means that we are one with the source of all love. To be with God is to be perfected in love.

---

35. Dalton, *Salvation and Damnation*, 30.

36. J. Walls, "Philosophical Critique," 122–23.

37. Walls also argues that "decline" doesn't necessarily imply "defeat" by pointing out that lots of things happen in this life that are against God's will, but that doesn't mean that God is defeated. I would disagree, and would make a distinction between temporary defeat and ultimate defeat. God is temporarily defeated in this age by the forces of sin and evil, not because God is weak, but because God has given power and freedom to his creatures. However, in the age to come, all temporary defeats will be redeemed by God's ultimate victory over evil and sin.

So how can people who are filled with divine-like love and compassion ever be fully happy knowing that some are forever lost? In speaking of the desire that he had to convert his fellow non-Christian Jews, the apostle Paul writes, "For I could wish that I myself were accursed and cut off from Christ for the sake of my own people" (Rom 9:3). This seems to be the perfect attitude of someone whose heart is filled with love. Paul cannot be happy with his own salvation apart from the salvation of all those that he loves. Love ties our personal identities with others together in an indissoluble bond. Wouldn't the inhabitants of heaven, people who are perfected in love, want to leave to rescue those who are in hell? In fact, one early Christian document entitled *The Shepherd of Hermas*, which was for a time considered to be a part of the New Testament, actually envisions a time when the apostles and church leaders will preach to those in the realm of the dead.[38] Even though this document eventually fell out of the biblical canon, it shows that at least for many early Christians there was a hope in the possibility of salvation for those who have died outside the Christian faith, and that there was a conviction that the church would somehow be a part of God's mission to reach them. In short, it is hard to see how the supreme happiness of individuals perfected in love can ever be made possible as long as some people are in eternal torment, whether divinely decreed or somehow humanly chosen.

Interestingly, this objection has not always been considered to have much weight at all. In fact, far from lessening the joy of the inhabitants of heaven, the sufferings of the residents of hell has traditionally been held to actually enhance the joy of those in heaven! Christian theologians such as Tertullian, Augustine, Aquinas, and Jonathan Edwards teach that the pains of those in hell are actually a source of delight for those in heaven. As a representative example, consider what the hugely influential thirteenth-century Catholic theologian Thomas Aquinas has to say: "In order that the bliss of the saints may be more delightful for them and that they may render more copious thanks to God for it, it is given to them to see perfectly the punishment of the damned."[39]

In fairness to Aquinas, he is not affirming that heaven is populated with sadists who enjoy watching the sufferings of others because in a perverse way seeing pain inflicted gives them pleasure. The reason that

38. See MacCulloch, *Harrowing of Hell*, 85–86. On the scriptural status of this document in the early church, see McDonald, "Integrity of the Biblical Canon," 123–25.

39. Aquinas, *Summa Theologica*, Supplement, 94:1.

he (and others) think that the sufferings of those in hell will enhance the delight of those in heaven is twofold. First, it will show them what they are missing out on, thus making them even more grateful for the grace shown to them. But again, while it may be natural to look at the calamities that others experience and be thankful that we are not them, this does not seem like the attitude of someone perfected in love. Perfect love compels us to join others in their sufferings, not to keep a safe distance and focus on our own happiness. The second reason Aquinas gives is that since God justly imposed the sufferings of those in hell, the saints will ultimately rejoice in God's justice that is manifested in the eternal punishment of the wicked. It is not suffering as such in which the saints rejoice, but the justice of God that the sufferings of those in hell represent. This, of course, is susceptible to the criticisms raised above about the justness of infinite punishment for finite sins. While I do believe that the saints will rejoice over God's justice being manifested in the age to come, and while I even think that some of this rejoicing will be over the wicked "getting a taste of their own medicine," it is far from clear how the inhabitants of heaven can desire that those in hell experience everlasting punishments that are purely retributive in nature. But if the saints in heaven can't be supremely happy while some are lost, then can God be?

How could God be satisfied while some of God's children are lost?

This is an enormous question for both of the views of everlasting hell we have considered. For the traditional view that is grounded in a divine decree of justice, it is difficult to see how God could be content to impose an eternal sentence of torture on God's children. For the revisionist view that is grounded in the value of human freedom that God must respect, it is hard to see how a God of love could ever give up on his children and be content with their eternal rebellion. In the Gospels, we are told that as Jesus rides into Jerusalem he weeps over the rejection he is about to experience from his people (Luke 19:41). If God looks like Jesus (John 14:9; Col 1:15; Heb 1:3), then it seems that an everlasting hell would mean everlasting tears flowing down the face of God.[40] It is impossible for me to

40. Some might argue that this is simply the consequence of God giving freedom to human beings, and a testimony to the vulnerable and suffering love of God. It seems, though, that this would undermine the biblical promises of a life in the age to come when all suffering is eliminated, and all tears and crying are no more (Rev 21:4).

believe that the God revealed in Jesus will at some point simply throw up his hands in defeat or harden his heart in retaliation.

To anticipate an issue we will discuss later on, why is death often seen as the deadline for receiving salvation? If God loves all people and desires for all to be saved, as scripture seems to clearly assert (1 Pet 3:9) and as most Christians (besides Calvinists) would agree, then why would God's attitude towards people change upon physical death? Why would God go from actively desiring and working for a person's salvation in this life, and yet be content to give that person over to the rebellion forever in the life to come? Why wouldn't God keep doing all that he could do to try to get through to that person?

Later we'll discuss some of the biblical passages that seem to point towards the possibility of postmortem conversion, but for now we will simply note that a God who gives up on some people is hard to square with the character of the God that Jesus reveals who keeps searching *until what is lost is found.*[41] N. T. Wright faces this objection and concludes that in the world to come evil will not be given any veto power over the heavenly celebration. He writes, "We do not have the choice to sulk in such a way as to prevent God's party going ahead without us. We have the right, like the older brother, to sit it out; God has the right to come and reason with us; but the fatted calf is going to be eaten whether we join in or not."[42] But it seems that Wright has missed the force of the parable he references here. After the prodigal son has come and the father has decided to throw a party, the older brother refuses to come in and so the father goes out to plead with him to come in. The story ends with the father outside the party pleading for the older son to come in. Are we to imagine that the father in this parable at some point will give up on the older brother and go back to the party? It seems that Jesus is telling us that God, precisely because his heart overflows with compassionate love, *cannot* rejoice and join the party until all his children are at home. As the contemporary theologian Miroslav Volf writes, "Neither the embrace of the prodigal nor the older brother's anger changes the fact that the older one 'is always' with the father, indeed that he is his father's dear 'child' and that 'all' that belongs to the father belongs also to the son (v. 31)."[43] It would seem to

---

41. Jesus tells three parables with this point in Luke 15.

42. N. Wright, *Evil and the Justice of God,* 147.

43. Volf, *Exclusion and Embrace,* 164.

deeply go against the grain of Jesus's story to envision the father changing his mind about the older son, becoming content to enter the party while his child remains in the hell of a self-imposed exclusion. The previous two parables of the lost sheep and lost coin make this very point. Just as the woman doesn't stop looking until she finds her coin, and just as the shepherd doesn't stop looking until he has found his lost sheep, the father too cannot rest content with a 50 percent success rate. For a divine party to happen, what is lost has to be found.

Conclusion

There is no more important question in Christian theology today than coming to terms with the doctrine of hell. While that may seem like a bit of an overstatement, regardless of what is said and preached about God being merciful and loving, if the doctrine of hell is not brought into this affirmation in a truly integrated way, then it will leave people wondering if God really is merciful and loving. If we cannot preach and teach about hell in a way that is coherent with the biblical affirmation that God is love, then the lingering image of a vengeful and angry God will get in the way of our proclamation. Here is what I have discovered: *Our vision of how things will end is actually what determines what we really think about who God is and what God is like.* To put it in words that would make my seminary professors proud, our eschatology determines our theology. This means our exploration of hell is actually nothing less than an exploration into the very heart and character of God.

So far I have laid out in broad strokes some of the main objections that a reflective Christian is bound to ask about the doctrine of everlasting punishment. But it wouldn't be fair to say that because the traditional view of hell has so many problems we should therefore adopt the universalist view. It has its fair share of objections to face as well. In what is to come, we will take a much deeper look into Christian universalism by way of addressing the six major objections that Christians often raise:

1. Universalists don't believe in hell.

2. Universalists don't believe the Bible.

3. Universalists deny human freedom.

4. Universalists think all religions are equally true.

5. Universalism undermines evangelism.

6. Universalism undermines holy living.

Approaching Christian universalism through this wide sweep of concerns from its detractors (i.e., most Christians!) will enable us to get a full and deep understanding of why Christian universalists believe what they believe. To refer back to a previous analogy, you are not being asked to throw away any of the biblical puzzle pieces as we go forward in our exploration. You are being invited now to examine whether or not those pieces can be put together to make a better picture, a picture in which the most pieces can fit, and in which the glory and grace of God can best be seen.

Chapter 2

Hell Hath No Fury?

Objection #1: "Universalists don't believe in hell."

I OFTEN HEAR MORE liberally-minded Christians say that a God of love would not judge anyone. God, it is thought, must be some sort of nice grandfatherly-like figure who just wants everyone to have a good time. While I am sympathetic to this popular reaction against a more harsh and fundamentalist view of an angry and punitive God, this way of thinking simply goes too far in the other direction. I suspect that the people who say this sort of thing have not seriously thought through the implications of this view. I would argue that in the kind of world we live in—a world where human beings inflict all sorts of monstrous harm on other human beings—divine love actually *requires* divine judgment. If God does not care about all the ways in which people suffer evil and injustice, and care enough about it to ultimately do something about it, then this God cannot be said to be just or loving.

The problem is that while many Christians rightly have this moral intuition that a God of love must care about justice and making things right, they wrongly assume that an everlasting hell is the only way that God can bring about this justice. As we noted in the previous chapter, it is very hard to see how this type of response from God can be seen as actually bringing about justice. Here it is important to see that we are not forced to choose between believing in either a God who punishes the wicked forever on the one hand, or in a God who is morally indifferent and nonresponsive to the evil and injustice in life on the other. Just because we are raising questions about the nature and duration of hell does not mean that we are abandoning any notion of divine justice or judgment. Indeed, most Christian universalists hold to a very robust and strong vision of divine judgment. Judgment need not be everlasting conscious torment in order for it to be very serious. This cannot be emphasized enough. Christian universalists do not deny the reality of judgment and hell, they simply contend that judgment and hell should be conceptualized and imagined in such a way as to be congruent with a God who is genuinely loving to all people and who therefore seeks what is best for all people. In this chapter, our goal will be to explore how Christian universalists can envision and imagine the reality and nature of hell. The imagination, not just the intellect, is important when it comes to thinking about the afterlife. Our collective religious imagination concerning what hell "looks like" must certainly take into account the teachings of the scriptures, but all views of the afterlife go beyond explicit scriptural declarations. The religious imagination shaped by the traditional view of everlasting torment, for example, has probably been just as much influenced by Dante's *The Inferno* and John Milton's *Paradise Lost* as it has by the Bible, knowingly or not.[1] To some degree this is inevitable, but self-awareness in this regard is critical. If you are inclined to criticize what is to follow by pointing out that I am letting my theological imagination have too much authority, I acknowledge that, yes, my view of hell is a human and imaginative construction, but this is simply the nature of all theological construction. While God's revelation in Jesus Christ, and in the scriptures that point to him, are the given "dots" in our theological thinking, the lines that we draw to connect the dots and the shapes that we make, are our own doing. Theology is always a matter of a divine-human dance, where the Spirit takes the lead and we try our best to follow.

While we will touch on only a few of the key biblical passages in this chapter very briefly, we will wait until the next chapter to engage in a fuller discussion of a wide range of the relevant biblical passages for this debate. For now, let's begin to see how hell can fit within the framework of the larger conviction that God desires to save all and is able to save all.

1. See Wray, *Bible Really Tells Us*, 100–4.

On Earth As It Is In Hell

While hell is undeniably taught to be a postmortem spiritual reality in the New Testament, there is also affirmation that hell isn't a place you can only experience when you die. Hell, like heaven, is a condition of life that we can bring on earth here and now. Jesus promised that following him and his Way of life would bring more of God's kingdom "on earth as it is in heaven" (Matt 6:10). In other words, as we walk with him in the way of self-sacrificing love, radical compassion, and genuine forgiveness, we bring a taste of heaven into our lives and into the lives of those around us. The goal of a follower of Christ is not simply to get into heaven when we die, but to get heaven into our life here and now, and we do that through trusting and obeying the Way of Christ.

The converse is also true. If we refuse to follow the Way of Christ, if we persist in living with ourselves at the center of the universe and treat everyone else as background props on a stage meant for us, then our lives bring a taste of hell into the here and now. Just as living a God-driven, other-centered life brings one a sense of fullness, community and joy, living a self-centered, ego-oriented life, inevitably brings one alienation, loneliness, and ultimately despair. This is what the apostle Paul was talking about when he contrasted the "works of the flesh" and the "fruit of the Spirit" (Gal 5:16–26). Our decisions and actions have very real consequences for determining whether or not our lives (and the lives of those we affect) will be joyful and wholesome or miserable and divisive. It is up to us to choose on which trajectory we want to live. As C. S. Lewis put it, "Every time you make a choice you are turning the central part of you, the part of you that chooses, into something a little different from what it was before. And taking your life as a whole, with all your innumerable choices, all your life long you are slowly turning this central thing into a heavenly creature or into a hellish creature."[2]

With each choice we make, we either bring a little more of heaven or a little more of hell into our lives. I realize that might sound like a bit of an overstatement. I know one could respond that there are lots of little choices in life that are morally and spiritually neutral, like deciding between coffee mugs. This is certainly, yet trivially, true, but it shouldn't detract from the importance of acknowledging that even many of the little choices that we make, such as the choice to be completely honest or

2. Lewis, *Mere Christianity*, 92.

33

to bend the truth a little to make oneself look better, are ultimately very important choices because they form us a little more in the direction of heaven or in the direction of hell.

Let's consider, for example, a seemingly little thing that Jesus said would bring a person into a hellish condition of life: lust. Because the reader may be tempted to roll his or her eyes at this example, let me say a few words before moving on. This is one of the seven deadly sins that most people today think of as simply the product of a sexually repressive church culture that need not be taken very seriously any more. Much of this kind of criticism is right on the money, in my estimation. It is certainly true that the church has struggled throughout its tradition to speak in a thoroughly positive way about human sexuality. Many of our top theologians hold that any sexual pleasure, even within marriage, is itself tainted with sin.[3] Lust is often thought of as any desire to experience sexual pleasure and intimate bonding for its own sake, apart from the desire to procreate. Much of the strong resistance to any sexual limits (other than consent) in our culture is what I see as an overreaction to a church culture that has held some pretty stupid and very damaging views of physical intimacy over the centuries. We have to remember, though, that Jesus came from a Jewish tradition that is much more positive about physical pleasure than subsequent Christian tradition that is tremendously influenced by the dualism of Greek thought that holds the soul to be good and the body to be bad. Anyone who doubts the affirming character of ancient Jewish thought toward sexuality need only to sit down with the Song of Songs for a few minutes!

Sexual desire as such is not sinful or dirty; it is a part of what it means to be a human being. Lust is not simply the desire to have sex. Lust is also not merely the experience of being sexually attracted to someone other than your spouse. As some wise person once said, "You can't keep the birds from flying over your head, but you can keep them from making a nest there!" So what is lust? Lust is a way of relating to another person sexually that reduces them to an object to be possessed. Maybe we could put it like this: Lust turns somebody into just some body. Lust turns a human being made in the image of God into a sexual object. It denies the other person's subjectivity, needs, and desires, and simply focuses on how they can be a means to our own end of sexual gratification. I can imagine

3. See Lawrence, *Sexual Liberation*.

someone protesting, "But what does it matter what stays in your mind? As long as you don't act on it, how can it be wrong?" Here is what Jesus has to say:

> You have heard that it was said, "You shall not commit adultery." But I say to you that everyone who looks at a woman with lust has already committed adultery with her in her heart. If your right eye causes you to sin, tear it out and throw it away; it is better for you to lose one of your members than for your whole body to be thrown into hell. And if your right hand causes you to sin, cut it off and throw it away; it is better for you to lose one of your members than for your whole body to go into hell. (Matt 5:27–30)

It seems to me that Jesus's main point here is that lust leads somewhere, and where it leads is not good, so it must be cut off as much as possible. Adultery doesn't start with an action. It begins with a thought, and then another thought, and then another, and so on. So Jesus tells his followers, in very vivid and graphic metaphorical language, to do all they can to root out lustful ways of relating to other people. As hard as that may seem to do, Jesus says that it is much better to experience the difficulty of resisting lust than it is to experience the destruction that comes from giving in to and allowing oneself to be ruled by lust. He says that the destination at the end of the path of lust is hell. To understand what he means by that we need to look at some crucially important background information on the word "hell" in the New Testament.

First, you may wonder why I said we need to look at the background behind the word "hell" only in the New Testament. That is because hell is nowhere taught in the Old Testament. For over a fifteen-hundred-year period, ancient Israel had no coherent belief system about the afterlife at all, and they didn't believe in hell.[4] Only a handful of vague glimpses into the possibility of an afterlife can be found in the Old Testament, perhaps with punishments and rewards, but there is no worked out theology of the afterlife.[5]

In the two centuries leading up to the time of Christ, the ancient Jewish people began to develop a much stronger belief, not only in an

---

4. Readers of the KJV are lead astray in this regard, as the Hebrew word sheol was mistakenly translated in many occurrences as "hell." Modern translations have correctly changed this to fit the original meaning, which is "grave" or "pit."

5. On the diversity, complexity, and ambiguity of the Old Testament and the afterlife, see Johnston, *Shades of Sheol*.

afterlife in the form of a resurrection, but they also began to believe in a postmortem judgment or place of condemnation. It is possible that external forces, such as beliefs about resurrection and judgment from ancient Persian religion may have impacted the development of Jewish belief in the afterlife.[6] However, the most influential historical factor that lead to this emerging belief was that the Jewish people were beginning to experience severe persecution that left them with the conviction that if God is just and if God is loving, then there has to be a life to come where those who are persecuted are rewarded and those who did the persecuting are punished. The belief in a world to come arose among ancient Jews shortly before the time of Jesus, then, primarily in response to severe suffering and injustice. It seemed like the only way to make sense of what they held so firmly to be true, that God is both good and just. So, many first-century Jewish people had a strong belief that there would be life after death, and that there is a place of judgment awaiting those who have turned against God and had turned on God's people. One of the main words they used to describe this place of judgment was the word *gehenna*, which has been translated from the Greek to English as "hell." Jesus uses this word eleven times in his teachings, as they are recorded in the Gospels.

Some background on *gehenna* is very important. In Jesus's day, *gehenna* was a specific location with a specific purpose. It was a strip of land, an actual, literal, physical place, on the southwest corner of Jerusalem. "*Gehenna*" was an abbreviated way of saying "Valley of Hinnom." This valley had a very dark history. King Ahaz encouraged child sacrifice to the Canaanite god Molech at this place (2 Kgs 16). After this, the real estate value bottomed out (to say the least) and it became the city's garbage heap that constantly burned.[7] This means that when Jesus was walking around and preaching, *gehenna* was a place of waste, despair, darkness, and destruction. In addition to being an actual place, it became a metaphor used by ancient rabbis to denote some type of an afterlife judgment and punishment.[8] The metaphor was very flexible and evocative, but the idea was not fixed.[9] *Gehenna* was used to refer to three different types of punishment. Some rabbis taught that the wicked would be

6. See Riley, *River of God*, 90–132.

7. See N. Wright, *Mark for Everyone*, 231.

8. See L. Bailey, "*Gehenna*."

9. See Milikowsky, "Which *Gehenna*?," 238–41.

forever punished, while others taught that they would be snuffed out of existence (annihilation), and yet others taught that the fires of *gehenna* were meant for a corrective purpose and would be temporary in nature, at least for some.[10] The imagery of fire, of course, lends itself to these three views. Fire can cause pain, it can burn something up, or it can purify. It is for these reasons that *gehenna* was a powerful attention-grabbing image of a severe divine judgment, but it was also a flexible image that could be taken in different directions.

When Jesus talked about *gehenna*, then, it would have been immediately clear to his first listeners that he was speaking of some type of present self-destruction that would lead to a postmortem judgment, but the precise and exact nature of this judgment would not have been immediately clear. From what we have of his teachings recorded in the Gospels, it takes some work to try to discern Jesus's view of *gehenna*. Did he think that it is for eternal vengeance, eternal capital punishment, or for purification and correction? Christians have disagreed over the best way to interpret him, and so throughout the history of the church there have been three main views that have been held and defended by Christians, as we noted in the previous chapter.

In the next chapter, we will examine more closely some of Jesus's teachings on hell, but for now we need to see how powerful this image of *gehenna* is in the warning against something so seemingly ordinary and "harmless" as lust. Lust deceives a person into thinking that following that path will lead to fulfillment and happiness, which is why it can be such a strong pull. Jesus pulls back the curtain and reveals that lust actually leads a person into a place of waste and self-destruction, and there can be no more powerful image to convey that than the place of *gehenna*. A person controlled by lust, Jesus is saying, will waste their life and be fit for the garbage dump. Jesus isn't warning his followers that if they experience sexual desire they will be in danger of being thrown into "the place down there" when they die. He is giving his followers the very perceptive and insightful teaching that if they handle their sexuality in an uncontrolled way that is dehumanizing and degrading, in a way that objectifies and exploits others, that this way of life will lead to despair and a sense of a life wasted. While heaven and earth come together a bit more every time one person treats another as the intrinsically and infinitely valuable daughter

---

10. See Powys, *Hell*, 171–73; Milikowsky, "Which *Gehenna*?," 241.

or son of God that they are, hell and earth come together a bit more every time one person reduces the value of another person down to what they can do for them. Hell, then, is not a bad place down there. Hell is right here and right now whenever and wherever the dignity of human beings made in God's image is violated or disrespected.

Lust is just one of the ways that God's will can be refused to be done on earth as it is in heaven. Anger is another primary human drive that pushes the kingdom of heaven further away. Jesus had this to say:

> You have heard that it was said to those of ancient times, "You shall not murder"; and "whoever murders shall be liable to judgment." But I say to you that if you are angry with a brother or sister, you will be liable to judgment; and if you insult a brother or sister, you will be liable to the council; and if you say, "You fool", you will be liable to the hell of fire. So when you are offering your gift at the altar, if you remember that your brother or sister has something against you, leave your gift there before the altar and go; first be reconciled to your brother or sister, and then come and offer your gift. Come to terms quickly with your accuser while you are on the way to court with him, or your accuser may hand you over to the judge, and the judge to the guard, and you will be thrown into prison. Truly I tell you, you will never get out until you have paid the last penny. (Matt 5:21–26)

The kind of anger Jesus speaks of here is the deep and smoldering contempt for another person; the kind of anger that, like lust, looks at another human being with a dehumanizing gaze. Anger and lust both cause us to see other people in a very flat, one-dimensional way. When someone offends us, we easily define that person by that action and reduce the complexity of their being down to an entity that we wish was not there. That, of course, is the impulse that stands at the beginning of a murderous desire. As with adultery, murder starts with a thought that another person is really subhuman and should not be shown the respect of a being that reflects divinity in their humanity. To walk down the road of contempt and resentful anger is to dehumanize another person, and in the process to dehumanize oneself by giving the reigns over to our most primitive drives. A person filled with this kind of anger is a person whose life is characterized by alienation, self-destruction, and a profound sense of frustration at their wasted energies. In other words, this person is in hell.

Jesus is very clear about the reality of hell, and he seems abundantly clear that the way we handle our most raw human drives and emotions determines whether or not we experience hell. Heaven and hell, for Jesus, are not simply postmortem destinations, they can be present realities. The Christian universalist, then, can strongly affirm that hell is a very real experience for people here and now who live self-oriented lives that dehumanize other people.

Hell for Christians

You may be surprised that the discussion has gone in this direction. You may be thinking to yourself, "Let's get away from the moralizing and the preaching and just get to the really important stuff about where people outside the Christian faith go when they die!" But if we are going to take Jesus seriously, then we need to see how he talked about hell and we need to pay close attention. Although evangelists most often preach about hell to try to convert people to Christianity, we need to reflect on the significance of the fact that Jesus never tried to scare people into the kingdom of God by threatening them with hell. The only people to which Jesus talked about hell were his own followers and especially to the self-righteous religious leaders of his day. We often assume that heaven is for good people and that hell is for bad people. But according to Jesus's message and ministry, it is the reverse: heaven is for bad people and hell is for "good" people.[11] Heaven is for people who know they are in need of large doses of grace, while hell is for people who alienate themselves from God and others through the self-sufficiency and self-centeredness of their own pride (Luke 18:9–14). Jesus didn't see those who were outside the bounds of proper religion as the ones in danger of hell. He saw the ones on the inside as being in the most spiritual danger, because when we are on the inside, it is easy to become complacent and presumptuous and turn our focus on making judgments about others. This is precisely what many of the Pharisees, the self-appointed spiritual and moral guardians of society, did in their day. They were so sure of their insider status with God that they turned their energies towards using threats of hell to those who didn't measure up the way they did. In most contexts, then, Jesus's teachings on hell took the Pharisees to task by turning their judgments

11. See Guthrie, *Christian Doctrine*, 396–99.

back on themselves. The threat of hell was primarily used by Jesus, not to encourage speculation about others in the world to come, but to encourage examination of our own lives here and now concerning all the ways in which our pride, greed, lust, anger, judgmentalism, and apathy may be leading us down a wide road to self-destruction (Matt 7:13–14).[12]

When it came to "outsiders," Jesus tried to love them into the kingdom of God. Jesus did not try to convert sinners by threatening them or heaping guilt or shame on them, as did many of the Pharisees (Matt 23:4). He tried to transform them by eating with them, by scandalously welcoming them into an unconditional embrace of love. This shockingly inclusive compassion that Jesus showed to notorious and egregious sinners like tax collectors and prostitutes was what magnetically drew the crowds of ordinary people to him, and at the same time enraged the religious leaders to conspire against him.

I am convinced that we Christians have for too long preached about hell as the Pharisees did, not as Jesus did. We have made it only about "them," not us. You see, when we make hell just about what happens to outsiders in the next life, we miss the fact that Jesus made his warnings about hell primarily in relation to what insiders do in this life. Personally, I would much rather sit around and theologize about what is going to happen to other people than to still myself in God's presence and take an honest look at the anger and lust (among other things) that reside in my heart and tempt to take me in a hellish direction. Debating what happens to other people is much easier than acknowledging that God really cares about how I handle conflict or what websites I visit. In fact, I can now see that as I have wrestled consistently with the issue of hell over the last decade, many of my reflections on what happens to other people when they die, especially back when I thought I knew for sure who was saved and who wasn't, have been driven by a desire to deflect attention away from myself and my own darkness that needs to be brought into the light. I am not saying that anyone who makes theological statements about other people going to hell is guilty of hypocrisy or dishonesty. I am saying that I have been guilty of this. Sometimes the way we try to solidify our own sense of being on God's side is to strongly define who is not on God's side. But this exclusionary attempt at self-definition, trying to define ourselves over against other people, is the complete opposite of what Jesus and the

12. See Travis, *Christ and the Judgement*, 323; Clark-Soles, *Death and the Afterlife*, 184.

apostles taught. They taught us to be defined by a grace much wider than the boundaries of our own selves or our own groups.

The Judgment of Love

Hell isn't just about them then, it is about us now. There is a way of being in harmony with God's good purposes and intentions, and there is a way of being out of joint with God's desires for us. Heaven is the first way, hell is the second. The Christian universalist has no problem in acknowledging the reality of hell on earth and in recognizing that we live in a moral universe where "we reap what we sow" (Gal 6:7). Theologically and exegetically, though, it would be unwise and unfair to try to limit a biblically-shaped view of hell to only what happens in this life. Even a cursory read of the New Testament forces us to be struck with the sense of a strong conviction that there will be judgment in the life to come. The key question is just what the nature and purpose of this judgment will be.

The traditional view of judgment and hell asserts that God's love and God's justice work in divergent directions. In other words, people end up in heaven because of God's love, while others end up in hell because of God's justice. One of the deep problems with this view is that it essentially splits God's personality in two. We end up with a schizophrenic God who is sometimes loving and sometimes just (or unjust, if one agrees with the criticisms in chapter 1). This goes against the majority of the Christian tradition that holds that God cannot be divided into different "parts," and that all of God's attributes must cohere and work together. Most importantly, though, it contradicts the message of Jesus that God is like a loving abba (the Aramaic word for "dad"). Jesus taught us to think of God primarily on the model of a loving parent. On one occasion he said, "Is there anyone among you who, if your child asks for a fish, will give a snake instead of a fish? Or if the child asks for an egg, will give a scorpion? If you then, who are evil, know how to give good gifts to your children, how much more will the heavenly Father give the Holy Spirit to those who ask him!" (Luke 11:11–13). Jesus is encouraging his followers to compare the character of God with the character of human parents. Merely decent human parents, who have a mixture of good and evil in their hearts, would not do anything to actively harm their children. Jesus says to take the basic goodness that a normal parent would show to their child and magnify it tremendously when thinking about how God relates to us. God, whose heart is only pure goodness, only wants to give God's children what is genuinely good for them. Francis Chan and Preston Sprinkle, in their follow-up response to Rob Bell's *Love Wins*, deny that we can subject God to human judgments of goodness and love. They write, "First, God is love, but He also defines what love is. We don't have the license to define love according to our own standards and sensibilities."[13] Actually, if we take Jesus seriously, we do have the license from him to think about God according to our own standards. God is much better than our human standards of goodness, which is Jesus's point, but if we throw away human standards of goodness when thinking about God, then the claim that God is better, greater, and higher than our goodness is rendered meaningless.

In applying this to the question of hell and judgment, I am not suggesting that since God is like a loving parent there is no judgment. What I am suggesting is that however we conceptualize and imagine the reality of hell, it must be consistent with the affirmation of Jesus that God relates to us as a loving parent, and loving parents only punish their children for the purpose of correction and restoration. If you are inclined at this point to object that I am limiting God by reducing God to the confines of good parenting on a human level, I would remind you that it was Jesus himself who taught us to think of divine goodness on the analogy of human parental goodness. If divine goodness is completely of a different kind than the goodness of a human parent, then Jesus's admonition wouldn't make any sense and there would be no use comparing the two. I don't think that can be emphasized enough.

Parental punishment can take different forms. It may take the form of an actively imposed sentence, like grounding, or, if the children are older, it may take the form of simply letting one's child experience the negative consequences of their actions. But the central contention here is that a loving parent will never punish their child simply for the sake of vengeance or retribution. Punishment will always have the goal of promoting what is genuinely best for the child. This would seemingly rule out conceiving of hell as annihilation or divinely-imposed everlasting conscious torment.

There are some defenders of an everlasting hell who would agree with everything I have said about how a loving God would punish, but

---

13. Chan and Sprinkle, *Erasing Hell*, 162 (italics original).

would contend that there will be some who will eternally resist the actions that God takes to bring a person to repentance and restoration. We will look more extensively at this view of hell as a humanly-chosen separation from God (rather than divinely-imposed) in a later chapter, yet we can already pose what is an enormous difficulty with this view. To put it bluntly, this free-will defense of hell has very little faith in the reconciling power of divine love and, conversely, very great faith in the alienating power of human sin. Paul's affirmation that "where sin abounds, grace abounds all the more" (Rom 5:20) then is effectively reversed to say "where grace abounds, sin abounds all the more." Christians should see as theologically suspect a view of judgment and hell that dethrones God and essentially enthrones human freedom as the ultimate power in the universe.

So what would hell in the life to come "look like" within a Christian universalist framework that refuses to budge an inch on the affirmation that God is love (1 John 4:8)? Any answer to this question, of course, requires some speculation and imagination. I am not claiming that I know with certainty what hell will be like in the age to come (and I hope I never do!). But since scripture describes God's wrath in this life as God letting us experience the consequences of our sin so that we will turn away from them (Rom 1:18, 24, 26, 28; 11:32),[14] it seems correct to say that hell, the ultimate expression of God's wrath, would be the most intense experience of having the consequences of our actions "brought home" to us. The purpose of this wrath would be to lead us to repentance and to kindle in us the desire to seek reconciliation and make restoration with those we have wronged, and ultimately with God. The United Methodist Bishop William Willimon describes the wrath of God as the ultimate encounter with the painful truth about ourselves. He writes, "Perhaps the wrath, the just judgment of God upon us is a kind of slaying, a kind of baptismal death to our illusions and lies, that pain that happens when we are given time to stare into the mirror of truth, the pain that is harsh but is also due to love?"[15] Hell is the most severe experience of the wrath of God, the horrible experience of having the painful truth of our sins revealed and the consequences of our sinful actions turned back on us. Hell is not a matter of God eternally shoving us out of his presence, nor is it a matter of God simply allowing us to remain in our rejection of God forever. Hell

14. See Green and Baker, *Recovering the Scandal*, 53–57.

15. Willimon, *Who Will Be Saved?*, 83.

exists because God refuses to let any of us escape the fire of God's holy love for us. The flames of love that burn in God's heart must melt away all the sin that has attached itself to us so that we can be united with God. If we love God, we will want nothing more than to be baptized in this fire of holy love that will set us totally free from our sinful nature so that we can be our true self that is hidden in Christ (Col 3:3–4; Mal 3:1–3; Zech 13:9; Matt 3:11). If we despise God, if we identify with our false self that is constructed on the lie of our own sovereignty, we will want nothing more than to flee these flames because they will feel like the destruction of our very being.[16] The judgment and wrath of God consists in the fact that, one way or another, we are headed towards the flames of love. Because "our God is a consuming fire" (Heb 12:29), heaven and hell are not two different locations. Heaven and hell are two different ways of being in the presence of God. As the Russian Orthodox theologian Sergius Bulgakov puts it, "The same fire, the same love gladdens and burns, torments and gives joy."[17] The evangelical theologian Donald Bloesch affirms that, "Hell is not parallel to heaven but preparatory to heaven . . . It is a searing word of judgment before the final word of grace."[18] For those who have turned away from God and brought misery into the lives of others, God's wrath consists in God's refusal to let that rebellion continue forever and in God's commitment to bring healing justice to the world (Rev 22:2). The wrath of God is not vindictive or punitive, but neither is it "soft on sin." God's love is a holy love, a love that refuses to tolerate the death-dealing powers of sin. Wrath is what happens when the inescapable holy love of God meets the life-destroying powers of sin. Wrath is not the opposite of divine love, it is the outworking of that love in a world infected and plagued by sin.

We should dwell on this biblical teaching on the wrath of God as the inevitable encounter with the consequences of our sin a bit longer. Oftentimes the phrase "wrath of God" conjures up images of a Zeus-like God

---

16. When the New Testament warns of "destruction" or "perishing" for those who turn away from Christ (e.g., 2 Thess 1:5–10), I believe it is the destruction of the sinful nature that is being threatened, not the destruction of the whole person. To those who still identify with the sinful nature (the "flesh"), and have not yet died to it, the destruction of the flesh will feel like a total destruction, hence the harsh sounding rhetoric in the New Testament that seems to threaten unqualified annihilation. On the ultimately restorative purpose of the destruction of the flesh, see 1 Cor 5:1–8 and 1 Tim 1:19–20. For an insightful analysis of these passages, see Marshall, Beyond Retribution, 152–55.

17. Bulgakov, Bride of the Lamb, 459.

18. Bloesch, Last Things, 238.

throwing thunderbolts at people. In the Bible, however, divine "wrath" is most often meant to refer to the divine decision to let people experience the negative consequences of their disobedience. Wrath is not a punishment that God imposes, nor is it an uncontrolled emotional outburst of anger, but rather it is simply the outworking of sin itself that God allows sinners to experience so as to turn them away from their sin and towards God.[19] It is important to note that even very harsh and vengeful-sounding language used in the Bible to describe God's wrath is consistent with this account of divine wrath. Take, for example, Ezekiel 22:31, which begins by stating, "Therefore I have poured out my indignation upon them; I have consumed them with the fire of my wrath." While that alone would lead to an image of a vengeful God full of anger, Ezekiel goes on in the very next sentence to explain precisely and clearly what is actually meant by this language of fiery wrath: "I have returned their conduct upon their heads, says the Lord God." This is by no means an isolated instance of this way of speaking about divine wrath. Terence Fretheim, one of the most widely and highly respected Old Testament scholars today, argues that there are over fifty such texts like this in the Old Testament that draw this link between divine wrath and the natural consequences of disobedience.[20] This kind of punishment is both retributive, in that we deserve it, but it is also restorative, in that God uses that experience to turn us away from sin and draw us to himself.[21] Eastern Orthodox Bishop Hilarion Alfeyev, in his analysis of the seventh-century mystical theologian Isaac the Syrian, writes, "All the afflictions and sufferings which fall to someone's lot are sent from God with the aim of bringing a person to an inner change. Isaac draws an important conclusion: God never retaliates for the past, but always cares for our future."[22] God's judgment is intended to bring sinners to repentance and to enable reconciliation, both among human beings and between human beings and God.[23]

---

19. One of the most consistent descriptions of God in the Old Testament is that God is "slow to anger and abounding in steadfast love" (e.g., Exod 34:6; Num 14:18).

20. Fretheim, *Creation Untamed*, 50.

21. For a helpful overview of how biblical justice contains a retributive element with an overall restorative goal, see Zehr, *Changing Lenses*, 126–57.

22. Alfeyev, *Spiritual World of Isaac*, 289.

23. See Volf, *End of Memory*, 179–81.

When Forgiveness Hurts Like Hell

This restorative view of divine judgment does not preclude the possibility of immense pain and anguish. Indeed, I would argue that this view of hell as God's most severe means of enabling a person to turn away from their sin could include the worst pain possible for a person to experience. Let me offer a story that I think illustrates this important truth. Several years ago I was asked to engage in a spiritual counseling relationship with a person who had just been released from prison. This man had become a Christian in prison, and was looking for someone to help him grow in his walk with Christ. He did not want to go to a church service, because he knew there would be children there, and being around children was off limits for him. He was a pedophile, convicted on multiple accounts of rape and sexual abuse. Reading this last sentence probably either sent a chill up your spine, turned your stomach in knots, or brought tears to your eyes. It did all three for me. It really is hard to imagine something more heinous and monstrous than this kind of tragic abuse of precious children. When I was told about this person and was asked to be his spiritual mentor, my first thought was, "Hell no!" But I prayed about it and came to the conclusion that if I refused to meet with him then I would be a huge hypocrite. I couldn't keep on talking about the boundless grace of God and at the same time write this person off. So I agreed to meet with him. I didn't really sleep at all the night before the morning of our first meeting. I kept praying, "Lord, help me to see the person as you see the person."

So the morning came and we met in my office. I was first surprised that he looked normal. I was expecting someone with greasy hair and red eyes, but I got an average-looking farmer in overalls. My next surprise came when we sat down and I began to talk. I have never had a conversation where I felt like the Holy Spirit was in charge as much as this one. As I began to talk to him, I felt an overwhelming love for him. I told him, "You know in your heart that God absolutely hates and weeps over what you have done with your life, but I want you to know in your heart that God has never stopped loving you and that you are God's child." After saying this to him, he began to weep. Through tears and sobs, he told me about a lot of the pain he had experienced in life. He had been horribly abused as a child himself. While in prison he had received numerous beatings. All of his friends had cut their ties with him. Pain, receiving it and inflicting it on others, was the defining feature of his life.

But do you know what he said was the most painful thing he has ever experienced? It wasn't being beaten, raped, or rejected. It was being forgiven. He said that being forgiven by God was the most painful thing he has ever experienced. The experience of being embraced by a divine love in the midst of his sinful mess of a life was for him both the most joyful and, at the same time, most painful thing imaginable for him. Before he opened his heart to the power of God's Spirit, his heart was hard and his mind was darkened. He could do horrible things and not experience sorrow or regret because he was blind to what was really going on. In a very real sense, he did not know what he was doing. Indeed, evil and sin always involve a deep kind of self-deception and ignorance. Recall that when Jesus was hanging on the cross, he prayed, "Father forgive them, for they do not know what they are doing" (Luke 23:34). But as God's Spirit began to take a hold of him, his heart began to soften and his mind began to clear. He was now seeing and feeling for the first time the horror of what he had done. And it hurt like hell.

I tell this story because it shows that forgiveness is not the equivalent of getting off the hook without facing any consequences. Paradoxically, it is only in being forgiven that a person can fully come to experience the pain of their wrongdoing.[24] Anyone who has hurt a loved one and then had that person forgive you and still choose to love you knows what I am talking about. The offer of grace and the opportunity of reconciliation are painful to receive because in being embraced by someone we have hurt our sense of the wrongness of our wrongdoing is intensified all the more. If we think a person hates us, it's easy not to feel bad about how we might have harmed them. If we know without a doubt a person loves us, and refuses to stop loving us, it's hard not to be cut to the heart at the thought of how we harmed them. Forgiveness frees us from the condemnation that we deserve for our sin, but it does not necessarily release us from all of the consequences that come from our sin. As I have said, in some ways the experience of profound forgiveness actually intensifies the painful consequences of our sin, in that it reveals the beautiful goodness of the forgiver, and because of that, the ugliness of our sin is seen in its proper light. Vengeance can cause pain, but only love can cut to the heart.

24. Talbott, *Inescapable Love of God*, 143–67.

Jesus once told a story about a father who had two sons (Luke 15:11–32).[25] The younger son demanded his share of the inheritance early, and he took it and went to a distant land and wasted it all. That was a very bad thing to do. He had disrespected his father in one of the worst ways imaginable for the folks in ancient Jewish culture, where respect for one's father was of paramount importance. After losing all his money and unable to find a job, he decided to try to come home to use his father again for the purpose of giving him something to eat and a place to live. Interpreters often take his journey home as an act of repentance, but that interpretation relies too much on the speech that the son prepares for his father ("I am no longer worthy to be called your son"), and not enough on his internal dialogue, which emphasizes the reason he is going home: he is hungry and there is plenty of food at his father's house. He hasn't yet repented. He has simply put together a pious-sounding speech in order to get food in his stomach, and he expects that without a big show of groveling and pleading for forgiveness that his father will never let him come back home.

What happens when he arrives at home shocks him and everybody else too. "But while he was still far off, his father saw him and was filled with compassion; he ran and put his arms around him and kissed him" (Luke 15:20). The son then starts to give the speech that he has prepared, but doesn't finish it. He doesn't finish it because he realizes he has misjudged the character of his father and there is no reason to try to cajole him into giving him food when he has already freely and shockingly given him much more than that before he has even done anything to make up for what he had done.

Theologian Gil Bailie articulates well the spiritual dynamics of this story regarding the relationship between acceptance, judgment, and repentance: "Jesus seems to have understood that the only real and lasting contrition occurs, not when one is confronted with one's sin, but when one experiences the gust of grace that makes a loving and forgiving God plausible."[26] Unconditional love and acceptance prompt genuine repentance, which in turn enables reconciliation. Because of this, I have to think that this hug from the father hurt like hell. I suspect that in some ways it would have been much less painful for the younger son if the

25. Much of the following interpretation of this parable relies heavily on K. Bailey, *Cross and the Prodigal*, 37–90.

26. Bailie, *Violence Unveiled*, 208–9.

father had rejected him and made him work for his food. At least that way he could have been confirmed in his rejection of his father in the first place. The father's grace, though, compels the younger son to experience the judgment of love. He had acted so thoughtlessly and hardhearted towards him, and now the person he wounded so deeply has run out to hug him and kiss him. Perhaps the entrance to hell isn't a door with the words "abandon all hope" inscribed above, as Dante imagined. Perhaps the entrance to hell is the wide-open arms of a God we have rejected and resisted. Hell is when God shines the light of divine love on all the dark places in our hearts and lives and makes things so clear to us that we can't help but turn away from the darkness and embrace the light. Hell is being told by God, "You know that I hate some of the things you have done, but I want you to know in your heart of hearts that you have never stopped being my child, and I have never stopped loving you." This way of thinking about the pains of hell as the flames of divine love that are purifying and reformative allows us to take seriously the severe and stark warnings of judgment in the scriptures, while at the same time not compromising one bit the affirmation that God is like a loving parent who always wills only what is genuinely best for us. Theologian Jan Bonda wonderfully describes the effects of the judgment of love:

> Never is there any other purpose than that the unbeliever return to obedience to God . . . If we keep this singular purpose of God in focus, we understand that eternal punishment is punishment that has as its only purpose an obedient return to the God of love; it is punishment that leaves no other escape than a radical break with the past, the total loathing of the evil of the past, that prohibits a return to the former disobedience.[27]

I cannot point out enough that this is not a distinctively modern way of envisioning hell. I can imagine some readers at this point may be thinking that I am trying to reinvent hell to fit modern sensibilities, so let me point out again that this view of hell as temporary in duration and healing and corrective in function has very ancient roots in the Christian tradition. (In the next chapter I will argue that the New Testament itself has several passages that point in this direction.) Both Clement and Origen, two influential theologians in the early church from Alexandria, very powerfully and compellingly articulated a strong view of divine

27. Bonda, *One Purpose of God*, 219.

punishment as medicinal in function and intended to cure us of the disease of sin. Even though Origen's writings were later labeled "heresy," the writings of Clement and Gregory of Nyssa, who articulated a very similar view of the nature and purpose of divine punishment, were never subjected to this charge. As we noted in the previous chapter, Gregory of Nyssa has been treated with the highest respect in the Christian tradition. Gregory strongly believed in the reality of postmortem judgment, yet he believed just as strongly that God's punishments are always in accord with God's love for people. In his work *On the Soul and the Resurrection*, Gregory (who attributes his teachings in this book to his brilliant sister and teacher Macrina) compares the pain of God's judgment to the pain of removing a nail that has pierced one's flesh.[28] On his view, sin has penetrated the human heart and God's work in judgment is to purge the heart of all sin so that the person will be able to fully enjoy the blessedness of living in God's unmediated presence.

I find this analogy to be very illuminating. When I was a kid I climbed a lot of trees and haystacks in my grandpa's barn, and in doing so I frequently got splinters in my feet and hands. I dreaded having to go to my dad to ask him to get them out, and I sometimes thought he was being mean to keep poking around with his needle or knife even when it hurt and I asked him to stop. What I couldn't really appreciate at the time was that he would have been being mean had he not done all that he could do to get it out, because to leave it in could cause infection and much more harm in the long run. Likewise, while God's judgment may be experienced as torturous and painful, it is most fundamentally an expression of a divine love that refuses to let sin infect and destroy God's good creation. As the Scottish preacher and author George MacDonald puts it, "For love loves unto purity . . . Therefore all that is not beautiful in the beloved, all that comes between and is not of love's kind, must be destroyed. And our God is a consuming fire."[29] Because God is for people, God must be against sin, because sin corrupts and distorts people so that they cannot receive the joy that God wants to give. Hell, then, for the Christian universalist, is God's refusal to simply accept our rebellion towards God. It is God's rejection of our rejection. It is God saying "No!" to our "No!" to God.

28. Schaff and Wace, *Nicene and Post-Nicene Fathers*, 450–52.
29. George MacDonald, "Consuming Fire," 28.

I confess that I am often baffled when defenders of the traditional view of an everlasting hell say things like, "God will not tolerate sinners."[30] I know this doesn't sound very nice to say, but it really makes me wonder if they have ever paid close attention to Jesus's life. If one thing is abundantly clear about Jesus's life, it is that he not only tolerated sinners, he loved them, ate with them, and accepted them into fellowship with himself, to the chagrin of the top religious leaders of his day (Luke 15:1–2). If we believe that Jesus reveals God more than anything or anyone else, as Christians have always believed, then how can we ever come to the conclusion that God cannot tolerate sinners? The Pharisees were the ones who thought that God could not tolerate sinners, not Jesus and his followers.

God loves sinners and wants to be with sinners (people like you and me). What God cannot tolerate is sin, because sin harms and destroys the good purposes that God has for people. Because God loves sinners, God hates sin. God's goal is not to damn sinners, but to destroy sin, and the way that God destroys sin is by drawing sinners close to his heart of holy love which burns like a refiner's fire. This is why Jesus graciously offered friendship to sinners (and why he still does), because he knows that only in coming close to the divine heart of welcoming love can people be really transformed to want to leave their sin behind, and the only way for sin to really be destroyed is for God to enable the sinner to destroy it. As MacDonald writes, "The only vengeance worth having on sin is to make the sinner himself its executioner."[31] Jesus sought to destroy the sin in people's lives by welcoming them into a transforming relationship with himself, and in welcoming them into his presence he was drawing them closer to the heart of God. Jesus revealed a God who is hell bent on destroying sin, not sinners. Hell, for the God of love that Jesus revealed, exists not because God hates sinners or because God is powerless to reach into people's hearts. Hell is God's refusal to let sin win. Heaven doesn't exist because God is loving and hell doesn't exist because God is just. God's love and God's justice require the same thing: the absolute destruction of sin.[32] It is for this reason that God's justice is merciful and God's mercy is just.

---

30. Mohler, "Salvation of the Little Ones."
31. George MacDonald, "Justice," 511–12.
32. Talbott, "Just Mercy of God," 241.

Conclusion

I realize at this point that what we have done in this chapter is very limited. I have tried to articulate the broad contours of how a Christian universalist can envision the nature and purpose of divine judgment and hell, both in this life and in the age to come. But it still remains to be shown if this view has any substantial biblical support. In the next chapter, we turn to examining the New Testament to see if this view can be anything like what Jesus and his first followers held.

CHAPTER 3

A Hell of a Problem for Biblical Interpretation

Objection #2: "Universalists don't believe the Bible."

IN THE PREVIOUS CHAPTER, we began to explore a way of envisioning the reality of judgment and hell that refuses to dilute or distort the claim that God is love. A view of hell as temporary in duration and corrective and healing in its purpose coheres with the image of God as a loving parent that Jesus reveals. But, we face a big problem with this claim. Jesus also seems to have taught that the punishment in the age to come will be *everlasting*. The same Jesus who teaches that God loves God's enemies (Matt 5:44) also teaches that some will be thrown into "the fires that will never be quenched" (Mark 9:48). What are we to make of this?

The problem runs even deeper. While there are numerous statements in the New Testament that seem to suggest everlasting punishment, there are also numerous statements that seem to go in the opposite direction by pointing towards the ultimate reconciliation of all people to God. Instead of attempting an exhaustive examination of every relevant passage, we will instead look at the three strongest passages for both Christian universalism and the traditional view of hell. Before engaging in a closer look at these passages, it will be helpful to simply see the contrast between these sets of passages laid out before us.

Key Traditionalist Passages

> When the Son of Man comes in his glory, and all the angels with
> him, then he will sit on the throne of his glory. All the nations

will be gathered before him, and he will separate people one from another as a shepherd separates the sheep from the goats, and he will put the sheep at his right hand and the goats at the left. Then the king will say to those at his right hand, "Come, you that are blessed by my Father, inherit the kingdom prepared for you from the foundation of the world; for I was hungry and you gave me food, I was thirsty and you gave me something to drink, I was a stranger and you welcomed me, I was naked and you gave me clothing, I was sick and you took care of me, I was in prison and you visited me." Then the righteous will answer him, "Lord, when was it that we saw you hungry and gave you food, or thirsty and gave you something to drink? And when was it that we saw you a stranger and welcomed you, or naked and gave you clothing? And when was it that we saw you sick or in prison and visited you?" And the king will answer them, "Truly I tell you, just as you did it to one of the least of these who are members of my family, you did it to me." Then he will say to those at his left hand, "You that are accursed, depart from me into the eternal fire prepared for the devil and his angels; for I was hungry and you gave me no food, I was thirsty and you gave me nothing to drink, I was a stranger and you did not welcome me, naked and you did not give me clothing, sick and in prison and you did not visit me." Then they also will answer, "Lord, when was it that we saw you hungry or thirsty or a stranger or naked or sick or in prison, and did not take care of you?" Then he will answer them, "Truly I tell you, just as you did not do it to one of the least of these, you did not do it to me." And these will go away into eternal punishment, but the righteous into eternal life. (Matt 25:31–46)

If your hand causes you to stumble, cut it off; it is better for you to enter life maimed than to have two hands and to go to hell, to the unquenchable fire. And if your foot causes you to stumble, cut it off; it is better for you to enter life lame than to have two feet and to be thrown into hell. And if your eye causes you to stumble, tear it out; it is better for you to enter the kingdom of God with one eye than to have two eyes and to be thrown into hell, where the worm never dies, and the fire is never quenched. (Mark 9:43–48)

Then another angel, a third, followed them, crying with a loud voice, "Those who worship the beast and its image, and receive a mark on their foreheads or on their hands, they will also drink the wine of God's wrath, poured unmixed into the cup of his anger, and they will be tormented with fire and sulphur in the presence of the holy angels and in the presence of the Lamb. And the smoke of their torment goes up forever and ever. There is no rest day or night for those who worship the beast and its image and for anyone who receives the mark of its name." (Rev 14:9–11)

Key Universalists Passages

For as all die in Adam, so all will be made alive in Christ. (1 Cor 15:22)

Therefore just as one man's trespass led to condemnation for all, so one man's act of righteousness leads to justification and life for all. (Rom 5:18)

Therefore God also highly exalted him and gave him the name that is above every name, so that at the name of Jesus every knee should bend, in heaven and on earth and under the earth, and every tongue should confess that Jesus Christ is Lord, to the glory of God the Father. (Phil 2:9–11)

Evaluating the Key Traditionalist and Universalist Passages

Being faced with two sets of passages that seem to point in radically different directions, we have three interpretive options available:

1. Simply affirm that the Bible is inconsistent on this issue.

2. Take the everlasting hell texts as primary, and interpret the universalist texts in light of the everlasting hell texts.

3. Take the universalist texts as primary, and interpret the everlasting hell texts in the light of the universalist texts.

The third option has been the road less traveled throughout the history of Christian theology. Most Christians, historically, have opted for the second option, while many Christians today would probably feel comfortable going with the first interpretive option. Let's look more closely at each one.

The first interpretative option claims that the Bible is simply inconsistent in what it has to say about the afterlife. This option takes very seriously the deeply human character of the Bible, which is essentially an anthology of various kinds of writings from multiple authors that span over a very long period of time. It is certainly the case that the Bible is inconsistent if one tries to read it as a divine textbook dropped from heaven. It is a thoroughly human book, written not by God, but by lots of different people who, although inspired by God, remained real people writing in real places and real times and with the real limits that come from being human. Even some very conservative biblical scholars who will claim the Bible is "inerrant" will qualify this claim by affirming that the divine revelation in the Bible is accommodated to the limited and sometimes mistaken human perspectives of the biblical authors.[1]

This first option may be the right way to go. It is possible for biblical authors to have different views on various subjects. It is also possible that a biblical author, such as the apostle Paul, might change his perspective over the course of his ministry, thus leaving inconsistent statements in his letters. However, I don't feel comfortable settling for this option on this issue for three reasons. First, it isn't just that there are apparently competing visions of the afterlife in different documents in the Bible, or even in documents from one person (like Paul) over a long period of time. Apparent traditionalist and universalist passages appear in the same documents in the Bible. It seems that we should assume that a particular author did not intend to contradict himself in the same document. Second, if the New Testament were to actually teach two very inconsistent visions of the afterlife, this would leave us without much guidance as to which one we should take as more definitive. Finally, I do not think the first option is the most compelling because, as I will argue, the third interpretive option has the best explanatory power for accounting for the seemingly wide range of biblical passages on this issue.

Most Christians accept the second option as their default position. In fact, this position is so standard that much of the time people do not even realize that they are actually giving interpretive priority to some biblical passages over others. N. T. Wright, one of the most brilliant biblical scholars to ever live, charges universalists with criticizing "one part of scripture on the basis of another," yet on the very same page of his article he goes on to do this very thing by asserting that when Paul makes apparent universalist statements, these must be interpreted in the light of other passages that affirm judgment and divine wrath.[2] One of the

---

1. For a defense of divine accommodation in biblical revelation, see Sparks, *God's Word in Human Words*.

2. N. Wright, "Biblical View of Universalism," 55. This is a very early article and may

interpretive principles that has guided the church over the centuries is that the "obscure" passages in the Bible should be interpreted in the light of the "clear" passages. Most Christians have *assumed* that the everlasting hell texts are so clear that the apparent universalist passages should be explained in such a way as to not contradict the everlasting hell passages. Consider, as another example, how easily and quickly even a theologian such as Clark Pinnock, who was a brilliant theologian willing to challenge traditional biblical interpretations in several ways,[3] can simply assume that the hell texts take interpretative priority over and set the parameters for the universalist texts. He writes, "Although certain texts taken in isolation could imply universal salvation, the warnings that occur in the same books must influence their interpretation."[4] It is fair to say that this is the overwhelmingly dominant reaction most Christians who think about this have to the universalist texts. They simply cannot mean what they appear to mean because other texts warn of judgment and punishment. In response, we could point out that a universalist vision does in fact have an integral place for judgment and even punishment in the age to come. But, more importantly, we need to point out the initial arbitrariness in the decision to unquestioningly give priority to the apparent everlasting hell texts rather than the apparent universalist texts. After all, the universalist can just as easily say, "Although certain texts taken in isolation could imply everlasting punishment, the declarations of universal salvation that occur in the same books must influence their interpretation."

This dominant interpretive move that gives theological priority to the apparent everlasting hell texts is really not as obvious as many Christians have taken it to be. For example, if a biblical author did want to affirm universal salvation through Christ, how exactly could they say it any more clearly than Paul did in the three passages quoted above? Think about that: if these passages are easily dismissed in the discussion as not really affirming universal salvation, then what *would* it take for you to be open to the idea that a biblical author taught universal salvation? If Jesus wanted to reveal to us that God relates to all people with unlimited

---

not reflect Wright's current thinking. However, Wright continues to only interact with liberal versions of universalism that reject wrath and judgment altogether, and in his more current work he seems to be unaware of the several recent works arguing for a robustly Christian vision of universal salvation. See Wright, *Surprised by Hope*, 175–82.

3. His theology of "inclusivism" will be explored in chapter 5.

4. Pinnock, *Flame of Love*, 190.

compassion and unbreakable love, how could he say it any more clearly than to say that God "is kind to the wicked and the ungrateful" (Luke 6:35)? A thoughtful reader of the key biblical texts under discussion could easily argue that the apparent universalist texts are just as "clear" as the apparent everlasting hell texts. There is no compelling reason why the everlasting hell texts should simply be assumed to be the clear texts that set the interpretive parameters for the supposedly "obscure" universalist texts. The apparent tension between the two sets of texts must not be relieved by mere acquiescence to uncritically held assumptions of tradition. We need to explore the texts on their own terms, and then make a decision about which set of texts provides the fuller and bigger picture within which the other texts should be interpreted.

As I see the debate, the traditionalists and the universalists both have a difficult interpretive task set before them. To put it concisely, the traditionalists have to try to explain why "all" doesn't really mean *all* when it comes to who will be saved, and the universalists have to explain why "eternal" doesn't really mean *eternal* when it comes to the duration of the punishment in the age to come. I will argue that I think the universalist position is more exegetically sound and theologically coherent than the traditionalist position, but before getting there, it is important to see that both positions have a similar predicament. Oftentimes Christians of a traditionalist perspective seem to think that the Christians who have a universalist perspective have the burden of proof on them. But, as we have argued, there is no good reason to simply assume from the start that the traditionalist passages should be taken as primary and more clear than the universalist passages. Certainly the weight of tradition leads many people to quickly filter out the universalist passages without much thought, but this is not a fair way to proceed in examining these texts. We should be willing to set aside, as best we can, our preconceived and inherited notions of which texts are really "clear," and see which position can do the best job of accounting for the other set of passages.

Does "all" mean all?

Let's look at how people who go with the second interpretive option attempt to account for the apparent universalist texts. As mentioned above, the central move that they must make is to explain how "all" doesn't really mean *all* in texts such as the following:

> For as all die in Adam, so all will be made alive in Christ. (1 Cor 15:22)

> Therefore just as one man's trespass led to condemnation for all, so one man's act of righteousness leads to justification and life for all. (Rom 5:18)

Traditionalists usually insist that the second "all" in these two sentences cannot be interpreted as all individuals, because elsewhere Paul is clear that faith in Christ is necessary for salvation. This response is inadequate, though, because the Christian universalist can agree that trust in Christ is necessary for salvation, but maintains that ultimately all will come to a saving faith in Christ in the age to come. While we will discuss the possibility of "postmortem conversion" in more depth later, for now we should note that it is commonly assumed that the scriptures clearly teach that when a person dies their fate is sealed. While this theological conviction is strongly and commonly believed, the assumption that a person's fate is determined forever at the point of death lacks virtually any clear scriptural support at all. Often traditionalists quote this passage from Hebrews, "it is appointed for mortals to die once, and after that the judgment" (9:27), as if this settles the issue. Universalists agree that humans die once and face judgment. There's no debate there. The important question, though, is just what does the judgment consist of and could God's judgment actually make it possible for a person to repent and turn to Christ? So, pointing out that elsewhere Paul requires that faith in Christ is necessary for salvation does not go very far in limiting the scope of "all" in these passages. Paul can logically (and theologically) affirm both a response of faith *and* an affirmation of universal salvation *if* one doesn't rule out from the start the possibility of salvation opportunities in the age to come.

Also, there is no restriction on the word "all" that is indicated by the immediate context of these passages.[5] Todd Miles argues to the contrary that, "[The universalist] argument would be persuasive if Paul did not restrict the meaning of 'all' who are saved to 'those in Christ.'"[6] This is

5. Bell, "Rom 5:18–19 and Universal Salvation," 426–27.

6. Miles, *God of Many Understandings?*, 108–9.

very misleading. It is true that Paul does affirm that all that are saved are in Christ, but the text does not give any indication that this class of people is somehow more restricted than the class of people who are "in Adam." Miles, and many others, often read this assumption into the text. Indeed, Miles even changes Paul's wording in his discussion of this passage. Miles has Paul saying that all "those in Christ" will be made alive, but what Paul actually says is that "all will be made alive in Christ." The so-called restriction is not in the text, but in the theology of the traditionalist interpreter.[7]

Other traditionalists will grant that "all" means all individuals, but will then attempt to argue, particularly in the case of the Corinthians text, that being "made alive" does not entail salvation, but rather only entails a resurrection to judgment where nonbelievers will then be assigned to an everlasting hell. This seems difficult to maintain, though, since Paul offers a sharp contrast between humanity "in Adam" and humanity "in Christ." The Romans passage makes this clearer where life in Adam is linked not only to death as such, but also to condemnation, and life in Christ linked not only with the mere act of being resurrected, but with being justified and given new life. In other words, in order for the contrasting parallelism between Adam and Christ to have the intended rhetorical power, it seems as though what happens through Christ must be the opposite of what happens through Adam. Being resurrected in Christ only to be thrown into an everlasting hell where sin reigns forever doesn't seem to be much of contrast between being "in Adam."

One final attempt at explaining how "all" doesn't really mean *all* is to argue that Paul is using the word "all" in the sense of *all types of people* (all without distinction), not *all individuals* (all without exception). Particularly in the Romans passage, scholars point out that one of Paul's main points in this letter is to undercut any distinctions between Jews and Gentiles in the church. So, when Paul says "all," he is really saying "Jews and Gentiles," and not intending to refer to every human being individually. He simply means to say that all kinds of people are given justification through Christ, without implying that absolutely all individuals will

7. Miles also argues that Rom 5:17 places a restriction on salvation because it affirms that only those who "receive the overflow of grace" are saved. Ibid., 112–13. The universalist can grant that receiving this grace is necessary, but simply contend that ultimately all will receive it. Again, just because Paul states a condition for salvation it doesn't necessarily follow that it implies a restriction on the number of people who will meet that condition.

experience this. This line of interpretation is, in my view, the strongest way of approaching these texts from the traditionalist perspective. I agree that one of Paul's main goals in Romans is to help heal the divide between Jews and Greeks in the church, and I believe that one of his primary intentions in using "all" language is to point out that all kinds of people, Jew and Gentile alike, stand in need of grace and are offered that grace by God in Christ. However, while the distinction between *all individuals* and *all kinds of individuals* is conceptually valid, the bifurcation of these options in relation to this text cannot hold up under closer inspection.[8] In fact, it seems that Paul can emphasize that *all kinds of individuals* need and are given God's justifying grace only because of the more foundational claim at work that *all individuals* need and are given God's justifying grace. For example, while one of Paul's main goals at the beginning of Romans is to affirm that Jews and Gentiles alike are sinners, this wouldn't, and certainly didn't, preclude Paul from affirming that all individuals are sinners. "All have sinned and fallen short of the glory of God," Paul writes in Romans 3:23. Tellingly, traditionalists never try to argue that Paul doesn't have in mind all individuals in this passage. To force Paul into meaning either *all kinds of people* or *all people* is a false dilemma that ignores the logic at work in Paul's argument. "All kinds of people" is a consequence of, not an alternative to, "all" meaning "all individuals." If all people are sinners and all people are given God's justifying grace, then one can take from this the point Paul wishes to focus on in Romans, namely, that no one group has an advantage over another because all individuals are in the same boat.

As a review and further explication of the points raised above, let's think through theologian John Sanders's statement, which is a very common response to the "all" texts from Paul. In a reference to Romans 5:12–21, he writes, "He asserts that Jesus' act of righteousness produced justification of life for 'all people'—by which he means 'Jews and Gentiles alike,' without distinction. That is to say, salvation is available to all people regardless of race or geography."[9] While Sanders's interpretation is one that is fairly standard among those who deny the universalist thrust of this passage, it is highly problematic. He makes two unwarranted moves in quick succession that need more careful examination. First, he

8. See Gregory MacDonald, *Evangelical Universalist*, 78–90.

9. Sanders, *No Other Name*, 107. Through personal correspondence, Sanders has shared with me that he now thinks the biblical case for universalism is stronger than he once thought.

assumes, without argument, that intending to use "all" in the sense of *without distinction* necessarily excludes Paul from intending to use "all" in the sense of *without exception*. Again, I would argue that Paul implies the former precisely because he is stating the latter. In other words, "Jews and Gentiles alike" is implied by the fact that Paul refers to all individuals when he uses "all." This is exactly Paul's logic when establishing the universality of a sinful condition, and he appears to apply the same logic to justification. The second questionable move that Sanders makes after unjustifiably limiting the scope of "all" is to then claim that this passage is saying that salvation is only "available" to people of all ethnic groups. To interpret Paul as saying that justification is only available to all human beings, and not that all human beings will be ultimately justified, is to ignore the clear parallel Paul makes between the *actual effects* of Adam's sin on human beings (death and condemnation) and the *actual effects* of Christ's life of obedience on human beings (justification). Adam's sin didn't just make sin universally available for human beings; it actually affects all human beings. The logic of Paul's argument depends on what has happened through Christ being much greater than what has happened through Adam. If Christ has only made justification a present universal possibility, not an ultimate universal actuality, then the flow of Paul's argument makes no sense. If Adam actualizes death and condemnation for all, but Christ only actualizes justification for some, then it is hard to see how the gift of Christ is really greater than the trespass of Adam, as Paul claims that it is.

These, then, are the three major interpretive moves that traditionalists generally apply to the "all" passages in the New Testament that seem to point in a universalist direction. Each of these approaches has problems of their own. It seems very difficult to deny that when Paul says "all," he really means *all*. The other key universalist text mentioned above from Philippians now needs to be examined on its own. I would argue that this passage is the most clear and compelling scriptural text to envision the ultimate reconciliation of all to God through Christ:

> Let the same mind be in you that was in Christ Jesus, who, though he was in the form of God, did not regard equality with God as something to be exploited, but emptied himself, taking the form of a slave, being born in human likeness. And being found in human form, he humbled himself and became obedient to the point of death—even death on a cross.

> Therefore God also highly exalted him and gave him the name
> that is above every name, so that at the name of Jesus every knee
> should bend, in heaven and on earth and under the earth, and
> every tongue should confess that Jesus Christ is Lord, to the glory
> of God the Father. (Phil 2:5–11)

Most biblical scholars agree that Paul is actually quoting an early
Christian hymn here in his letter to the church at Philippi. Paul may have
written it himself, or someone else may have written it. (Scholars believe
it is a hymn because of its rhythmical prose form.) In this hymn, Paul
makes the claim that "at the name of Jesus," that is, when Jesus comes
again in glory and his name will echo throughout the universe, "every
knee" will bow and "every tongue" confess that Jesus Christ is Lord. Taken
at face value, it seems like Paul is clearly saying that on that day all people
will be drawn to confess Jesus is Lord. Some have tried to argue against
this straightforward interpretation by proposing that even though everyone will acknowledge that Jesus is Lord, this doesn't mean that everyone
will offer this confession *in a saving way*. They argue that some will simply
be forced to acknowledge this against their will, similar to the way that in
the Gospels we see that demons recognize Jesus as Lord, but they don't
profess a genuine faith in him as Lord. There are several problems with
this line of interpretation.

First, the verb that Paul uses which is translated "confess" (*exomolo-
geo*) is a Greek word that is used throughout the Greek translation of the
Old Testament, especially in the Psalms, in a way that always suggests vol-
untary consent, praise, and thanksgiving. If forced and inauthentic praise
is what Paul has in mind, then he picked a bad word to convey it. Also,
Paul explicitly uses the phrase "confess Jesus Christ is Lord" elsewhere to
describe conversion (Rom 10:9), and he unequivocally affirms that one
cannot "confess" this without the Holy Spirit (1 Cor 12:3). In addition,
Paul is quoting from Isaiah 45, where the context clearly conveys an authentic, saving confession[10]:

10. Isaiah 25:4 goes on to say that "all who were incensed against him shall come
to him and be ashamed." Some have taken this statement about the enemies of God
experiencing shame in God's presence as an affirmation that some will not experience
salvation. The text by no means requires this. As we have seen, universal salvation is
very much compatible with, and indeed requires, that some be brought to an experience
of shame over their sins so that they will want to leave them behind. The experience of
shame and the reception of salvation are not incompatible. See Bonda, *One Purpose of
God*, 203–8.

Turn to me and be saved, all the ends of the earth! For I am God, and there is no other. By myself I have sworn, from my mouth has gone forth in righteousness a word that shall not return: "To me every knee shall bow, every tongue shall swear." (vv. 22–24)

Third, how exactly could forced, inauthentic praise give Jesus Christ glory? This whole hymn is about God's self-giving and humble love revealed in the life and death of Jesus. The imagination must strain to read this as saying that God gets glory by forcing people, against their will, to worship him. This reminds me of a former roommate who was a college linebacker and would sometimes twist my arm behind my back until I said glowing things about him. A muscled-up yet insecure linebacker (if that person is reading this please be gentle next time you see me!) might take this approach, but it is impossible to see how a God who reveals strength by dying on a cross could get glory from a forced submission.[11]

It is very interesting that Paul expands on what he means by "every knee" by adding the line: "in heaven and on earth and under the earth." What does he mean by "under the earth"? His meaning isn't abundantly clear, but "under the earth" was the way that first-century Jews thought of the place of punishment in the age to come. As the New Testament scholar Fred Craddock writes concerning the message of this hymn, "There is no place in the universe, no created being, beyond the reach of the redeeming act of the servant Christ."[12]

The second interpretive option, as we have seen, attempts to offer *implicit* limits on what seem to be *explicit* statements of universal salvation. These attempts all have shortcomings, but it is up to you to decide if these are insurmountable problems or if there may be other ways of interpreting these texts in such a way as to continue to affirm an everlasting hell. Personally, I cannot find such a way to legitimately limit the apparent meaning of these texts. How a Christian universalist can interpret the key traditionalist texts in such a way as to fit in the universalist framework is yet to be seen. We now turn to that task.

---

11. Eugene Boring acknowledges that this kind of submission to Christ is alien to Paul's theology, but contends that the universalist conclusion is not necessary because Paul is not speaking of salvation, but rather the lordship of Jesus Christ. This distinction does not strike me as relevant since, according to Paul's theology, an authentic confession of Christ's lordship will lead to salvation. See Boring, "Language of Universal Salvation," 282.

12. Craddock, *Philippians*, 42.

Does "eternal" mean eternal?

We begin with the text that is seen throughout the Christian tradition as the most definitive statement in the New Testament of the reality of an everlasting hell, the parable of the sheep and the goats that ends with the ominous pronouncement, "Then he will answer them, 'Truly I tell you, just as you did not do it to one of the least of these, you did not do it to me.' And these will go away into eternal punishment, but the righteous into eternal life'" (Matt 25:45–46). At first this doesn't seem very promising for a universalist. After all, it clearly says that some will go into "eternal punishment." However, the word translated "eternal" is the Greek word *aionios*, and although it can sometimes mean "forever," in the sense of unending sequential duration, biblical scholars across the board acknowledge that it doesn't always mean that, and most often doesn't.[13] *Aionios* literally means, "pertaining to an age" and was often used by ancient Jews and Christians to refer to the age to come. In the ancient Jewish and early Christian way of envisioning the world, there are fundamentally two "ages." The current "age" is one characterized by death, suffering, and sin (Gal 1:4). The next "age" is when God's loving and liberating rule is fully realized and thus all sin, death, and suffering are overcome by God's healing grace and merciful justice. Scholars widely agree that *aionios* was used primarily in this context to speak of the age to come, without necessarily implying anything about the duration of that age. So, the last sentence in this parable should probably be rendered "punishment in the age to come" and "life in the age to come."

The Greek word for punishment used here is *kolasis*, which was used to refer specifically to remedial or corrective punishment. The late New

---

13. Romans 16:25–26 is one clear example where this word cannot mean unending duration. The same thing can be said for the Hebrew word *olam,* which is sometimes translated "forever" in the Old Testament. See, for example, Jonah 2:6. For a recent in-depth study of this term, see Ramelli and Konstan, *Terms for Eternity.* They summarize their exhaustive research by affirming, "*Aionios* corresponds to the uses of *aion,* which means a lifetime, a generation, or an entire age or epoch . . . in Christian writings, *aion,* may refer to the temporal age prior to creation, to this present world, or, most often, to the epoch to come in the next world. *Aionios* may also acquire the connotation of strict eternity, particularly when it is applied to God or divine things: here the sense of the adjective is conditioned by the subject it modifies" (p. 237). Millard Erickson, a highly regarded conservative evangelical scholar who is a supporter of the traditional view of everlasting punishment, acknowledges that "the adjective *aionios* may refer simply to an age rather than having its customary meaning of eternity" ("Principles, Permanence," 322.)

Testament and Greek scholar William Barclay pointed out that this word actually originally didn't have anything to do with punishment at all, but was an agricultural term used to refer to the practice of pruning trees so that they would put forth more fruit.[14] If this line of reasoning is right, then Jesus is saying that those who refuse to learn to love in this lifetime (love being something that shows up in tangible actions of mercy), will have to be taught a very difficult lesson in the age to come so that they will learn the value of bearing the fruits of love. Physicist and theologian John Polkinghorne makes this wise observation on this passage:

> We are neither wholly sheep nor wholly goat. Perhaps then, judgment is not simply a retrospective assessment of what we have been but it includes the prospective offer of what we might become. Perhaps judgment is a process rather than a verdict. Perhaps its fire is the cleansing fire that burns away the dross of our lives; its sufferings the consequence of the knife wielded by the divine Surgeon who wounds to heal. Perhaps judgment builds up the sheep and diminishes the goat in each one of us.[15]

If the basis for divine judgment is how we have responded to those in need, as Jesus says it is in this parable, then we must acknowledge that none of us are 100 percent sheep or 100 percent goat. We have all acted like sheep at times, and like goats much of the time as well. The line between sheep and goat really doesn't run between two separate groups of people; it runs down the middle of every human heart.[16] I have picked up a homeless man before and taken him to eat lunch with me, but just about an hour ago, on my way into the library, I turned away from a homeless man wanting help and I was filled with annoyance that he was even there. (My goat level is pretty high today.) The only honest way of interpreting and applying this passage to our own lives is to see that we are all a mixture of goat and sheep, of good and bad, and that Jesus is challenging us by saying that God's goal for us is to burn up the goat-like apathy and evil

---

14. Barclay, *Spiritual Autobiography*, 66. Barclay's proposal may be a bit one-sided. Some have argued persuasively that this word also carried more retributive connotations. However, even if Barclay's assertion is questionable, not much is lost from a Christian universalist's perspective, because a corrective goal for punishment does not preclude a retributive element. *Kolasis* could refer to a corrective punishment that is deserved. See the criticisms from Fudge, *Fire That Consumes*, 138.

15. Polkinghorne, *God of Hope*, 130.

16. See Bulgakov, *Bride of the Lamb*, 462.

within us and to enhance the sheep-like compassion and care for others in our lives. For some of us, this may take a lot longer than this lifetime.

The classic objection to limiting the duration of punishment in the age to come is that the word "eternal" cannot mean one thing when applied to "life" and something different when applied to "punishment." Put bluntly, if the punishment isn't forever, then life with God isn't forever either. From Augustine to today, defenders of the traditional view of everlasting damnation have seen this as a definitive rebuttal to those who would deny that hell is everlasting. Although this objection makes for a good rhetorical punch, there is little logical substance to it. Follow me here: although the age to come where God reigns is everlasting, that doesn't require that punishment in the age to come be everlasting. The punishment occurs in an age that is everlasting, but the punishment itself does not have to be everlasting. The duration of life with God or punishment from God is simply not the focus of the parable. We know from other scriptural passages that the life with God in the age to come is forever (1 Pet 1:4), and so our conviction of the eternality of life with God doesn't depend on how we translate the word *aionios* in this passage. To repeat, Jesus is here asserting a dual destiny in the age to come, but the duration of these two destinies is not addressed in this passage. *Aionios* can be taken here to simply refer to the next age, while leaving open the question of the chronological duration.

The forgoing discussion is not likely to convince everyone that this is the best way to interpret this passage. Although I think this exegesis is solid, I acknowledge that it is not a watertight case. So, let me offer another way of thinking about this passage that accepts the traditionalist interpretation of the meaning of "eternal punishment" as everlasting torment in hell. Even if these words are interpreted in the harshest sense possible as a retributive punishment that will last forever, it still is possible to avoid the traditionalist conclusion by arguing that Jesus is speaking in prophetic hyperbole in order to really grab the attention of his audience and to elicit a response of repentance from them.[17] Jesus stood in a long line of prophets who used very colorful and shocking language to break through to people and to get them to see the severity of their rebellion against God and the gravity of the consequences of their actions. The prophets didn't refrain from using the harshest sounding language

17. See Baker, *Razing Hell*, 134–35.

possible to describe God's pain and anger over the disobedience of God's people. Consider the following examples from Jeremiah:

> By your own act you shall lose the heritage that I gave you, and I will make you serve your enemies in a land that you do not know, for in my anger a fire is kindled that shall burn forever. (17:4)

> I am going to send for all the tribes of the north, says the Lord, even for King Nebuchadnezzar of Babylon, my servant, and I will bring them against this land and its inhabitants, and against all these nations around; I will utterly destroy them, and make them an object of horror and of hissing, and an everlasting disgrace. (25:9)

Based on these words from Jeremiah, it seems as though God will forever be angry at Israel and will punish them with everlasting pain and humiliation. But if we were to keep reading in Jeremiah, we would find the following a few chapters later:

> For the days are surely coming, says the Lord, when I will restore the fortunes of my people, Israel and Judah, says the Lord, and I will bring them back to the land that I gave to their ancestors and they shall take possession of it. (30:3)

What seemed so absolute and unchanging was in fact not absolute and unchanging after all. God did not give up on his people. But because the role of the prophet was to confront the people with the starkest and most shocking imagery available to them to help jolt the people out of their slumber of disobedience, they did not refrain from using even the language of "forever" and "everlasting" to describe the gravity and severity of God's wrath towards their course of sinful action.[18] But this language, while intended to be taken very *seriously*, was not meant to be taken *literally*. If it is taken literally in the sense of unending chronological duration, it contradicts the later word of the prophet that God is not finished with them. As Jan Bonda writes, "When Jesus refers to this punishment as eternal, he simply underlines, as the prophets had done, the total seriousness—the eternal seriousness—of God in pursuing his one and only purpose."[19]

---

18. For another example, see Isa 32:14–15.
19. Bonda, *One Purpose of God*, 219.

The hyperbolic and metaphorical use of this type of language from the prophets is not completely unfamiliar to us. When the person after church says, "The sermon seems like it went on forever today," she doesn't mean to make a comment about the duration as much as her experience of it, which in this case is that it was somewhat dull and boring. Language that seems to be about time can often function to describe *qualitative experience* rather than *quantitative duration*. Similarly, when a mom yells at her teenager, "You're grounded forever!" she doesn't mean that literally, but she does mean it to seriously convey the depth of her displeasure. In interpreting Jesus's "forever" language as hyperbolic language to be taken seriously, but not literally, we are not straining at all to reinterpret his meaning. This line of interpretation is deeply rooted in the prophetic tradition of the Bible, and it accords with more universal ways of employing this type of language rhetorically to drive home a point. So, even if one is convinced that in the parable of the sheep and the goats Jesus intends to describe the punishment as "everlasting," as opposed to "the age to come" as suggested above, it doesn't necessarily follow that Jesus intends this to be taken literally. After all, Jesus frequently employs shocking hyperbolic language to drive home a point, such as telling people to cut off body parts that lead them into sin. All of us, no matter how conservative, instinctively interpret teachings like that in the Bible as metaphor and hyperbole, because to take it literally seems absurdly harsh and unrealistically punitive. How much more should we apply that interpretive logic to the idea of a punishment that lasts forever! Sometimes taking Jesus literally results from not taking him seriously enough as a prophet and preacher who uses all the attention-grabbing and soul-penetrating images and words that he can find to captivate people and lead them deeper into the heart of God.

Speaking of attention-grabbing words, that leads us into the next key traditional passage.

> If your hand causes you to stumble, cut it off; it is better for you to enter life maimed than to have two hands and to go to hell, to the unquenchable fire. And if your foot causes you to stumble, cut it off; it is better for you to enter life lame than to have two feet and to be thrown into hell. And if your eye causes you to stumble, tear it out; it is better for you to enter the kingdom of God with one eye than to have two eyes and to be thrown into hell, where their

worm never dies, and the fire is never quenched. For everyone will be salted with fire. (Mark 9:43–49)

If you are perceptive, you will notice that I have added a verse to this passage since previously quoted. Oftentimes when folks from the traditionalist perspective quote this passage in support of an everlasting hell, they leave off verse 49.[20] This is exegetically indefensible, because this sentence begins with a word ("for") that connects it with the previous sentences. Jesus's statement that "everyone will be salted with fire" is intended to be an explanation for his previous warnings, and understanding it in this light can allow for a whole new meaning to emerge.

Jesus is warning people in vivid metaphors that if they do not take steps to cut off the sin in their life, however painful and difficult that may be, they will face a much more painful experience of judgment in hell. This passage gives us a window into how Jesus talked about hell (*gehenna*). He talked about hell in a much different way than most Christians and preachers. As mentioned earlier, hell is not used by Jesus as a *threat for outsiders*, but as a *challenge for insiders*. Anytime Jesus talks about hell, he is talking either to his own disciples or to religious people who see themselves as insiders. Jesus never once threatened hell as a means of gaining converts. Instead of scaring people into the kingdom of God, he loved people into the kingdom of God. Jesus used hell as a vivid metaphor for the kind of destruction that we can bring into our life and into the world around us if we let sin have free reign in our heart and life. *Gehenna* is meant to be a powerful challenge to cut our ties with sinful ways of living so that our lives don't end up fit for a garbage dump.

This is the only place where Jesus follows up a teaching involving hell by giving some sort of description of the nature of the punishment of hell. He says, "For everyone will be salted with fire." "Salted with fire" is a curious phrase, probably intended to be an image of purification. In ancient Israel salt was used as a purifying agent on sacrifices as they were burned and made holy for the Lord (Lev 2:13). Interestingly, Jesus says "*everyone* will be salted with fire." So, if purification is what is intended by this image, then Jesus is essentially saying that purification from sin will either happen now or it will happen later for everyone, and it will be much better for it to happen now than later. The deeper the thorns of sin are stuck into our hearts, the harder they will be to pull out and the

20. For example, Piper, *Jesus*, 35.

more it will hurt. All of us will need to go through the cleansing fire of God's holy love in order to be able to be at home in God's presence (1 Cor 3:10–15), yet hell can be spoken of as the most severe expression of this fire and the most painful experience of this perfect love that embraces us in the midst of our imperfections.[21]

Before leaving this passage, it is worth pointing out the arbitrariness with which most traditionalist scholars read this passage. I have never come across a conservative biblical scholar who attempts to maintain that we should literally cut off body parts and that there is a literal worm somewhere in the universe that will never die, but many conservative biblical scholars are willing to defend the idea that the flames of hell are literal fires that never go out. Why be so selective in a literal interpretation? It is fascinating how in the span of these short verses some think that Jesus is speaking hyperbolically and metaphorically about cutting off body parts and an eternal worm (remember, *gehenna* was a perpetually burning garbage dump, so this is where the imagery of worms and fire comes from), yet then maintain that he is slipping back into straightforward, literal language when he talks about fires that do not ever go out. It seems much more consistent, coherent, and compelling to interpret this whole passage as a serious warning from Jesus about the consequences of living out of harmony with God and God's good intentions for our lives that employs the most vivid images and language available for a first-century Jew.

The final key traditionalist passage we will look at in this chapter comes from the book of Revelation. Everything we have said so far about Jesus's prophetic use of hyperbolic images and metaphors needs to be remembered as we approach the most severe sounding hell text in the Bible, which is from the book of Revelation. The author, John, also claims to be a prophet who is writing in a style of literature known as apocalyptic writing, a genre characterized by otherworldly symbols and images. Here is the passage, again, that often gets used as a "killer" hell text:

21. This account of hell I am proposing is very similar to some contemporary Roman Catholic thinking about the nature of purgatory, which has shifted from a punitive to a more purifying function. See Rolheiser, "Purgatory Revisited." While Roman Catholic theology holds that the function and purpose of purgatory and hell are radically different, with the former being purification and the latter being punitive punishment, I am arguing that punishment that is merely punitive in nature (and especially endless in duration) is inconsistent with the claim that God's essence is love. For a rigorous contemporary Protestant defense of purgatory, see J. Walls, *Purgatory*.

> Then another angel, a third, followed them, crying with a loud voice, "Those who worship the beast and its image, and receive a mark on their foreheads or on their hands, they will also drink the wine of God's wrath, poured unmixed into the cup of his anger, and they will be tormented with fire and sulphur in the presence of the holy angels and in the presence of the Lamb. And the smoke of their torment goes up forever and ever. There is no rest day or night for those who worship the beast and its image and for any-one who receives the mark of its name." (14:9–11)

This sounds horrible because it is meant to sound horrible. John is writing this document to churches at the end of the first century in the Roman Empire that felt pressured to assimilate to the priorities and values of the empire, which would have involved things like worshiping the emperor (referred to as "the beast") and participating in the exploitative economics of the empire. For many Christians, it must have been a huge temptation to want to "fit in" the empire so as to have an easier life, or to keep having life at all! One of John's main goals in this enigmatic text is to motivate his fellow Christians to stand strong against the corrupting influences of their culture. He paints a picture of gruesome destruction and punishment to motivate his brothers and sisters in Christ to be fully devoted to Christ no matter what the cost. In saying this, I do not mean to suggest that John doesn't really believe in a judgment to come, and that he is just making stuff up to frighten people into conforming to Christian teaching. What I am suggesting is that John's vivid language in this passage (like the language used throughout the whole document) is meant to point towards the reality of judgment and the pain of infidelity to God without giving a literal description of what this entails. His "forever" language, like the language of the prophets and Jesus, is intended to be more *motivational* than *informational*. I realize that one cannot draw a hard and fast distinction between these two, because it is only motivating insofar as one believes it is informing one of the way things really are. However, the distinction is important because John's aim is not to provide a detailed blueprint for the afterlife; his aim is to tell people enough and in such a way as to illicit a response of repentance and obedience. To press the details for dogmatic definitions would be to press his writings to do something they were not intended to do.

It is also worth giving closer attention to just what John could mean by people being tormented "in the presence of the Lamb." Jesus Christ is referred to as "the Lamb" twenty-six times in the book of Revelation, and it is clearly the controlling metaphor for the message of this book.[22] The image is meant to highlight the vulnerable, humble, sacrificial, and self-giving love of Christ. Even though John uses traditional apocalyptic images of divine violence, the meaning of those images is deeply transformed and subverted by his central metaphor of Christ as the Lamb who was slaughtered (5:6). Christ is declared to be the conqueror over all forces of evil, hence the graphic imagery of violence. Yet, the way he actually "conquers" is through the non-retaliatory, sacrificial love put on display on the cross.[23] This is crucially important to keep in mind, because many people take this imagery at face value and conclude that the second coming of Jesus will be much different than the first coming. John Dominic Crossan, one of the most brilliant historical Jesus scholars of our time, puts the dilemma before us: "The First Coming has Jesus on a donkey making a nonviolent demonstration. The Second Coming has Jesus on a war horse leading a violent attack. We Christians still have to choose."[24] Fortunately, we really don't. Crossan misses the way in which the violent imagery in Revelation is transformed, not only by the central metaphor of Jesus as the Lamb, but also by the details of the supposed "violent attack" that Jesus leads. Even when Christ is pictured as a warrior on a white horse (19:11–16), it is highly significant that Christ's robe is dipped in blood *before* the "battle" (which is never actually described), indicating that it is his own blood, not that of his enemies. Also, the sword that he "fights" with is coming out of his mouth, indicating that actual violence from Christ is not what is being described. The judgment that Christ brings is the penetrating message of sacrificial divine love that can leave the hardest of God's enemies feeling "cut" to the heart. When read carefully, with attention to the details and to the central message of Revelation as the unveiling of the One on the throne as the Lamb that was slain (Rev 4–5), we are not forced to choose between competing conceptions of Christ's character. The apocalyptic Jesus is not the alter ego of the incarnational Jesus.

So, when we read this harsh and shocking language of people being tormented forever in the presence of the Lamb, we should not forget the

22. On the centrality of the Lamb metaphor for the theology of the book of Revelation, see Grimsrud, "Biblical Apocalyptic"; Rossing, *Rapture Exposed*, 109–14.

23. See Bauckham, "Language of Warfare."

24. Crossan, *God and Empire*, 218.

significance of how John invests new and fresh meaning into traditional apocalyptic images of violence by characterizing the One who sits on the divine throne as the slaughtered Lamb. What kind of torture and torment could come from being in the presence of this Lamb? I don't think John intends for us to imagine Christ undergoing a personality change in the age to come and turning into a sadistic tyrant who delights in torturing people. The character of Christ will always remain the same (Heb 13:8). The Christ who is revealed as a slaughtered Lamb that conquers with self-giving love will not become a bloodthirsty warrior that destroys with vindictive violence.

As I suggested earlier, I think the torments and the torture that will come to the unfaithful and the rebellious will be from being in the presence of perfect love while still being deeply imperfect. A clear vision of the Lamb, of the divine love that has never turned away from us, will make our turning away from God feel all the more painful and regretful. John's juxtaposition of torture images along with identifying Christ as "the Lamb" compel us to seek an interpretation that doesn't ignore either dimension. Traditional images of Christ torturing people simply ignores and denies the fact that even in judgment John refers to Christ as the Lamb, as the vulnerable, self-giving Savior. I strongly believe that our unfaithfulness will cause great torment to us when we are in the pure, unmediated presence of the One who is faithful and true, but this torment isn't something that Christ actively causes. It is simply something that happens when we are in his presence; and it is what we most deeply need, regardless of how painful it might be. John describes the risen Christ as having eyes "like flames of fire" (Rev 1:14). The grace in his gaze will burn away all that is false and deceptive within us and will destroy the masks that we hide behind. We will be fully known while being fully loved. Therein lies the pain of judgment, which will come from having the light of love shine brightly on the darkness of our sin. John Polkinghorne writes, "The concept of judgment as the painful encounter with reality, in which all masks of illusion are swept away, is powerful and convincing. It is also basically a hopeful image, for it is only in the recognition and acknowledgement of reality that there can reside the hope of salvation."[25] The torment that comes from being in the presence of the Lamb, I believe, is the torment of coming to see the futility and absurdity of our sinful

25. Polkinghorne, *God of Hope*, 131

ways, and the harm that we have done to others. The flames will burn as hot and as bright as they need to in order to purify us and restore us to God and one another, but they are flames of love, and although they may hurt like hell, they will fit us for heaven. The pain of coming to terms with reality and being compelled to see and feel the consequences of one's wrongdoing may be intensely torturous,[26] but it is a pain that heals and leads to hope, because restoration to God and reconciliation with others can only happen through repentance, and repentance can only happen when reality truly hits home.

One more thing about this passage that is important to see is that the book of Revelation doesn't end at 14:11. This isn't the last word about those who are tormented in the flames. To read this passage and to stop here would be like reading Jeremiah's warnings, stopping there, and not reading on to see the promise of restoration. John offers sharp warnings about the fate of the faithless, to be sure, but he doesn't stop there. As we will see, he goes on to offer a promise of restoration and reconciliation. When we turn to the end of Revelation, we find a most startling description of the heavenly city:

> And the city has no need of sun or moon to shine on it, for the glory of God is its light, and its lamp is the Lamb. The nations will walk by its light, and the kings of the earth will bring their glory into it. Its gates will never be shut by day—and there will be no night there. (21:23–25)

Throughout the book of Revelation the "kings of the earth" are presented as the ultimate bad guys. If John were writing a Western novel, the kings of the earth would be the whiskered guys wearing the black hats. In previous chapters, they are depicted as buzzard food at the banquet of the Lamb, their names are not found in the Book of Life, and so they are among those who are thrown into the lake of fire. Yet here we see them making their way into the heavenly city that has gates that are never closed. Why would the gates never be closed? In the spiritual geography of John's vision, there is the lake of fire and the heavenly city. That's it. It is hard to imagine that they would be open so that the inhabitants of the city

---

26. Although I wouldn't want to press the evidential value of this too much, this way of envisioning judgment accords with the experience of many who have had a near-death experience in which they experienced a "life review" where they felt the good and the bad that they did from the perspective of the other person. See Long and Perry, *Evidence of the Afterlife.*

could leave, so they must be open so that those in the lake of fire can make their way in. Since John is clear that nothing can enter the heavenly city without being cleansed of sin, this could reasonably lead one to conclude that the lake of fire ultimately has a corrective and purifying function.

Some would argue that the images of punishment in Revelation are very retributive, and so it is a stretch to imagine that the lake of fire is meant to be restorative. Here I think it is important to point out that we do not have to draw a hard and fast line between retributive punishment and restorative punishment. Even if one thinks that all of God's punishments have a restorative purpose, as I do, that doesn't mean that these punishments are not also severely painful and deserved by the person experiencing this correction. They are retributive in that the person really does *deserve* to have their illusions and self-deceptions ripped way so that they can see and feel the wrongness of what they have done, so that they will be in a position to repent and seek reparations and reconciliation. In other words, although it may seem strange at first glance to put it this way, sinners deserve to be reunited with God, because being reunited with God is what makes genuine and ultimate justice possible. To go back to the example given earlier, the man who sexually abused many children deserves to have his heart softened and his vision cleared so that he can fully know the depths of the horror and tragedy he inflicted on others. As I suggested earlier, this type of pain goes much deeper and is more intense than any pain that could be externally inflicted on him. This is why I said in the opening chapter that Christian universalism can actually envision a more painful destiny for Hitler than the traditional view of hell. On the traditional view, Hitler's heart remains forever hardened and his vision forever darkened. He will never really fully know the wrongness of his actions based on the traditional view. On the Christian universalist view, Hitler will be compelled to experience first-person the horror that he inflicted on all his victims, and he will be compelled to experience these pains so deeply because God will be working to soften his heart and clear his vision. What makes it possible for him to experience the worst pains imaginable is also what will make it possible for him to repent and be reconciled to God and others. As the philosopher Thomas Talbott puts it, "Only someone on the road of redemption, only a forgiven sinner, can fully appreciate the horror of even the most monstrous acts."[27] So in order

27. Talbott, *Inescapable Love of God*, 167. See also Moberly, *Ethics of Punishment*, 345–47.

for a person to be properly punished, on this view of justice, he must be brought to repentance.[28] God's active involvement in drawing people to repentance is not to be thought of as an activity that is separate from God's activity of punishing people for their involvement in wrongdoing, as is often assumed by many traditionalist Christians. God does not punish people *instead* of saving them from their sins, but, if the foregoing picture of divine punishment is true, God punishes people (by showing them the essential ugliness of their sins) *so that* God can save them. As the theologian Jurgen Moltmann puts it, "Transforming grace is God's punishment for sinners."[29] Retributive rhetoric and even vengeful images of punishment are not incompatible with a restorative goal to those punishments. One can take very seriously the harsh and painful images of punishment in the book of Revelation, and still make room for the hopeful and restorative goal of such punishments that seem to be strongly implied by the vision of the open-gated heavenly city.

All of this, however, assumes that God can ultimately enable everyone to choose God, and that people have freedom to do this not only in this life, but also in the age to come. Most Christians highly question these two assumptions. In the next chapter we will explore how humans can be really free if God is going to save all, and if there is any good reason to think that there is the opportunity to repent and choose God in the age to come.

---

28. This view of justice that has repentance and restoration as its goal is a deeply Hebrew and Pauline way of thinking of justice. See Marshall, *Beyond Retribution*, 34–93.

29. Moltmann, "Logic of Hell," 47.

CHAPTER 4

A Hell of a Choice

Objection #3: "Universalists deny human freedom."

CLARK PINNOCK, A CONTEMPORARY defender of the annihilationist perspective, articulates a central objection that many people have to Christian universalism: "How would it even be possible for God to save everyone if not by forcing some to be saved who do not want that? Some would have to be saved against their will."[1] Those who stand in the Arminian tradition usually make this objection because this theological tradition holds that human freedom is genuine and immensely valuable. They would hold that hell exists essentially as a monument to human freedom and that God would never create a system whereby all will be saved, because to do so will require God to override this freedom. This is something God will never do, because a relationship of love requires the capacity for free choice. So, since God can't ensure that all people will freely choose God, everlasting hell is a very real possibility. C. S. Lewis, one of the most influential proponents of this view of hell and human freedom, writes, "The gates of hell are locked from the inside."[2] On this view, God's hands are tied by the choices human beings make and God must eternally accept the consequences of human decisions to reject God. An everlasting hell, then, is a tragically necessary consequence of creating human beings with genuine freedom.[3]

1. Crockett, *Four Views*, 128.
2. Lewis, *Problem of Pain*, 127.
3. For contemporary defenses of this view of hell, see J. Walls, *Hell*; Sanders, "Freewill Theist's Response."

We should note that this view of an everlasting hell, while very popular today, is out of sync with most of the Christian tradition. That doesn't make it false, but I point this out because it is somewhat ironic that those who offer a free-will defense of hell often quickly accuse universalists of being heretics that go against the grain of established tradition. Universalism, however, has deeper roots in the Christian tradition than the free-will defense of hell. Throughout most of church history, the theological justification for an everlasting hell was a view of divine justice that required it as the retributive punishment for sinning against a holy God. Only in very recent times have theologians begun trying to justify an everlasting hell with an appeal to human freedom.[4] I am not suggesting that the free-will defense of hell should be dismissed because it is recent. In fact, if I were to hold to a belief in an everlasting hell, this would be the line of reasoning I would go with (and I did for several years). I am simply suggesting that those who embrace the free-will defense of hell should not be closed to a view like universalism simply because it is a minority position, since their position is very much in the minority as well, historically speaking.

Human Freedom, Postmortem Conversion, and the Bible

Christian universalism deeply values human freedom, so much so that it holds that God will not even take it away in the age to come. Freedom to choose God does not end at death on this view, as it does for traditionalists. In addition to extending human freedom in the age to come, the Christian universalist can also criticize the free-will defense of an everlasting hell for failing to take into account several important features about the nature of human freedom. In this chapter, we will explore how the account of human freedom offered in a free-will defense of everlasting hell fails to consider two very important things: the power of God to change a human will, and the inherently socially-embedded and constrained nature of human freedom. In other words, the free-will defenders of an everlasting hell do not give enough credit to the power of divine love, and they give too much credit to the power of human choices. Before exploring these two main contentions, though, it would be good for us

4. See Walker, *Decline of Hell*, 29–31; Blocher, "Everlasting Punishment"; Almond, "Changing View of Heaven."

to go deeper into the claim that human beings maintain the freedom to choose God even after death. Much of the Christian tradition assumes that death is the deadline for getting right with God, and if this is true, then the Christian universalist's case is destroyed, since obviously in this life not everyone is reconciled to God through Christ. But is it possible that there is the opportunity to choose God in the age to come?

Mark Galli, Senior Editor for *Christianity Today*, asserts, "There is no talk anywhere in the New Testament of people ever leaving hell."[5] Francis Chan and Preston Sprinkle boldly claim, "No passage in the Bible says that there will be a second chance after death to turn to Jesus."[6] While these are misleading overstatements (we have already seen in the previous chapter how the book of Revelation envisions the open gates of heaven and the "kings of the earth" making their way from the lake of fire into the heavenly city), it is certainly true that there is very little in the New Testament that explicitly points in the direction of postmortem opportunities for conversion.[7] It is also true that there seem to be some teachings of Jesus, especially several parables, which strongly deny the possibility of further chances for repentance. Jesus tells some parables, for instance, where the story ends with a powerful image of rejection that has a tone of finality, such as a door being slammed shut and people that are left on the outside (Luke 13:23–30). Isn't that a definitive message that there are no more chances after death?[8]

Not so fast, because Jesus also tells other parables where the "God-figure" doesn't give up looking until he or she has found what was lost (Luke 15). Some parables vividly and starkly affirm the reality of God's judgment, while other parables strongly and shockingly affirm the relentless compassion of God that transcends human barriers. When reading the parables of Jesus, it is of the utmost importance to remember that they were not intended to be mini essays in systematic theology. We cannot look at any one parable of Jesus and derive from it an all-encompassing theological vision. Jesus's parables function like jokes, in that they usually have one powerful "punch line," while the rest of the details are meant to

---

5. Galli, *God Wins*, 78.

6. Chan and Sprinkle, *Erasing Hell*, 35.

7. Of course, the converse is also true. There is very little that explicitly denies such opportunities as well.

8. See Tiessen, *Who Can Be Saved?*, 221.

support that central thrust. This is why it is dangerous to derive doctrinal affirmations out of the particular narrative details of parables.

For example, the parable of the rich man and Lazarus (Luke 16:19–31) presents the rich man in a state of torment in the afterlife from which he cannot escape, and this is sometimes taken to be Jesus's affirmation of the eternality of hell and the impossibility of someone leaving hell to enter heaven. Evangelical theologian J. I. Packer goes so far as to claim that this parable makes it "unambiguously clear" that hell is an unending source of "ongoing pain."[9] However, the point of this parable is not to provide details about the afterlife, but to criticize the religious people in this life who are greedy and apathetic towards those in need. Even Robert Peterson, a staunch defender of everlasting damnation, approaches with the caution that "we must be careful not to derive from this parable things God never intended," and encourages interpreters not to "press all the details of the parable, as if it were a detailed description of the afterlife."[10]

In this parable, Jesus is actually taking the framework of a well-known folk story to make a very direct point about how wealth is not a guarantee of divine favor and how refusal to help those in need reveals a heart closed off to God.[11] To take the narrative details of this parable and to use it to justify the traditional view of hell is misleading and inconsistent.[12] The parable of the sheep and the goats, for example, is often pressed into service to justify the eternality of hell, yet this parable also teaches that one's salvation is based on how one responds to people in

9. Packer, "Universalism," 185.

10. Peterson, *Hell on Trial*, 66.

11. See N. Wright, *Jesus and the Victory*, 255.

12. Even if, however, we do make the mistake of pressing the detail about the "chasm that is fixed" (Luke 16:26) as giving definitive information about the afterlife, it does not clearly or necessarily follow that this shows that there are no opportunities for salvation in the afterlife. This would only show that it is impossible for a person to leave hell before the purging work of the flames of God's love is finished. Since the rich man has clearly not repented over his sinful apathy and indifference to the beggar Lazarus (indeed, he still considers him as beneath him, as evidenced in the fact that he only thinks about what Lazarus can do for him and he doesn't address Lazarus directly), the fixed chasm "is a gap only in the sense that unrepentant sin constitutes a formidable barrier to salvation" (Bloesch, *Last Things*, 227). Universalists have no problem acknowledging that there will always be a great divide between God and unrepentant sinners, and that unrepentant sinners cannot leave hell, but hold that ultimately all will repent. Interpreters of this passage also need to take into account Rev 21:5, which clearly teaches that the gates of heaven will always be open.

need. By Packer's interpretive method, one could just as easily claim that the parable of the sheep and the goats makes it "unambiguously clear" that salvation has nothing to do with God's grace, but is something that is earned through acts of mercy. Parables, especially the narrative details, are shaky ground on which to develop or support an entire theological vision. They have very context-specific motivational goals, rather than providing timeless and general theological information.

Some of Jesus's parables were meant to comfort the afflicted, and some were meant to afflict the comfortable. Jesus's parables that draw a picture of a harsh finality are meant to motivate people to get serious here and now in living in tune with God and in harmony with God's good purposes. There is a time and a place for telling someone in a spiritual slumber as sharply and vividly as you can, "You have got to stop living this way. There is no more time to waste!" There is also a time and a place for reminding someone that God is patient and compassionate beyond belief. Jesus tells a variety of parables to address people in a variety of spiritual conditions. To focus on any one of them to the exclusion of the others distorts the depth and the breadth of Jesus's mission and message.

Although we will look at a few passages that directly suggest post-mortem opportunities for salvation in just a moment, it is important to see that the case for the possibility of postmortem conversion does not rest solely, or even primarily, on these few passages. The strongest argument for this possibility lies in the more general consideration of what the scriptures teach us about the character of God. Over and over again throughout the Bible we are told that God is a God of steadfast love, the kind of love that refuses to surrender or ever give up. Judgment followed by mercy is a consistent pattern throughout the biblical storyline, from beginning to end. In the beginning, Adam and Eve disobey God, but God doesn't follow through with the threatened punishment of death. Instead, in judgment God kicks them out of the garden of Eden, but mercifully makes clothes for them to wear as they leave. In the end, those who reject and rebel against God are thrown into the lake of fire, the flames of God's holy love, yet the gates to the heavenly city are then opened wide for them to come in.

Between these opening and closing visions of judgment then mercy, the biblical plot is filled with instances of this type of divine response. Perhaps one of the most startling examples of this in the Old Testament is the prophet Isaiah's vision of God's desire to reclaim and restore two nations who are the archenemies of God's chosen people: Egypt and Assyria.

> The Lord will strike Egypt, striking and healing; they will return to the Lord, and he will listen to their supplications and heal them. On that day there will be a highway from Egypt to Assyria, and the Assyrian will come into Egypt, and the Egyptian into Assyria, and the Egyptians will worship with the Assyrians. On that day Israel will be the third with Egypt and Assyria, a blessing in the midst of the earth, whom the Lord of hosts has blessed, saying, "Blessed be Egypt my people, and Assyria the work of my hands, and Israel my heritage." (Isa 19:22–25)

When the ancient Israelites heard this they must have thought Isaiah was crazy! Egypt and Assyria had ruthlessly oppressed the Israelites. Yet here Isaiah envisions a time when there will be a great event of reconciliation to follow God's judgment. Notice that Isaiah says that God will strike Egypt, but it is for the purpose of healing them and restoring them to a right relationship with God and his people. Egypt will not escape the just judgment of God, but this judgment has an ultimately restorative purpose. God refuses to give up on even the people who have brutally dominated God's own people. Isaiah is proclaiming that ultimately all people are God's people and God will not give up on them. Even though earlier in the biblical storyline judgment seemed like the last word for Egypt, it wasn't.

A similar instance occurs in the story of the city of Sodom. Sodom has become a virtual synonym for divine judgment because of the fire from heaven that we are told destroyed this wicked city (Gen 19:1–28).[13] Yet, what is less well known is that this was not God's final word for Sodom. The prophet Ezekiel spoke these words about their future:

> I will restore their fortunes, the fortunes of Sodom and her daughters and the fortunes of Samaria and her daughters, and I will

---

13. This story is the also the source of a long, yet unfortunate and inaccurate, tradition of referring to homosexual persons as "sodomites." The story involves attempted homosexual rape; it is irrelevant in discussions of the morality of homosexual relationships between consenting adults. If we read a story about heterosexual rape, we wouldn't therefore conclude that all heterosexual relationships are wrong. In addition, in later biblical tradition, homosexuality is not cited as being the fundamental perversity of the people of Sodom. Instead, inhospitality and violence towards marginalized people is given as the essence of their sin (Ezek 16:49). Ironically, then, the real "sodomites" are those who speak and live inhospitably towards gay and lesbian people.

restore your own fortunes along with theirs . . . As for your sisters, Sodom and her daughters shall return to their former state, Samaria and her daughters shall return to their former state, and you and your daughters shall return to your former state. (16:53–55)

Judgment was not God's last word for Sodom. Even through severe judgment, God desires to restore them. Some may object that the examples of Egypt and Sodom are about God's judgment towards nations in this life, not individuals in the next life. This is certainly true, because, as we noted earlier, ancient Israelites did not even have a strong and coherent belief in an afterlife for individuals. But these passages are relevant for our discussion insofar as they reveal to us the character of God and how God's judgment, regardless of how severe, is never the last word. There is judgment, then mercy. As James, the brother of Jesus, puts it, "Mercy triumphs over judgment" (Jas 2:13). Also, two New Testament authors actually took the story of Sodom as a "type" or foreshadowing of the judgment in the age to come (2 Pet 2:6; Jude v. 7), giving us scriptural warrant for incorporating this story into our theology of postmortem judgment. Just as judgment was severe, but not final for Sodom, so will judgment be severe, but not final, for those who in this life rebelliously resist God's truth and spurn God's grace.[14]

In the New Testament, we see the steadfast love of God take on flesh and blood in the person of Jesus of Nazareth. Jesus is consistently misunderstood, disobeyed, maligned, and ultimately killed by the people he has been trying to reach, and yet he never decides to strike back. Even after being betrayed and abandoned by his closest disciples, the risen Jesus doesn't choose to call new followers. This may be the most miraculous thing about the resurrection stories! Instead, he forgives and empowers his frail and fault-filled disciples with his life-giving Spirit to carry on his mission. When God becomes human it becomes abundantly apparent that there is nothing, absolutely nothing that we can do that can change God's heart of love towards us. We can mock and murder him, and he still longs to forgive us. The love of God in Christ is shown to be the most unbreakable substance in heaven and earth.

So if God's love is relentless, unstoppable, unchanging, unconditional, and never ending, then why will physical death change all of this? Take the tragic case of a college student who dies in a car wreck on the

14. See Bonda, *One Purpose of God*, 48–53.

way home from school. Let's suppose this young adult has become disillusioned with church and has decided that God is just a fairytale and that Jesus may have been a good moral teacher, but certainly not the Son of God who can work miracles and be raised from the dead. In other words, she rejects the Christian faith. According to many Christians, while she is alive God is filled with love for her and is doing all that God can to reach out to her and save her, but after she dies, all this changes and her fate apart from God is sealed. This strikes me as absurd, not to put it too bluntly. I can see no reason why a God of steadfast love will stop trying to reach out to a person after their physical death. Many early Christians couldn't either.

For the first four hundred years of the Christian church, many Christians believed that there would be postmortem opportunities for salvation.[15] St. Augustine effectively closed the door on such opportunities, and ever since the dominant Christian position has been that only in this life does one have the chance to choose God. It is interesting that the majority of Christians since Augustine have taken this view as so fundamental and even beyond question, even though there is little to no biblical support for the idea that death is the deadline for God's grace. The passages that are usually brought out to make this claim are those that affirm God's judgment for the individual after death. Probably the most frequently cited text in this regard is Hebrews 9:27, which states that "it is appointed for mortals to die once, and after that [face] the judgment." The assumption that passages like this clearly foreclose on the possibility of conversion after death is highly questionable. In order for it to do what the traditionalists claim that it does, one has to read into the text the idea that the result of judgment is an eternal separation from which there is no escape, which clearly goes beyond what the text actually says. Christian universalists have no problem affirming that people die once or that after death people face God's judgment. But universalists affirm that judgment is for the purpose of leading people to repentance and reconciliation with God. So quoting texts that simply affirm postmortem judgment does not suffice to limit the capacity to choose God to this life only.

15. See Trumbower, *Rescue for the Dead*.

Postmortem Conversion and the Age of Accountability

Most Christians, including those who would strongly deny the possibility of postmortem conversion, affirm a doctrine that has come to be known as the "age of accountability." This doctrine basically affirms that human beings are not under the judgment of God until, as it is put in the words of the Southern Baptist Convention's official statement of faith, they are "capable of moral action."[16] Today, there is a commonly held view, although nowhere officially defined, that this age of moral accountability is around thirteen years of age. Before this age, if a child dies it is believed that this child automatically goes to heaven.

I want to be clear that this doctrine makes all the sense in the world to me, and I am glad that most Christians now hold it. What makes it relevant in this discussion is that this doctrine is nowhere explicitly supported in scripture, yet most Christians embrace it out of a deep conviction that a God of love and justice will not eternally condemn children to hell. As Rachel Held Evans writes, "The age of accountability is a concept born from the compassion of the human heart, from a deep and intrinsic sense that a loving, good, and just God would not condemn little children or the mentally handicapped to such suffering when they could certainly bear no responsibility for their faith."[17] The belief in an age of accountability is ultimately grounded, not primarily in specific scriptural declarations, but in more general scriptural affirmations about the character of God and in our deep moral sense of what is right and wrong. In that sense, it is a doctrine with a similar status as the belief in the possibility of postmortem salvation. I am tempted to say that a belief in postmortem conversion and a belief in an age of accountability are on equal theological grounds, because neither is strongly and clearly rooted in an abundance of specific scriptural texts, while both depend on broader biblical convictions to support them. However, the belief in the possibility of postmortem conversion actually has stronger support in church tradition and scripture than the belief in the age of accountability. While there are no texts that can be used to directly support an age of accountability as most contemporary Christians conceive it, there are several texts that can be marshaled in support of postmortem conversion.

16. Southern Baptist Convention, *Baptist Faith and Message,* art. 3.
17. Evans, "Rob Bell."

Christians who easily and quickly dismiss the possibility of post-mortem conversion because of a lack of clear and direct scriptural support, and at the same time hold to a belief in an age of accountability, are being inconsistent in their scriptural criteria for theological truth. They are demanding a level of scriptural support for one doctrine that they are not for another. They are holding others to a standard that they themselves are not willing to follow. This is not only a logically fallacious way of arguing, but it also violates the Golden Rule.

As a case in point, consider some of the remarks made by Albert Mohler, a well-respected leader in the Southern Baptist Convention, on the issue of what happens to infants and young children when they die. He affirms that all "young children and infants" automatically go to heaven when they die, but he isn't content to acknowledge this simply as an implication of affirming that God is good and just.[18] He goes so far as to claim that he has clear scriptural support for this belief and cites in his defense Deuteronomy 1:39, which states, "And as for your little ones, who you thought would become booty, your children, who today do not yet know their right from wrong, they shall enter here; to them I will give it, and they shall take possession of it." This passage comes from Moses's first speech in Deuteronomy to the people of Israel as they are ready to enter into the promised land after forty years of wandering in the wilderness. As punishment for disobedience, the adult generation will be kept from entering the land, while the "little ones" will be able to enter since they did not know right from wrong, and so shouldn't be punished. Mohler claims that this passage "bears directly on the issue of infant salvation," because it shows that before moral awareness we are not punished for sin.

Before I offer some critical remarks about Mohler's inconsistencies, let me again emphasize that I have no qualms at all with Mohler's larger claim. I have been with parents when they have had to bury their little ones, and I am so glad that even most fundamentalist Christians today, contrary to much of our church tradition, hold that these little ones are safe in the arms of Christ. My problem is with the scriptural double standard that Mohler and many others employ regarding the issue of post-mortem salvation. When considering the proposal that people will have a chance in the afterlife to encounter Christ in a saving way, he quickly and decisively dismisses it by saying, "The problem with this position is

---

18. Mohler, "Salvation of the Little Ones."

that Scripture teaches no such post-mortem opportunity. It is a figment of a theologian's imagination, and must be rejected."[19] He claims that there is no scriptural support for postmortem conversion, while also claiming that there is direct scriptural support for an age of accountability. Let's revisit that support.

Remember, Mohler derives from Deuteronomy 1:39 the claim that "infants and young children" are not held morally accountable by God, and therefore automatically go to heaven. He doesn't offer an age at which someone stops being a "young child," and in fact, he claims that, "The Bible does not reveal an 'age' at which moral accountability arrives." What is truly fascinating about this claim is that Mohler is either ignorant of or ignores more specific information from Moses's speech found in the earlier version of Numbers 14:

> Say to them, "As I live," says the LORD, "I will do to you the very things I heard you say: your dead bodies shall fall in this very wilderness; and of all your number, included in the census, from twenty years old and upwards, who have complained against me, not one of you shall come into the land in which I swore to settle you, except Caleb son of Jephunneh and Joshua son of Nun. But your little ones, who you said would become booty, I will bring in, and they shall know the land that you have despised." (vv. 28–31)

This passage clearly considers the "little ones" to be anyone under twenty years old, not just infants and young children. I suspect that Mohler has ignored this version of Moses's speech because it doesn't accord with the way most Christians, himself included, have understood the age of accountability to be a much younger age. In the light of this passage, it should be clear that to take Deuteronomy 1:39 and make it support the age of accountability as it is most often conceived (applying to only infants and young children), is strained at best, and simply disingenuous at worst.

This little excursion into the way the doctrine of the age of accountability is defended by someone who strongly denounces the possibility of postmortem conversion has been to show that sometimes Christians operate with a double standard when it comes to theological beliefs. Mohler is clearly much more willing to bend scripture to fit his theological agenda than he is to even acknowledge the potential scriptural

19. Ibid.

support that does exist for a theological claim of which he disagrees. Of course, this is something that all of us are susceptible to, and I don't at all mean to attribute intentionally deceptive motives to Mohler. Once we get a theological conviction locked into place in our minds, it becomes very easy for us to filter out any scriptural affirmations that go against our convictions, as well as to see support for our convictions in scriptures that really may have nothing to do with them. This is very important to keep in mind as we think about the Bible and the possibility of postmortem conversion. Many of us have been trained to filter out these passages or immediately interpret them in such a way as to support our prior conviction of the denial of this possibility.

I have brought up the issue of the age of accountability as a way of helping us get this in a proper perspective. Because most of us who have grown up in church have been conditioned to think that there is an age of accountability, we are willing to take one passage that is extremely loosely connected to the doctrine and claim it as direct support. On the other hand, we have also been so conditioned to think that death is the deadline for accepting God's grace, that when we run across the handful of passages that seem to deny that, we are willing to explain them away in a hurry. Those who believe in an age of accountability (which is virtually all Christians today) shouldn't be so quick to dismiss the hope of salvation opportunities in the life to come. As we'll see, even though the possibility of postmortem conversion is not one of the most consistently and clearly revealed truths in the scriptures, it is rooted in the same theological and moral intuitions that gave rise to the belief in an age of accountability, and it actually contains much stronger scriptural roots.

Scriptural Affirmations of Postmortem Conversion

Having made the point that God's character of steadfast love seems in and of itself to point towards the possibility of a postmortem conversion, we can go on now to look at the handful of texts in the New Testament that seem to endorse this possibility. We have already looked at one of these texts from Revelation that envisions a heavenly city where the gates are never closed (21:25), strongly implying that it is possible for those on the outside in the lake of fire to come in. This is perhaps the most significant text to be brought to bear on this issue, yet it is often dismissed all too easily. Revelation also affirms that God will one day unite heaven and earth and will "make all things new" (21:5). Many people argue that since Revelation speaks of the lake of fire burning forever, that it is clear that not all will enter through the open gates, and so not all things will actually be renewed and restored. In addition to the considerations in the previous chapter about the rhetorical power of metaphorical uses of "forever" language, we should note that this logic of interpretation is arbitrarily applied to the texts. One can just as easily argue the reverse position, namely, that since Revelation asserts that all things will be restored to God, the passages asserting that the lake of fire last forever cannot be taken literally. While I would not go so far as to say that Revelation unequivocally and unambiguously affirms universal salvation, it undeniably at least holds up as a possibility, and along with that possibility, the opportunity to turn to God after death. Keep in mind that in addition to the scriptural passages we are about to look at, the passages we have already examined that seem to support Christian universalism, also implicitly support a belief in postmortem conversion. If all are going to be saved through Christ, and since it is obvious that not all come to explicitly know Christ in this life, then it follows that there will be a saving encounter with Christ in the age to come.

There are two related texts in the New Testament that many traditionally believe to be the foundational biblical support for the belief that there will be opportunities for receiving salvation in the afterlife. These passages are found in 1 Peter:

> For Christ also suffered for sins once for all, the righteous for the unrighteous, in order to bring you to God. He was put to death in the flesh, but made alive in the spirit, in which also he went and made a proclamation to the spirits in prison, who in former times did not obey, when God waited patiently in the days of Noah, during the building of the ark, in which a few, that is, eight persons, were saved through water. (3:18–20)

> For this is the reason the gospel was proclaimed even to the dead, so that, though they had been judged in the flesh as everyone is judged, they might live in the spirit as God does.[20] (4:6)

20. The New International Version translates this as "For this is the reason the gospel was preached even to those who are now dead." The NIV Study Bible acknowledges that translators added the word "now," which isn't originally in the text. They reason that it is necessary to add this word so that the verse doesn't have the impression of allowing for

There is hardly anything noncontroversial about these passages, and if this were all we had to go on to support the possibility for conversion in the afterlife, then the argument would admittedly be weak. While I think that the best argument for such a possibility is the broader consideration of the character of God's steadfast love, these passages are not without some force of their own. There is tremendous debate among biblical scholars about the precise meaning of these passages, and the prospect of a consensus seems impossible.[21] The three main interpretive questions can be summed up like this: To whom did Christ preach? What was the effect of the preaching? Was this a one-time event or something that continues to happen? Multiple answers have been given to each question, and those various answers have been put together in different ways to draw diverse overall messages from this passage. If you ever read someone claiming what "all scholars agree on" about this passage, they are making it up, I promise you. All scholarly commentators on this passage, wherever they are on the theological spectrum, acknowledge that this passage is one of the most opaque and difficult to interpret in the New Testament. Any honest interpreter of this passage will add their agreement with the evaluation given by Martin Luther: "This is a strange text and certainly a more obscure passage than any other passage in the New Testament. I still do not know for sure what the apostle meant."[22]

We will not wade into all of the details of the debate, because I am not arguing that this passage must be interpreted along the lines of Christ offering salvation to people in hell. However, I do think that one can legitimately interpret this passage from 1 Peter as teaching this. This interpretation enjoys as much scholarly support as any of the others, and it is in accordance with a very large branch of church tradition going back to the beginning of the church that has concluded from these texts that the

---

opportunities for salvation in the afterlife, which is clearly wrong in their view. On this interpretation, the people preached to were alive, but now they are dead. This is simply a case where a prior theological conviction not only distorts the interpretation of a text, but it actually leads translators to add a word in order to make it say what they think it should say. Of course the Bible doesn't offer us the hope for salvation in the afterlife if the verses that point in that direction are changed!

21. For the historical range of interpretations and theological directions taken with these passages, see Pitstick, *Light in Darkness*, 30–60; Trumbower, *Rescue for the Dead*, 91–108; Alfeyev, *Christ the Conqueror of Hell*, 43–104; MacCulloch, *Harrowing of Hell*, 45–66.

22. Quoted in Clark-Soles, *Death and the Afterlife*, 192.

author is making an affirmation of the rescuing power of Christ to reach even into the depths of hell.[23]

With the previous caveats in mind about the interpretive difficulties of this passage, let me briefly share why I think that this passage teaches the decent of Christ into hell for the purpose of proclaiming the gospel to set people free. That Peter speaks of the "patience" of God, uses the term "gospel," and describes Christ's activity in the prison as that of "proclamation," a word that is used throughout the New Testament to describe preaching the gospel for the purpose of conversion, all fit together nicely with the interpretation I am proposing.[24] The only detail that seems to throw off this way of looking at it is the reference to the generation of Noah. Did Christ just preach to that generation, and, if so, why? It turns out, though, that what at first seems a weakness of this line of interpretation is actually a sign of its strength and coherence. The generation of Noah came to be regarded in ancient biblical tradition as the most-wicked generation ever with no chance of finding redemption. The flood was seen as a definitive sign of its hopelessness. In naming this generation in particular, Peter seems to be affirming that there is absolutely no group of people outside the scope of God's will to save. If there is hope for them, there is hope for anybody!

Besides the details of this specific passage cohering well with this interpretation, it also fits integrally with what comes after, and with the overall message of this section of the letter. Right after Peter mentions the generation of Noah, he says that the flood "prefigures" the Christian practice of baptism (3:21). While the flood was seen originally as a sign of judgment alone, Peter says that the flood, like baptism, ultimately had a restorative purpose—to wash away the dirt of sin. The flood was a sort of "baptism" by which those in Noah's generation were "put to death in the flesh but made alive in the spirit" (4:6), which happens now in the life of the baptized believer. This interpretation also can cohere with the general thrust of this section of the letter, which is to give courage and hope to

23. Archbishop Hilarion Alfeyev argues persuasively that the majority of the Eastern fathers embraced this interpretation. See his *Christ the Conqueror of Hell*, 43–81.

24. See the discussion and list of New Testament references in Sanders, *No Other Name*, 187. William Dalton argues that Jesus's proclamation (kerysso) doesn't necessarily mean to preach for the purpose of conversion, but can simply refer to the announcement of judgment. Dalton, *Christ's Proclamation*, 158. I believe this interpretation relies too much on pressing the analogy of Noah's purpose in preaching, and not enough on how this word is regularly and consistently employed by New Testament authors.

Christians who are suffering persecution for their proclamation of the gospel. Peter is saying, in effect, "You may be going through hell, but don't forget that Christ has been through hell and he didn't stop preaching!" So, while other interpretations have been strongly advanced and widely accepted, I believe this one makes the most sense.

This passage has been the foundational and primary scriptural basis for the doctrine of Christ's descent into hell, a doctrine that, while controversial, has been a firmly entrenched feature of Christian theology throughout history. The Apostles' Creed for much of its history has included an affirmation of the belief that "he was crucified, died, and was buried. He descended into hell. On the third day he rose from the dead." The line concerning Christ's descent has unfortunately been removed from many modern editions of the creed, and so many Christians do not affirm it in worship. There has always been debate about this line in the creed. The Apostles' Creed, unlike the Nicene Creed, was never affirmed and codified at an ecumenical council. In all probability, it began its life as a baptismal creed in Rome in the mid-second century, and evolved over a period of several centuries. Church historians point out that this line is not included in many of the early versions of the creed, and when it was included there was always some debate about exactly what it meant.[25] Some interpreted it as simply describing the hellish suffering Christ endured on the cross, while others interpreted it as just a redundant way of saying that Christ really died, without implying an actual "visit" to hell.

It is highly unfortunate that this line has simply been removed because of its interpretive difficulties. For much of church history, this was seen as an affirmation of the all-encompassing nature of Christ's victory over the forces of evil and sin. Not even in hell are people outside the rescuing and saving power of Christ. One of the pieces of evidence that the early Christians held to this hope in the power of Christ to break through the gates of hell is found in the catacombs in Rome where the dead were buried. Christians often drew art on the walls of the catacombs to express their faith, and several paintings have been discovered that depict Christ as the Good Shepherd. What is startling is that some of them

---

25. Although, some argue that the early Roman baptismal creed might have contained such a line. This line of argument depends on 1 Peter being written in Rome and influencing the development of the baptismal creed. See Scaer, "He Did Descend To Hell," 94.

depict Christ, not with a sheep on his shoulders, but a goat.[26] Although the significance of this shouldn't be overblown to say that this necessarily reflects the belief of most Christians at that time, it also shouldn't be underestimated. The belief in Christ's power to save "goats" in the age to come was a live option for the early Christians, and a belief in Christ's descent into hell was one of the ways they expressed that hope.

The practice of praying for the dead was also a common feature in a wide variety of early church liturgies, which supports the idea that most Christians did not believe death was a firm barrier to God's grace and the cutoff for the opportunity to repent and seek moral and spiritual transformation.[27] There is also strong evidence of the early Christian belief that Christ can rescue people from the depths of hell found in the earliest extant Christian hymnbook from the early second century called the Odes of Solomon.[28] Ode 42:10–20, the last hymn in the collection, very beautifully describes Christ's descent into hell in the first person:

> I was not rejected although I was considered to be so, and I did not perish although they thought it of me . . . I made a congregation of the living among his dead; and I spoke with them by living lips; in order that my word may not fail. And those who had died ran toward me; and they cried out and said, "Son of God, have pity on us. And deal with us according to your kindness, and bring us out from the chains of darkness . . . May we also be saved with you, because you are our Savior." Then I heard their voice, and placed their faith in my heart. And I placed my name upon their head, because they are free and they are mine. Hallelujah.[29]

While, of course, there isn't good reason to think this is a transcript of what Christ actually said, it very powerfully articulates the early and widespread Christian hope that the freedom to repent and turn to Christ doesn't end at death, and it poetically conveys the deep conviction that Christ is Lord over all realms of reality, hell included.

The belief in Christ's descent into hell to offer salvation to those imprisoned there has played a much larger role in the Eastern Orthodox Church's theology of the afterlife than it has in the Roman Catholic and Protestant churches of the West. In the iconography of the Eastern

---

26. Hanson, *Universalism*, 21.

27. See Sanders, *No Other Name*, 182–83; Von Balthasar, *Dare We Hope?*, 48–49.

28. See Trumbower, "Early Visions of Hell," 31.

29. Charlesworth, *Old Testament Pseudepigrapha*, 771.

Church, Christ's rescue mission into hell is depicted as integral to the saving significance of Christ's death and resurrection. Eastern Orthodox Archbishop Hilarion Alfeyev, after surveying the broad and deep support of early church theologians for an understanding of Christ's decent into hell as signifying an offer of salvation for all in the age to come, concludes by writing,

> On the basis of what has been said above, we may say that after death the development of the human person does not cease, for existence after death is not a transfer from a dynamic into a static being, but rather continuation on a new level of that road which a person followed in his lifetime . . . We do not know if everyone followed Christ when He rose from hell. Nor do we know if everyone will follow Him to the eschatological Heavenly Kingdom when He will become "all in all." But we do know that since the descent of Christ into Hades the way to resurrection has been opened for "all flesh," salvation has been granted to every human being, and the gates of paradise have been opened for all those who wish to enter through them. This is the faith of the Early Church inherited from the first generation of Christians and cherished by Orthodox Tradition. This is the never-extinguished hope of all those who believe in Christ Who once and for all conquered death, destroyed hell and granted resurrection to the entire human race.[30]

A belief in Christ's descent to hell to preach the gospel doesn't necessarily lead to a universalist conclusion, but it does set forth the possibility. At a minimum, it affirms the genuinely universal offer of salvation to all people who have ever lived, not just those who have received the Christian gospel in this life.[31] In the words of the German theologian Wolfhart Pannenberg, "The meaning of the Christian acknowledgement of the conquest of the kingdom of death and Jesus Christ's descent into hell lies in the universal scope of salvation."[32] This scriptural and creedal affirmation of Christ's descent, though admittedly surrounded by controversy and ambiguity, points us in the direction of a hope in the power of Christ to redeem anyone from the grips of sin and death.

30. Alfeyev, "Descent of Christ."

31. I can see no reason to limit the scope of Christ's offer of salvation to the righteous in the Old Testament, as has been done for most of the Roman Catholic tradition, especially since 1 Peter emphasizes that Christ went to preach to the dead who were disobedient.

32. Pannenberg, *Apostles' Creed*, 95.

The conviction that there is no realm of existence in which Christ cannot break through with saving grace and healing justice is not limited to these two passages alone. It is also found in the writings of the apostle Paul:

> (When it says, "He ascended," what does it mean but that he had also descended into the lower parts of the earth? He who descended is the same one who ascended far above all the heavens, so that he might fill all things.)[33] (Eph 4:9–10)

Although there is some debate about what exactly Paul means by "lower parts of the earth," one reasonable interpretation is that he is referring to the place of punishment for the dead, since within his religious worldview we live in a three-tiered universe of heaven-earth-hell. Likewise, John also affirms that Christ has the power to reach into the depths of hell:

> I was dead, and see, I am alive forever and ever; and I have the keys of Death and of Hades. (Rev 1:18)

While I agree with C. S. Lewis that the gates of hell are locked from the inside, I also agree with John that Christ has the power to open those gates with the keys of his omnipotent love.[34] If Christ has conquered the power of death, as all Christians believe, then why still hold that death can keep a person from Christ? To refuse to believe that a person can come into a saving relationship with Christ in the age to come is to deny the foundational truth of the gospel that nothing, not even death, can separate us from the love of God in Christ Jesus (Rom 8:35–39). Such a refusal does not take seriously enough the victory over death that was achieved in Christ's resurrection. Because the tomb is empty, to assume that death is the deadline for grace gives death a power that it no longer has.

I fully realize that this discussion of the possibility for human beings to retain the freedom and the opportunity to choose God in the life to come is not sufficient to make it a watertight case. But I do believe that

---

33. See also Rom 10:7.

34. Although "Hades" originally referred to simply the realm of the dead, without necessarily implying a place of punishment, by the New Testament period it kept this general meaning while also acquiring the more specific meaning of a place of postmortem punishment, and it is that more specific sense that is probably intended in this passage. One of the stronger arguments for this is that if John only meant the realm of the dead in a more generic sense, then he would be redundant by stating "of Death and of Hades."

these considerations show that the denial of this possibility is far from being as clear as some detractors would make it seem. For authors to assert that there is nothing in the New Testament to support this claim is simply and demonstrably false. Besides the deeply important and more general consideration of the steadfast nature of divine love, there are several texts across the writings of Peter, Paul, and John that have traditionally been and can still be reasonably and faithfully interpreted as affirming the reality that the saving power of Christ is not bound by the power of death, and that human beings retain the freedom to turn away from themselves and turn towards God in the life to come.

Human Freedom and Divine Power

Christian universalism goes further than just claiming that it is possible for people to enter into a saving encounter with Christ in the life to come; it affirms that ultimately everyone will experience such a saving encounter with Christ. But if human beings are free, then how can God ensure that this will happen without violating human freedom? Contemporary philosopher and Christian apologist William Lane Craig makes the point starkly,

> Those of us who have unbelieving family and friends no doubt often feel that if they will not freely give their lives to Christ, it would be worth it if God would simply overpower their wills and save them in spite of themselves . . . But as strong as such feelings are, they do not change the fact that such an action on God's part amounts to salvation by divine rape. For God to subvert the will of someone who chooses to reject His grace would be to violate their personhood; and that God necessarily will not do.[35]

For Craig, it seems that the only way he can envision God bringing about the salvation of all would be to force himself on people who want nothing to do with him, and this would amount to divine rape. J. I. Packer asserts that in order for universalism to be true, God would have to "brainwash" many people.[36] This objection that God must use illegitimate force in order to save all is one that is repeated consistently in the literature dealing with this topic, both in scholarly and popular works. It certainly has at least a

---

35. Craig, "Talbott's Universalism Once More," 502.
36. Packer, "Universalism," 174.

surface-level degree of plausibility to it. We all know that a relationship of love must be entered into freely, and that a love that is forced is really no love at all. We simply cannot make people love us. Love is a risk, whereby one party extends an invitation that must be embraced by the other. Most of us know to some extent the pain and frustration of rejection, and our ultimate inability to control the response of other people towards us. This type of human experience makes it seem reasonable to assume that God also is bound by the freedom of others and cannot ensure that someone will embrace the divine love revealed in Christ with a positive response.

This objection, however, suffers from what I see as a fatal flaw. It fails to take into account important features of the psychology of religious conversion. God isn't limited to forcing people against their will to repent and be reconciled to him. God has the power, according to mainstream Christian theology, to change the human will to see the ugliness and destructiveness of sin, and to turn away from it and embrace the grace that is freely given by God. Take the apostle Paul, for example. On the road to Damascus, as he is on his way to persecute Christians, Christ reveals himself to Paul in such a way as to cause Paul to see the harm that he is doing and the pain that he is causing Christ (Acts 9:1–19). This compels him to turn away from his violent way of life and open himself up to the light of Christ's forgiveness and empowerment to become a new person (2 Cor 5:17). Paul wasn't seeking to choose Christ. He had chosen to reject Christ and to try to stamp out those who had accepted Christ as the Messiah.

So, to those who say that God cannot ensure that someone will choose God, I ask them this: Did God do something wrong to Paul on the road to Damascus? Did God "rape" or "brainwash" Paul? I don't think so. Out of love, God overwhelmed Paul with a vision of truth that left Paul in repentance and a desire to love Christ. Christ didn't make Paul love him and serve him against his will; he changed his will to set him free to want to love and serve him. If God can do this for Paul, this hardened murderer of Christians who scripture says is the "chief of all sinners" (1 Tim 1:15), then why can't God do this for anyone? According to John the revelator, when Christ returns, "every eye will see him, even those who pierced him; and on his account all the tribes of the earth will wail" (Rev 1:7). John seems to be affirming that God will ultimately do for all people who remain hardened to God exactly what God did for Paul. Just as God gave Paul a powerful vision of the pain that he was causing God and the love that God still had for him, so God will ultimately reveal to all the crucified love of God that is pierced and wounded by our sins. This vision of God's vulnerable and sacrificial love will both judge and melt the hardest of hearts from all tribes and cause people to cry out in repentance to be cleansed.[37] It is true that the word "wail" itself doesn't necessarily have connotations of repentance, and can even possibly refer to the kind of grief that comes from destructive judgment (as it does in Rev 18:9). However, the Old Testament context that John is drawing from for this image settles the issue of what kind of "wailing" is mentioned here. John is drawing from Zechariah 12:10—13:9, which makes clear that the kind of "wailing" that is being spoken of is that which comes from being broken over sin and desiring the cleansing grace of God. John doesn't change the meaning of the original passage in Zechariah, but he does universalize it. In the original passage only the house of David will wail, but in John's vision this becomes "a pointer to the conversion of the nations."[38]

When we think about how God could bring it about that all would ultimately choose to repent and be reconciled to God, we are not limited to thinking that God will have to twist people's arms behind their backs or beat them into submission. A foundational Christian belief is that God has the power to break into people's hearts and lives and change them from the inside out and make them new people.[39] God has the power to dispel our illusions and set us free from the bubbles of self-deception in which we often live. In the age to come, when we are immersed in the divine presence, surrounded by the unmediated and pure holiness and love of God, the light will shine on the ugliness of our sin and on the beauty of God's love for us. God will not externally force anyone to do

---

37. See Von Balthasar, *Prayer*, 177; Sachs, "Current Eschatology," 245.

38. Travis, *Christ and the Judgement*, 312.

39. In the Christian theological tradition, the technical term for this is "efficacious grace," which refers to the power of God's grace to transform a person's will so that they desire God. Most major theologians, Protestant and Catholic, assume some version of this doctrine. While Arminians hold that divine grace is necessary for salvation, they argue that it is not sufficient, and can always be resisted by human free will. While I stand in an Arminian theological tradition as a United Methodist, and believe that God's ordinary and penultimate means of interacting with people leaves room for freedom to resist the promptings of God, I also hold that it would be better for God to ultimately bestow efficacious grace on a person if he or she would not choose God otherwise. For a rigorous philosophical analysis of human autonomy and efficacious grace, see Kronen and Reitan, *God's Final Victory*, 127–51.

something they do not want to do. Rather, we can trust that God has the power to internally compel all people to see the truth about themselves and the truth about God in such a way that will leave them without any motivation to cling to their sin, and every motivation to throw themselves onto the mercy of God.[40]

The eighteenth-century Cambridge theologian Thomas Burnett writes that our sinful dispositions and habits "cannot be so deeply rooted but Fire will purge it out: a Remedy as searching as it is powerful and strong . . . Moreover, in another life, when the Wicked shall see Christ come in His Glory . . . Concupiscence will be no more, and the Food for Vices, for unlawful pleasures . . . be taken away; why therefore, and with what Motives can they adhere forever to their Sins?[41] For human freedom to be meaningful and worthy of respect, it must be rational. Take a drug addict, for example. We don't respect such a person by allowing them to make completely irrational and irreversibly self-destructive decisions. Instead, we do all that we can to help them be restored to a healthy and rational state of being so that they can truly be free to choose what is best for them. A person who chooses to "adhere forever to their sins," who is addicted to their sinful rebellion against God, is blinded by self-destructive and self-deceptive illusions about what is best for them. God would not be loving if he let such persons damn themselves forever because of illusions about where their true good lies. God would be loving and just to remove those illusions and set them free to see that their true good really lies with God.

If this seems to you to be too much divine intervention to allow for real human freedom, consider the fact that in a very real sense our deepest moments of freedom are also those moments where we feel most compelled. Not to be too mushy about it, but even though I freely chose to marry Andrea, at the same time I felt like I had to do it. I felt compelled from within to take that course of action, but I didn't at all experience this as somehow dehumanizing me by taking away my freedom to decide differently. Being free and feeling compelled from within to do something are totally consistent. I think that we are most free when we are being compelled by the love of God (2 Cor 5:14), and that becoming a "slave of Christ" is how we find our deepest freedom (Rom 1:1).

40. See Reitan, "Human Freedom."
41. Walker, *Decline of Hell*, 164.

At this point, one could object by saying that even if God does this, even if God does all that he can do to reveal the ugliness and destructiveness of sin, and the fullness and joy to be found in being united with God, some may choose to remain stubborn or rebellious where they would rather be eternally miserable without God than be eternally happy with God. This is an important objection that takes seriously just how deeply entrenched human self-centeredness can be. However, I do not think it is a possibility that does much to weaken the universalist position. John Hick, one of the most influential twentieth-century philosophers of religion, makes the following claim:

> It seems morally (although still not logically) impossible that the infinite resourcefulness of infinite love working in unlimited time should be eternally frustrated, and the creature reject its own good, presented to it in an endless range of ways. We cannot say in advance how God will eventually free all created souls from their bondage to sin and establish them in love and glad obedience towards Himself; but despite the logical possibility of failure the probability of His success amounts, as it seems to me, a practical certainty.[42]

It seems that this comes down to whether or not we should have more confidence in the power of human sin, or the power of divine grace. I'm going with divine grace. Paul writes that "where sin abounds, grace abounds all the more" (Rom 5:20). At the end of the day, I believe that God's love for us will be more relentless than our rejection of him, and that is why I am a universalist. I do not at all underestimate how deeply rooted self-centered and sinful patterns of living can be, but at the same time I do not think we should underestimate the power of God's just and holy love to pull the roots of sin out of our hearts.

If I am proven to be wrong about this, if some will forever hold out against God, then I think God will not be offended if I put too much confidence in the power of divine love. Even if one doesn't go all the way in affirming that God will ultimately heal every human heart and transform every evil will through destroying all sin with the fire of his holy love, it seems to me that every Christian should at least have hope in the possibility of this happening. Jesus, after all, told us that, "with God, all things are possible" (Matt 19:26). We should take careful note of the fact

---

42. Hick, *Evil and the God*, 380.

that when Jesus said this he was explicitly referring to the power of God to save even those who seem impossible to save from a merely human perspective (Matt 19:23–26). When it comes to who can be saved, our hope is in divine possibility, not in human probabilities.[43]

The Limits of Freedom

There is another reason why I have come to think that the free-will defense of an everlasting hell is ultimately not that plausible. I would argue that it assumes an overly idealistic and excessively individualistic conception of human freedom. In other words, while we do have the freedom to play the cards we have been dealt in different ways, we do not get to choose the cards we are dealt. All of our free decisions happen within a web of factors that are beyond our control and for which we are not responsible.

What first alerted me to the significance of this fact was my experience over a decade ago working with teenagers in an institutional "home." They were in the foster care system, but were too violent to be placed in foster homes or even attend public school. The teenagers that I worked with were unmanageable, unpredictable, and were filled with rage and violent anger. From the outside looking in, it would be easy to judge these young people. I know because that is what I did at first. On the inside, I would get angry at them for their behavior and would instinctively blame them or internally label them as "no good" or "rotten to the core." As I got to know them, however, all of that changed. I heard their stories of abuse, and how some had even witnessed one parent murdering the other. After getting to really know them, I could only feel sorrow and compassion for them, even when they tried to physically hurt others or myself. Their minds, hearts, and wills were so thoroughly wounded and distorted by events and actions over which they had absolutely no control. Yes, in a sense they were choosing to do many of the bad things that they were doing. But in a deeper sense, their choices were constricted and distorted by much greater factors over which they had no freedom to control.

While their life situations were uniquely difficult, their situation highlighted for me the universal condition of human freedom. Human freedom is inherently socially-embedded, psychologically-impaired, and

---

43. Perhaps it is also worth noting that right after Jesus speaks of God's power to save anyone, he speaks of the "renewal of all things" at his return (Matt 19:28).

metaphysically-circumscribed by influences that we did not choose. We are inherently social creatures, and so our identities and character are inextricably bound up with the lives and choices of other people. We do not simply relate to other people as we are. We are who we are in relation to other people. Our individual identities are not simply the product of the choices we make; in large part, they are the result of choices that other people have made for us.

Acknowledging this seems to have two ways of impacting our current discussion about human freedom as it relates to our salvation. First, it brings into question the idea of being judged by God as individuals, since who we are cannot really be separated from the influences from others. Although the scriptures do affirm a judgment for individuals, we should note that in the biblical world there was a much greater sense of social solidarity and communal identity than there is in Western cultures today. Individuals were seen and judged by their relation to a large whole of which they were a part. It is perhaps not without significance that the parable of the sheep and the goats envisions nations coming before the throne to be judged rather than distinct individuals (Matt 25:32).[44]

Second, and perhaps more importantly, it reveals how impaired human freedom really is. Our freedom really isn't all that "free" after all. This is actually one of the key insights of the traditional doctrine of original sin. We do not come into the world as a blank slate. Instead, we are all born into a network of influences that are both good and bad. I do not believe that we inherit guilt, as Augustine held, but it certainly makes sense to say that we are born into a world where the cards are stacked against living a life in tune with God. While we do have some level of freedom, the wisdom of the scriptures insists that we are not truly autonomous creatures, but instead, our natural condition is that we are blinded by ignorance and enslaved to the power of sin. The traditional Christian view of humanity is not that we are born on "neutral ground" with the opportunity to choose God or reject God, as the free-will defense of hell seems to imagine. It seems that the free-will defenders of an everlasting hell come very close to committing themselves to the Pelagian heresy that asserts that human beings have the power in and of themselves to choose

---

44. Clark Pinnock writes that "the Bible is more concerned about structural redemption than the fate of individuals in contrast to ourselves" (Wideness in *God's Mercy*, 152). On the essential unity of humanity in the judgment, see Bulgakov, *Bride of the Lamb*, 457–58.

God without God's aid or intervention.[45] The contemporary theologian Jurgen Moltmann makes this strong criticism of the logic behind the free-will defense of an everlasting hell:

> The logic of hell seems to me . . . extremely atheistic: here the human being in his freedom of choice is his own lord and god. His own will is his heaven—or his hell. God is merely the accessory who puts that will into effect . . . Is that "the love of God"? Free human beings forge their own happiness and are their own executioners. They do not just dispose over their lives here; they decide on their eternal destinies as well. So they have no need of God at all . . . Carried to this ultimate conclusion, the logic of hell is secular humanism.[46]

We are made to find our fulfillment in God, yet the blinding power of sin keeps us in the illusion that living self-centeredly and self-sufficiently is where our true good lies. If this is true, then God isn't in the position of simply needing to respect our current "freedom" to choose between good and bad. God is in the position of needing to enable us to be truly free from the power of sin so that we may see clearly and have the genuine freedom to choose what we are made for, which is a life in union with God. As the theologian John Sachs puts it, "human freedom is . . . the capacity for God, not the capacity for either God or something else. Human freedom is created for one end alone: God. Only God finally 'defines' the person."[47] We are made for God, and so God values us, not by letting us forever reject him, but by working with us and in us to enable us to see where our true freedom lies. The contemporary philosopher of religion Marilyn Adams, after reflecting deeply on the nature of human freedom and all the ways it is actually impaired by life's circumstances, writes,

> First, . . . impaired adult human agency is no more competent to be entrusted with its . . . eternal destiny than two-year-old agency is to be allowed choices that could result in its death or serious physical impairment; and second, . . . the fact that the choices of such impaired agents come between the divine creator of the

---

45. Pelagius was a fourth-century British monk who debated with Augustine on the relationship between divine action and the human will. Since then, any view that highlights the role of human freedom to the exclusion of the need for divine intervention is usually labeled "Pelagian."

46. Moltmann, "Logic of Hell," 44.

47. Sachs, "Current Eschatology," 247 (emphasis original).

environment and their infernal outcome no more reduces divine responsibility for the damnation than two-year old agency reduces the responsibility of the adult caretaker.[48]

Adams's critique insightfully highlights what is most troublesome about the free-will defense of an everlasting hell. It attempts to set God free of any responsibility for our damnation while placing all of the responsibility on us. But as Adams points out, this is not the kind of responsibility that can reasonably be expected of creatures like us. God doesn't "respect" our freedom to reject God by choosing not to intervene, any more than a mother "respects" the freedom of her young child to run out into the road by choosing not to reach out and stop her. Our freedom to choose or reject God is an important part of our development as a human being, to be sure. In the end, though, we can trust that God's freedom to save us will be more powerful than our freedom to damn ourselves. That, at least, is the foundation of hope for the Christian universalist. The United Methodist Church Bishop William Willimon makes this point eloquently: "The love of Christ does not extinguish God's gift of our freedom as human beings. And yet our refusal is cast into doubt, as if it cannot be the ultimate word on things. The 'ultimate word on things' is always God's word, not ours."[49]

Conclusion

One of the most frequently raised objections to the belief in universal salvation through Christ is that it will require that God override the human freedom that God has given humanity. After an excursion into exploring the possibility of human beings retaining the freedom to choose God in the age to come, we went on to probe this issue by highlighting the psychology of religious conversion, and how God can internally compel people to come to repentance without treating them in a dehumanizing, arm-twisting sort of fashion. We then went on to examine the socially-embedded and spiritually-enslaved nature of human freedom and the implications this has for the free-will defense of hell. We are not neutral or blank slates when we come into the world. We inherit a whole host of negative factors from which we must be set free in order to see and

48. Adams, "Problem of Hell," 313. See also her *Horrendous Evils*, 36–38.
49. Willimon, Who Will Be Saved?, 83.

choose clearly. God doesn't respect us by leaving us to our enslavement to sin. God loves us by setting us free.

In our discussion so far, we have held to a very Christ-centered vision for how to think about the ultimate reconciliation of all things to God. However, Christian universalists are consistently accused of denying that Jesus is the only Savior, and of affirming that every spiritual path leads to God. In the next chapter, we will focus in more depth on the issue of God's saving work through Christ and how this cannot only be accommodated within a universalist framework, but is actually highlighted and enhanced.

CHAPTER 5

Stairways to Heaven or Highways to Hell?

Objection #4: "Universalists think all religions are equally true."

One of the biggest mistakes we make
is to believe there is only one way.
There are many diverse paths leading to God.

—OPRAH[1]

OPRAH SUMS UP ONE of the most popular ways of responding to religious diversity in our culture today. We live in an age where people who make grand and absolute claims about religious truth are looked upon with deep suspicion and fear. Many people see it as extremely arrogant to insist that one's own religious tradition might be truer than other religious traditions. Not only is this claim seen as arrogant, it is also seen as very dangerous. After all, history is full of examples of people who have committed moral atrocities because they were absolutely certain that God was behind what they were doing. Wouldn't the world be better off if religious people stopped insisting on the absolute truth of their claims, and instead recognized that all the world's religions are valid ways of connecting to the divine? In this chapter, we will explore three of the dominant ways in which Christians think about the truth of the Christian faith in a world with a plurality of religions.[2]

---

1. Quoted in Taylor, *Christianity Today*, "Church of O."

2. The threefold classification of viewpoints we are considering has been a fairly standard taxonomy among theologians since the early 1980s. While this scheme of classification is not without its tensions and inadequacies, the approach remains useful to

Three Christian Approaches to Religious Diversity

Pluralism

One of the most popular ways of dealing with this situation is to go with Oprah in saying that all religions essentially boil down to the same thing and that we should accept one another's different paths to God. This position is usually given the name *pluralism*.[3] Pluralists believe that the way to live with respect and tolerance towards others is to affirm that no religion is inherently better than any other. Each of the world's great faiths is a legitimate means of accessing the sacred reality we call "God."[4] One of the most common images used to explain pluralism is that of a mountain with many different roads that lead to the top. The parable of the elephant and the blind men (not in the Bible, by the way) is another story that is often used to explain this position. According to this parable, three blind men come across an elephant, but, being blind, cannot see that it is in fact an elephant. One of the men feels a leg and concludes it must be a tree. Another man feels the snout and concludes it must be a snake. The other blind man feels the side of the elephant and concludes it must be a sturdy wall. The moral of the story is supposed to be that each religion sees only a part of the big picture, and goes wrong when it assumes that the part it has grasped is really the whole.

There is much to be praised in the pluralist outlook, especially the motivation that often leads to adopting this position. Many people are so put off by the arrogance and narrow-mindedness of religious believers that they find this outlook to be a cure for the dangerous poison of religious certainty. It is safe to say that religious wars have never been started

---

understanding Christian responses to religious diversity at a broad level. For a helpful overview and a more nuanced approach to understanding this taxonomy, see Morgan, "Inclusivisms and Exclusivisms." For a critical evaluation of this taxonomy, and an even further nuanced approach to the options, see Tiessan, *Who Can Be Saved?*, 31–47.

3. The label "pluralism" can be used in either a sociological or theological sense. "Pluralism" as a sociological label simply describes a society marked by a diversity of religious perspectives. Here the term is being used in the theological sense, which is a label for a position that prescribes how one should think about and respond to the fact of religious diversity.

4. The religious philosopher John Hick has been one of the strongest advocates of this theology of religions. See, for example, his *God Has Many Names*. For an appreciative but critical evaluation of Hick's work, see Netland, *Encountering Religious Pluralism*.

by religious pluralists. They are mostly motivated by a desire to transcend religious squabbling, to promote understanding and acceptance, and they often work to unite people of all faiths to work towards the common good.[5] Pluralists also adopt this position out of a genuine sense of moral outrage at the thought of all non-Christians being punished forever in hell. For them, a God of love could never be so stingy as to reserve the blessing of salvation for the people of one religion only.

That said, the pluralist vision does have some setbacks that should give pause before fully embracing and closing ourselves off to any other alternatives. Let's return to the image and the parable mentioned above in order to see two serious difficulties with this approach to religious diversity. The pluralist sees the religious traditions of the world as different roads that all lead up the same mountain. The problem with this view, though, is that after one has learned about the actual content of the religions of the world, it is hard to hold. Although there is a great deal of commonality to be found, especially among the mystics of each tradition and in the fundamental moral guidelines in each faith,[6] there are also some very real differences among the religions of the world that are perhaps too easily glossed over in the pluralist perspective. From a practical standpoint, the religions of the world do not appear to simply be different roads going up the same mountain. They appear to be very different mountains. Ironically, even though this viewpoint is often held out of a desire to respect the diversity of religion, it actually ignores or fails to take account of the genuinely diverse particularities of each tradition, and in doing so, ultimately disrespects the unique claims to be found in each major faith. For someone to maintain that Buddhism and Christianity are simply different paths that lead to the same place would be incoherent.[7] To make such a claim would ignore the way each tradition specifically describes the human predicament and the solution for it. So, while on the surface this position seems tolerant and respectful, upon further

5. The seeds of modern pluralism were actually planted about four hundred years ago in response to the religious wars that plagued Europe. See Netland, *Encountering Religious Pluralism*, 95–100.

6. Knitter, *Introducing Theologies of Religion*, 125–47.

7. This is not to say that a Christian cannot greatly benefit from the wisdom and spirituality of Buddhism, or vice versa. I am simply claiming that honesty compels us to acknowledge that ultimately Christianity and Buddhism envision the spiritual goal, and the path to that goal, in genuinely different ways. For a concise and fair description of the points of convergence and divergence, see Yandell and Netland, *Buddhism*, 175–212.

inspection it seems as though it inadvertently disrespects the diversity of religious traditions by trying to make them all fit into one mold. I am not claiming that people who claim to be pluralists are not tolerant and respectful people after all. I am claiming that if they are, it is ultimately in spite of where their viewpoint logically leads at its deepest level.

In fact, pluralists cannot consistently hold up tolerance and respect as key virtues in the arena of religious pluralism. The fact is that many religious traditions do not see inclusive love and universal respect as most important. So when a pluralist criticizes a religious tradition for being too dogmatic or exclusionary, on what ground are they standing? If all religious paths are equally valid cultural constructions leading to the same God, how will one make genuine moral criticisms of any other faith tradition? If the pluralist is to ever make a moral protest against another religious tradition's sanctions, he or she must privilege some religious truth claims over others, and that goes against the grain of the pluralist model of religious truth.[8]

Ironically, while pluralists are, in my experience, most often motivated by a praiseworthy, moral sensitivity towards others outside their own traditions, pluralism itself offers little to no conceptual resources for making moral judgments and theological evaluations about systems of thought that are actually harmful to people. Often, Christians are convinced that if God is love then God must want to bless and save all people, regardless of their religion, and so they adopt a pluralist mode of thinking out of love for others. While that motivation is right on, one cannot consistently and coherently let the distinctively Christian claim that God is love be their guide, while at the same time affirming that all paths are equal. Christians think the path of unlimited love, incarnated in Jesus, is the supreme path to God. If unbounded love is our guiding conviction, then we need to be honest about where that conviction comes from; not from a universal religious consensus, but from Jesus of Nazareth. It is because of Jesus that we believe that God is love.[9] If we are going to use a ladder to get to the roof, we shouldn't then kick the ladder down and pretend that we didn't need it to get there.

To return to the parable of the elephants and the blind men, we can certainly affirm one of the key points of this story, namely, that none of us

8. See Newbigin, *Gospel in a Pluralist Society*, 162. See also Netland, *Encountering Religious Pluralism*, 243–46.

9. See Pinnock, *Wideness in God's Mercy*, 44–46.

have a complete and total grasp of the truth about God. However, there is one main flaw to this story. The story intends to show that no one sees the whole truth, yet the story is told from the perspective of someone who sees the whole truth, which is that the object they are touching is, in fact, an elephant. This is significant because people are often motivated to adopt pluralism because they think it is arrogant to make the claim that one religion has more truth than another. However, the person who says that all religions are equally true is like the person telling the story of the blind men and the elephant. They assume everyone else has only a partial grasp of the truth, while they themselves are actually claiming to know how things really are. In other words, it is no less "arrogant" to say that one religion has more truth than the rest, than it is to say that every religion is true. Both people are making claims about reality, and truth claims by their very nature are exclusive, that is to say, they exclude the converse of what they affirm. I can see no reason why it is necessarily arrogant to affirm that one way of seeing the world is true and another isn't. Again, pluralists, in making a claim about the truth of all religions, are in fact excluding the possibility that one religion can have more truth than another. They are claiming to know reality as it is; to see an elephant that no one else can see.[10] So, while I am extremely sympathetic to some of the main motivations behind pluralism, I find it to be religiously inadequate and intellectually incoherent. It can also be, unintentionally, even very practically dangerous if it causes us to overlook real differences between others and us.[11]

Although I deeply resonate with the pluralist desire to avoid religious arrogance, I see arrogance as less about what a person believes, and more about how they hold that belief. For example, I can believe that Jesus is the only way, and I can hold that belief with a smug sense of self-righteousness and arrogant certainty, or I can hold it with a sense of intellectual humility and hopeful assurance. Truth claims are not arrogant. People are arrogant. I don't think it is arrogant when a Buddhist friend tells me that although she finds Jesus to be full of wisdom, she really thinks the Buddha has a lot more to say to humanity. I don't think it is arrogant to say that the Buddha has more truth than Jesus. That's just how she sees things, and I respect that. I would say that although the Buddha

---

10. On this point I am indebted to Keller, *Reason for God*, 8–10.
11. See Prothero, *God is Not One*, 4.

has tremendous insight into the workings of the human mind that we can all benefit from knowing, I still think that Jesus reveals the fullness about God and about the best kind of human life that can be lived with God. That's how I see things, and she respects that. Arrogance isn't limited to any specific religious outlook. In fact, pluralists can be just as arrogant as traditional religious believers if they look upon such believers with a sense of superiority because they think they know something that others don't know.

Exclusivism

The second major position that Christians take on the question of religious diversity is the exact opposite of pluralism, and it goes by the label *exclusivism*.[12] A religious exclusivist believes that their religion is the only true religion that contains the light of revelatory truth, while all the rest are mostly in the dark. A specifically Christian exclusivist believes that Jesus is the only Savior, and that to be saved by him one must hear the gospel message and explicitly confess Jesus is Lord in this lifetime. A Christian exclusivist, therefore, believes that any non-Christian who dies is eternally excluded from fellowship with God.[13] This position enjoys tremendous popularity because it seems to have the clear support of a number of texts in the New Testament, such as:

> I am the way, the truth, and the life. No one comes to the Father except through me. (John 14:6)

> There is salvation in no one else, for there is no other name under heaven given among mortals by which we must be saved. (Acts 4:12)

The greatest strength of the exclusivist position is that it takes very seriously the scriptural claims of the uniqueness of God's saving revelation in Jesus Christ. The early Christians lived in a culture that was

12. This position also sometimes is labeled "restrictivism" or "particularism." Some theologians want to make nuanced semantic distinctions between these labels, but exploring these distinctions is not necessary for our purposes here. See Sanders, *What About Those?*, 12–13; Pinnock, *Wideness in God's Mercy*, 12–15.

13. Most exclusivists, though, do not believe this to be absolutely true, as they will make exceptions for small children or mentally impaired people who cannot comprehend the gospel message.

characterized by great religious and philosophical diversity, and the dominant civil mood towards religions was one of tolerance. The Roman Empire was very open to a wide variety of religious cults and the worship of many gods, as long as religious devotion didn't interfere with one's ultimate allegiance to the emperor. Worship of the emperor and the swearing of ultimate allegiance to him united the empire in a civic religion. The pledge of allegiance in ancient Rome was "Caesar is Lord." The early Christians, however, did not see allegiance to Jesus as just another religious option that one might try on for size. They understood and proclaimed that "Jesus is Lord"; that he is the true King of kings who is worthy of worship from all people. This is why the early Christians often found themselves in jail or the subjects of persecution. They believed that the highest throne wasn't occupied by the emperor in Rome, but by Jesus in heaven (Rev 4–5). Because of this foundational belief, they understood their mission in life to announce the good news to all people that Jesus is the true King of the world and that his kingdom is a kingdom of love.

Christianity, as understood and lived out by the earliest followers of Jesus, was never a matter of a mere therapeutic religious option that one might add on to their life if they were so inclined. The first Christians believed that God had revealed the divine heart decisively and supremely in the person of Jesus of Nazareth, and that therefore all people are called to repent, to change their thinking about God to match up with whatever Jesus reveals, and to seek to live in harmony with that revelation by the power of Christ's Spirit. To be faithful to the New Testament witness to the significance of Jesus, one must affirm that Jesus is not simply one among many revealers of the character and nature of God, but that Jesus is the fullest and clearest revelation of God's saving love that the world has ever seen. The early Christians had such a high view of the person of Jesus, that they didn't even shy away from including Jesus within the very identity of God. Although Jesus's first followers were all Jewish monotheists, they allowed their experience of Jesus and his Spirit to reshape and reform their understanding of the very nature of God. They couldn't talk about God anymore without also talking about Jesus in the same sentence. Look, for example, at how Paul reshapes the ancient Jewish confession of belief in one God:

> Indeed, even though there may be so-called gods in heaven or
> on earth—as in fact there are many gods and many lords—yet for

> us there is one God, the Father, from whom are all things and for
> whom we exist, and one Lord, Jesus Christ, through whom are all
> things and through whom we exist. (1 Cor 8:5–6)

This experience and conviction is the seed of the doctrine of the Trinity
that will develop over the next few centuries. But we should note that
even though the doctrine of the Trinity developed over centuries, the
foundation of this doctrine, which is the conviction that Jesus should be
somehow identified with God, was there from the beginning.[14] Although
it has become somewhat fashionable to insist that in the beginning Jesus
was only thought of as a great moral example and spiritual leader, only
to be later turned into a god by power-hungry church leaders, this claim
simply does not fit the historical evidence at all. The earliest Christian
documents in existence that we know of are Paul's letters, and his writings
are permeated with what scholars call a "high Christology," that is, a view
that insists that Jesus defines God. Any authentically Christian faith must
somehow place Jesus square in the center of our thinking about God and
God's purpose for the world.

The exclusivist vision of salvation certainly does a much better job
than the pluralist vision of preserving a sense of the uniqueness of Jesus
and the particularity of the Christian claim that "God was *in Christ* reconciling the world to himself" (2 Cor 5:19). My suspicion is that most
people who are exclusivists are not so because they are uncaring and un-
troubled by the thought of billions of people burning in hell forever. It
is highly unfair to accuse such folks of being ignorant or hardhearted in
order to quickly dismiss the exclusivist position with a few *ad hominems*.
I think most exclusivists are so because they are convinced that Jesus is
the world's only true Savior, and that in order to hold on to this claim one
must also embrace the exclusivist view of salvation. *What I want to point
out is that one can hold on to the affirmation that Jesus Christ is the exclusive means of salvation, without concluding that salvation is exclusively
limited to those who profess faith in Christ in this lifetime.* The failure to
properly distinguish between these two claims is probably at the root of
much of the motivation for most Christians to either hold too tightly to
the exclusivist position, or to reject any uniqueness to Christ and embrace
the pluralist position.

14. See Hurtado, *Lord Jesus Christ*; Bauckham, *God Crucified*; C. Wright, *Uniqueness
of Jesus*, 100–104.

The biggest and most glaring problem with the exclusivist view is that God seems so unloving and unjust to damn people who never had an opportunity to respond to the gospel. Christians have struggled with this question and have come up with a number of proposals. Most often, though, exclusivists will simply tell us that we have no right to question God and we should just be thankful that God has provided a way for some of us to be saved because God didn't have to do anything to save us, and God doesn't owe us anything.[15] Let's think about this claim for a moment: *God doesn't owe us anything.* There is one important sense in which this is certainly true. None of us have done anything to earn God's blessings and God's love. The fact that we even exist is sheer grace. Life is a pure gift from a generous God, and our forgiveness and salvation are likewise pure gifts. Creation and redemption flow from the grace of God. In that sense, it is true to say that God owes us nothing, in that ideas of earning or merit have no place in our thinking about our relation to God.

However, there is another sense in which this statement can be misleading. When exclusivists claim that we have no right to question God's decision to consign to an everlasting hell all those who are not Christians because God owes us nothing in the first place, they are making an unwarranted logical leap. To say that God owes us nothing is one thing, but to infer from this that God then has the right to create billions of people who will experience everlasting torment because they have not heard the gospel message and accepted it in this lifetime is another. To say that God owes us nothing is not the same as saying that God has the right to do anything. My children did not do anything to earn their existence or to earn my love for them, and so in that sense I do not "owe" them anything. However, because they exist, and simply because they exist as precious people made in the divine image, they are owed the respect and love from me that being made in the divine image warrants. In an important sense, I do "owe" my kids the love and respect they deserve, not because of anything they have done, but simply because of who and what they are. I believe the same applies to God. God, Christians assume, was under no external compulsion to create a world, and God is not externally obligated to anyone else. At the same time, it does make sense to talk about God being internally compelled to always act in accord with the nature of divine goodness and love. In that sense, God does owe us certain things,

15. See, for example, Edgar, "Exclusivism," 95.

not because of what we have done, but because of who God is and who God made us to be.

I recall several years back having a conversation with a friend who is a Calvinist exclusivist. This position holds that only those in this lifetime who accept the gospel are saved (exclusivist), and that God actually determines who will and will not accept the gospel (Calvinist). In response to my protests against the injustice of this, he gave me the following analogy. Suppose that there are a hundred men in a homeless shelter, each of which is in desperate need of help. Then suppose that there is a rich man who comes to town who takes pity on thirty of the men, and decides to give each of them a new home and enough money to pay their bills for the rest of their life. Who would be so arrogant and rude as to say that the rich man is unjust for not choosing the other seventy? Instead, he should be praised for what he did for the thirty men, considering the fact that he didn't have to do anything for any of them in the first place. This is how my friend saw the issue of why God doesn't save more people than just Christians. God doesn't have to, and in not doing so, there is nothing unfair about it.

There is one huge detail that is wrong with this analogy. In order for the story to accurately reflect the issue at hand, we would need to suppose, not just that there is a rich man who can help, but that there is a rich man with *infinite riches* at his disposal. God, presumably, doesn't have to worry about running out of grace. If there were a rich man with infinite riches at his disposal, and this rich man arbitrarily picked thirty men to help without offering any help to the other seventy, then this infinitely rich man could certainly be criticized for being unjust in the distribution of his riches. Even if you still are resistant to calling that unjust, then at a minimum you should agree that this isn't what a *perfectly loving* and infinitely rich man would do. (Also, on the Calvinist view, the analogy should be adjusted to say that the rich man was actually the one who made them homeless in the first place!)

Another attempt to salvage the exclusivist position against the charge of injustice is to say that all those who have never heard the gospel would have never believed the gospel anyways had they heard it.[16] This strikes me as highly absurd. Are we really to imagine that the gospel message is so weak and non-compelling that in every culture that has

16. Ibid.

existed without the gospel, no one who would have responded positively? Those of a Calvinist bent may modify this argument to say that God has arranged the world in such a way as to guarantee that all of the elect will have an opportunity to hear the gospel. This response, though, only gets the exclusivist out of the frying pan and into the fire concerning a charge of injustice. If God elects (that is predestines or determines) some to salvation and some to damnation, then this God is not in any meaningful sense loving towards all. Once again, the exclusivist will revert back to saying that we are in no position to question God. I will remind him or her that it isn't God I am questioning. I am questioning the coherence and intelligibility of a humanly constructed theological system that makes it impossible to tell the difference between God and the devil.

The exclusivist viewpoint, when pressed, has a supreme irony, or shall I say contradiction, at the heart of its claim. It claims that God so loved the world that he gave his only Son, yet for the people who do not know about how much God loves them, God will subject them to never-ending suffering. While this view certainly highlights the central role of Christ in our salvation, it ultimately paints God as something of an arbitrary tyrant rather than the loving parent Jesus describes.

Inclusivism

Fortunately, there is a third option available to us that preserves what is good about pluralism and exclusivism, while avoiding the pitfalls that come with both of these views. This view is known as *inclusivism*. According to this view, Christ is the only way to God, yet the saving work of Christ is not limited to people who in this life knowingly and intentionally put their trust in Christ. On this view, Christ can reach through to people in this life without them necessarily knowing about him, or Christ can encounter people in the life to come to welcome them into a reconciled relationship with God. This stance, we should note, can embrace a fully orthodox understanding of the saving and revelatory significance of Jesus. This position affirms that in Christ we see the fullest and clearest image of God, yet it also takes a more positive view towards glimpses and rays of divine truth and goodness being found in other religions as well. On this view, the cosmic Christ that fills the universe (Col 1:15–20) is at work in the world beyond the church and can reach through to people with his love and grace in a wide variety of ways, such as through the common truth among the world's religions, the light of moral conscience, the glory of nature, visions and dreams, and even an encounter with Christ in the life to come.

Perhaps we can clarify the essence of the inclusivist position by comparing it to the others. Exclusivism holds that Jesus is the one way to God, and that there is only one way to go through Jesus to God, which is an explicit confession of faith in him in this lifetime. Pluralism holds that Jesus is one among many ways to go to God. Inclusivism holds that Jesus is the one way to God, but that there is a wide plurality of ways that people can go through Jesus to God.

Exclusivists may be tempted to dismiss inclusivism as a modern theological invention that has developed simply out of pressure from our pluralist religious culture in the West. However, this way of understanding the dynamic tension between God's *universal* love and desire to save all people, and God's *particular* revelation of the divine nature that culminated in Jesus of Nazareth, is one that actually has deep and pervasive roots in the mainstream historical theological tradition.[17] The Roman Catholic Church accepts it as their official view,[18] most Protestant denominations widely accept it as their position, and several very influential and highly revered evangelicals, both past and present, support it. The following quotes suffice to show how even Christian thinkers with impeccable evangelical credentials can embrace the inclusivist perspective:

> Of course it should be pointed out that, though all salvation is through Jesus, we need not conclude that he cannot save those who have not explicitly accepted him in this life. —C. S. Lewis[19]

> We can safely say (i) if any good pagan reached the point of throwing himself on His maker's mercy for pardon, it was grace that brought him there; (ii) God will surely save anyone he brings thus far (cf. Acts 10:34f; Rom 10:12f); (iii) anyone thus saved would

---

17. This includes theologians such as Justin Martyr, Clement of Alexandria, Erasmus, Martin Luther, Ulrich Zwingli, Jacob Arminius, and John Wesley (see below). See the brief history provided by Tiessan, *Who Can Be Saved?*, 48–70. Tiessan prefers the term "accessibilism" rather than "inclusivism."

18. See Pope Paul VI, *Lumen Gentium*, 2.16.

19. Lewis, "Christian Apologetics," 102.

learn in the next world that he was saved through Christ. —J. I. Packer[20]

I have never been able to conjure up (as some great Evangelical missionaries have) the appalling vision of the millions who are not only perishing, but will inevitably perish . . . I cherish and hope that the majority of the human race will be saved. And I have a solid biblical basis for this belief. —John Stott[21]

I think everybody that loves Christ, or knows Christ, whether they're conscious of it or not, they're members of the Body of Christ . . . He's calling people out of the world for His name, whether they come from the Muslim world, or the Buddhist world, or the Christian world or the non-believing world, they are members of the Body of Christ because they've been called by God. They may not even know the name of Jesus but they know in their hearts that they need something that they don't have, and they turn to the only light that they have, and I think that they are saved, and that they're going to be with us in heaven. —Billy Graham[22]

I am not going to stand in the way of anyone whom God wants to save. I am not going to say "he can't save them." I am happy for God to save anyone he wants in any way he can. It is possible for someone who does not know Jesus to be saved. But anyone who is going to be saved is going to be saved by Jesus: "There is no other name given under heaven by which men can be saved." —Dallas Willard[23]

God will judge the unreached on the basis of their response to His self-revelation in nature and conscience . . . Now this does not mean that they can be saved apart from Christ. Rather it means that the benefits of Christ's sacrifice can be applied to them without their conscious knowledge of Christ. They would be like people in the Old Testament before Jesus came who had no conscious knowledge of Christ but who were saved on the basis of his sacrifice through their response to the information that God had revealed to them. And, thus, salvation is truly available to all persons at all times. —William Lane Craig[24]

---

20. Packer, *God's Words*, 210. Packer, however, is not very optimistic about this happening, but holds it as a possibility. See Morgan, "Inclusivism and Exclusivisms," 31.

21. Stott and Edwards, *Evangelical Essentials*, 327.

22. Schuller, interview of Billy Graham, "Hour of Power" radio show.

23. Willard, "Apologetics in Action."

24. Craig, "Can a Loving God?"

> Christians are asked to proclaim the good news . . . Yet we must
> never think that it is by preaching the gospel that we are somehow
> making salvation available or possible. It is God who makes salva-
> tion possible through the work of Christ and who uses preaching
> of the gospel as a means of actualizing that salvation. But it is not
> the only means. —Alister McGrath[25]

As a United Methodist pastor, I am glad that our Wesleyan tradition
has always embraced a very wide and broad view of God's saving power.
In a cultural context marked by a recent history of religious wars among
Christians, John Wesley (1703–1791) stood out as one who preached that
God's love could not be monopolized by any one religious group. Keep in
mind that Wesley had as much evangelical passion as anyone who ever
lived. He made it his life's mission to preach the gospel and make disciples
of Christ with every ounce of energy he had, and yet this strong passion
did not keep him from a very wide understanding of God's ability to save
people outside the specific channels of Christian preaching and evangelism. It is worth quoting from some of Wesley's sermons at length, so that
we can see how deep evangelical passion can be united with a humble
acknowledgment of God's mysterious power to save people in ways that
go beyond our understanding. For a complete understanding of Wesley's
words, I offer a few historical and linguistic notes. "Mahometan" was an
old-school English way of referring to Muslims. "Heathen" traditionally
referred to people who were not Christian, Jew, or Muslim. Also, remember that in Wesley's world, Protestants saw Catholics as deeply heretical,
and Catholics returned the favor, and the two sides had a history of trying
to settle disputes by killing each other.

> "On Living Without God"—I have no authority from the Word of
> God "to judge those that are without." Nor do I conceive that any
> man living has a right to sentence all the heathen and Mahometan
> world to damnation. It is far better to leave them to him that made
> them, and who is "the Father of the spirits of all flesh;" who is the
> God of the Heathens as well as the Christians, and who hateth
> nothing that he hath made.[26]

> "On Faith"—It cannot be doubted, but this plea [lack of knowl-
> edge] will avail for millions of modern Heathens. Inasmuch as to
> them little is given, of them little will be required. As to the ancient

25. McGrath, "A Particularist View," 179.

26. Wesley, "On Living Without God," 14.

Heathens, millions of them, likewise were savages. No more therefore will be expected of them, than the living up to the light they had.[27]

"On Faith"—But with Heathens, Mahometans, and Jews we have at present nothing to do; only we may wish that their lives did not shame many of us that are called Christians. We have not much more to do with the members of the Church of Rome. But we cannot doubt, that many of them, like the excellent Archbishop of Cambray, still retain (notwithstanding many mistakes) that faith that worketh by love.[28]

"On Faith"—It is not so easy to pass any judgment concerning the faith of our modern Jews . . . it is not our part to pass sentence upon them, but to leave them to their own Master.[29]

"Imperfection of Human Knowledge"—We cannot account for his present dealings with the inhabitants of the earth. We know, "the Lord is loving unto every man, and his mercy is over all his works." But we know not how to reconcile this with the present dispensations of his providence. At this day, is not almost every part of the earth full of darkness and cruel habitations . . . But does not the Father of men care for them O mystery of providence![30]

"On Living Without God"—Perhaps there may be some well-meaning persons who carry this farther still; who aver, that whatever change is wrought in men, whether in their hearts or lives, yet if they have not clear views of those capital doctrines, the fall of man, justification by faith, and of the atonement made by the death of Christ, and of his righteousness transferred to them, they can have no benefit from his death. I dare in no wise affirm this. Indeed I do not believe it. I believe the merciful God regards the lives and tempers of men more than their ideas. I believe he respects the goodness of the heart rather than the clearness of the head; and that if the heart of a man be filled (by the grace of God, and the power of his Spirit) with the humble, gentle, patient love of God and man, God will not cast him into everlasting fire prepared for the devil and his angels because his ideas are not clear,

---

27. Wesley, "On Faith," 1.4.
28. Ibid., 2.3.
29. Ibid., 1.6.
30. Wesley, "Imperfection of Human Knowledge," 2.4.

> or because his conceptions are confused. Without holiness, I own,
> "no man shall see the Lord;" but I dare not add, "or clear ideas."[31]

While Wesley certainly believed in an everlasting hell for those who would forever refuse to turn towards God, his views on hell and who goes there was grounded in his central conviction that God's essence is holy love.[32] This conviction is what led him to question a very narrow exclusivist understanding of who can be saved, and to embrace the position that now bears the label "inclusivism."[33]

We should pause to point out that this current discussion is on the question of *how* people are saved, not *how many* people are saved. Most inclusivists are not universalists. They would hold that even though God through Christ can reach into people's lives in any number of ways, it will still be the case that some will forever refuse this offer. Inclusivism is a position on how people are saved, while universalism is a position on how many will be saved. If Christian universalism is true, then Christian inclusivism is necessarily true, but Christian inclusivism can be true even if Christian universalism is false. On the inclusivist view, non-Christians can be saved even if not all non-Christians are saved. The position that I am arguing in this book could then be called *Christian inclusivist universalism*. Inclusivist describes the means of salvation (Christ), while universalism describes the outcome (all people).

Because inclusivism must be true if universalism is true, then any of the previous arguments you have found convincing for universalism also support the case for inclusivism. However, since universalism requires inclusivism to be true, I will argue for Christian inclusivism as such at more length. Because I find pluralism to be deeply incongruent with the reality of genuine religious diversity, and because I find exclusivism to be deeply theologically inadequate because of the narrow view of God it espouses,

31. Wesley, "On Living Without God," 15.

32. On this central Wesleyan belief, see Dunning, *Grace, Faith, and Holiness*, 192. For a Wesleyan critique of Wesley's view of hell, see Truesdale, "Holy Love vs. Eternal Hell."

33. Although Christian universalism was not John Wesley's view, and is not the official view of the United Methodist Church, I believe that the kind of Christian universalism outlined in this book can flow organically out of the key convictions of Wesleyan theology, without subverting or distorting any of the key doctrines of the UMC. In my own theological development, it has been Wesley's insistence that love is God's "reigning attribute," along with his conviction that love and justice cannot be separated in God, that lead me to explore and ultimately embrace the hope of Christian universalism. On these points, see Jones, *United Methodist Doctrine*, 107; Maddox, *Responsible Grace*, 53.

I think that inclusivism provides a very valuable set of lenses through which Christians can evaluate the fact of religious diversity, even if they don't go all the way with the universalist argument. Inclusivism allows the Christian to hold on to the uniqueness of Jesus Christ in God's plan of redemption for the world, while avoiding the incoherence and relativism of the pluralist position, on the one hand, and the unjust and unloving view of God found in the exclusivist position, on the other hand. Let's examine what reasons there are for thinking that inclusivism is true.

We have already examined, in the previous chapter, the possibility of postmortem conversion, which is usually featured, at least as a hope, in most versions of inclusivism. Although there are a handful of passages that can be interpreted as pointing in the direction of this possibility, the strongest argument in favor of this proposal rests on the character of God's steadfast love who looks for lost sinners until he finds them (Luke 15). There is simply no compelling reason to assume that God's posture towards someone changes at their death. There are also no explicit scriptural declarations that a person's fate is definitively sealed at death. Often those who deny the possibility of postmortem conversion point to passages that affirm that human beings face judgment when they die (Heb 9:6; 1 Cor 5:10), but these passages do not spell out what judgment consists of and what is made possible by the judgment. These passages do not say that judgment leads to an eternally-dualistic outcome, but this assumption is often read into these texts. Supporters of the possibility of postmortem conversion will certainly agree with these scriptural affirmations that all people face divine judgment when they die, but they will also affirm that God's judgment is designed to illicit repentance and foster reconciliation. Appeals to postmortem judgment, again, do not suffice to close the door on the possibility of postmortem salvation.

Another key aspect of the argument for inclusivism is the broad scriptural theme of God's saving love that reaches out to the whole world. From the beginning of the biblical story of redemption, God reveals himself to be a God who is not concerned with only a small set of people in the world, but rather with all the people of the world. In fact, God's particular election of the people of Abraham is for the universal purpose of drawing all people into the blessing of God (Gen 12:1–3).[34] The Christian tradition has mostly missed this point in a huge way, and has instead

34. See Pinnock, *Wideness in God's Mercy*, 23–25.

talked about "election" as pertaining to the *salvation of some instead of others*. But in the biblical story, election is about a *calling for the sake of others*. Election is not a matter of God favoring some people over others. Election is a matter of God choosing some people to be instruments of blessings to the rest of the people. It is never about God choosing some individuals for redemptive privilege, but rather it is about God choosing a group of people for missional service. Throughout Israel's history as it is told in the Old Testament, this point is consistently overlooked, as God's people had a tendency to think of themselves as special or immune from judgment because of their "chosen" status. The prophets were a group of people that had to continually remind the people of Israel that they were called to be instruments of divine blessing, not recipients only, and that "their" God is really the God of all people. The Lord speaks through the prophet Amos to the people of Israel, "'Are not you Israelites the same to me as the Cushites?' declares the Lord. 'Did I not bring Israel up from Egypt, the Philistines from Caphtor and the Arameans from Kir?'" (Amos 9:7). Although the storyline of the Old Testament focuses on God's relationship with Israel, here we are reminded that God is also involved in the lives of people and nations outside of Israel. The whole book of Jonah is written to criticize the religious stance of the ancient Israelites that seeks to keep God for themselves instead of sharing the mercy of God with other nations. The real miracle in the book of Jonah is not a man being swallowed by a whale; it is the miracle of a God who stays with a group of people even in the face of persistent refusal to live out the outward-focused, servant-oriented mission that they were given.

In the New Testament, Jesus is presented as the climax and culmination of God's revelation in the world. The gospel writer John says of Jesus,

> In the beginning was the Word, and the Word was with God, and the Word was God. He was in the beginning with God. All things came into being through him, and without him not one thing came into being. What has come into being in him was life, and the life was the light of all people . . . The true light, which enlightens everyone, was coming into the world . . . And the Word became flesh and lived among us, and we have seen his glory, the glory as of a father's only son, full of grace and truth . . . No one has ever seen God. It is God the only Son, who is close to the Father's heart, who has made him known. (John 1:1–4, 9, 18)

The word "Word" here is *logos,* from which we get our word "logic." This word is very rich and deep and has many nuances and meanings. It can also mean "communication," "reason," "expression," or "word." A "word" is something that when used properly reveals what is on the inside. A word takes what is on the inside and brings it out into the open. Words express and reveal, but sometimes spoken words are insufficient to communicate what is on the inside. Several years back I was meeting with a couple who was trying to put things back together after an act of infidelity. The husband was very sorrowful and full of regret for what he had done, and he kept saying over and over, "I am so sorry." She, understandably, didn't really believe him, and so at one point he said, "I wish I could just take my heart out and show it to you." The foundational and core claim of our faith is that in Jesus, God took his heart out and showed it to us. Jesus, John claims, speaks for God. Jesus is God's Word. According to John, Jesus defines God.

I certainly agree with John, and can't think of a better way to summarize the heart of Christianity as I understand it and seek to live it out. Yet, John also affirms that the God *defined* by Jesus is not *confined* to Jesus. The light that shone brightly through the life of Jesus is a divine light that is in some way capable of enlightening everyone (1:9).[35] This needs to be kept in mind when we read what Jesus later says in John 14:6. The Way, the Truth, and the Life incarnated in Jesus is one that is to some degree universally available to all people through the divine light within them. The light of Christ, while revealed decisively in Jesus of Nazareth, is present throughout the universe.[36] This is why the apostle Paul assumed that the people to whom he preached about Jesus were not completely ignorant of God and were capable of already seeking God to some degree (Acts 14:16–17; 17:22–30).

---

35. The second-century Christian philosopher Justin Martyr carried forward this line of theological reasoning. For a concise summary of his view, see McDermott, *God's Rivals,* 93–97.

36. John's affirmation ultimately causes the distinction between "general revelation" and "special revelation" to break down. On most theological definitions, general revelation is what can be discerned about God from outside of special revelation, which is defined as what can be discerned about God from God's decision to reveal himself through the history of ancient Israel, the life of Jesus, and the ongoing story of the church, as this is narrated and witnessed to by the scriptures. John affirms that ultimately all authentically divine revelation is mediated to the world through the *logos* and light of Christ.

There are many who would agree with all of this said about God's desire for all to be saved (1 Tim 2:4; 2 Pet 3:9), and God's revelation of himself throughout the broader world. But they would also hold that outside of explicit knowledge about Jesus, people know enough to be condemned for their sin, but not enough to be saved. In response, we can point out that this will negate the "holy pagan" tradition within the Bible, where we frequently are reminded that there are people outside of God's chosen group who appear to be authentically and rightly connected to God (Melchizedek, Abimelech, Job, Jethro, Balaam, Naaman, Rahab, the Roman centurion whose slave was healed, and Cornelius).[37] We certainly seem to have several cases within the Bible where people who are outside the channels of God's special revelation through Israel, Christ, and the church are presented as rightly related to God. While some of the examples that are brought forth are stronger than others, it is impossible to deny that none of these were actually rightly related to God. Interestingly, even some (perhaps most) who would self-identify as an exclusivist still make exceptions for these "holy pagans" in the Old Testament, along with Jews before the time of Jesus. William Edgar, a contemporary defender of the exclusivism, writes of these two groups, "They were saved by Christ though not having full knowledge of his person and work."[38] Although Edgar and other exclusivists would see this as simply a small qualification of their position, this admission is actually a much bigger deal than that. If people seeking after God can be saved by Christ without explicitly knowing about Christ, then how is this not really inclusivism? If that is how God judged people before Christ's coming, then why would this change after Christ's coming? How is someone from three thousand years ago who lives in a culture that hasn't heard the gospel any different than someone who lives today in a culture that hasn't heard the gospel? This type of admission seems to me to expose a large crack in the foundation of the exclusivist position.

It could also be said that a God who gives people enough information to damn themselves, and yet not enough information to be saved, is not a loving and just God. How is that a fair deal? As the influential (and somewhat controversial) Southern Baptist preacher and professor Dale Moody asks, "But what kind of God is he who gives man enough

37. For a critical evaluation of this tradition, see Kaiser, "Holy Pagans." For a more positive appraisal, see McDermott, God's Rivals, 31–33.

38. Edgar, "Exclusivism," 96.

knowledge to damn him but not enough to save him?"[39] Exclusivists often appeal to Romans 1:18–25, where Paul argues that human beings have rejected what has been revealed about God in creation and the moral law within (what theologians call "general revelation"). This text, however, does not demand this interpretation. While it is true as a general indictment on humanity as a whole, it doesn't necessarily follow that every human being persistently and irrevocably rejects what God has revealed to them. In fact, Paul goes on in the very next chapter to make it clear that it is possible for people to respond positively to the general revelation of God that has been given to them. He writes, "For he will repay according to each one's deeds: to those who by patiently doing good seek for glory and honor and immortality, he will give eternal life; while for those who are self-seeking and who obey not the truth but wickedness, there will be wrath and fury" (Rom 2:6–8).[40] In commenting on this passage, the popular Christian apologist and philosopher William Lane Craig writes, "But the Bible says that the unreached will be judged on a quite different basis than those who have heard the gospel. God will judge the unreached on the basis of their response to His self-revelation in nature and conscience . . . The Bible promises salvation to anyone who responds affirmatively to this self-revelation of God (Rom 2:7)."[41] It makes much more sense to suppose that God will judge people based on what they have been given, not on what they haven't been given (Luke 12:48).

In response to this, I know that many passages of scripture come to mind about the importance, indeed the necessity, of faith in Christ. I believe that faith in Christ is necessary for salvation. But on the inclusivist vision of salvation, saving faith in Christ doesn't necessarily require a correct cognitive understanding and explicit acceptance of the Christian gospel.[42] Faith in Christ is ultimately more about a condition of the heart

---

39. Moody, *Word of Truth*, 59.

40. I find it very interesting that in a recent major evangelical defense of the exclusivist view (Morgan and Peterson, *Faith Comes By Hearing*), there is no interaction at all with this passage, even though, based on the index entries, Romans is cited and discussed more than any other biblical book.

41. Craig, "Can a Loving God?"

42. See Rom 2:6–16. Sanders, a leading contemporary proponent of inclusivism, claims that on this view, "What God requires is a right disposition towards God and a willingness to do God's will" ("Hell Yes! Hell No!," 151). Also, remember that even most exclusivists grant that this is true in the case of small children and the mentally handicapped. Exclusivists try to maintain that this doesn't compromise their view that persons

than a position in the head. It is more about a way of life than a system of belief (Matt 7:21). To have faith in Christ is to open our heart up to being animated by the power of divine love and compassion. This is the kind of faith that Jesus was interested in cultivating in people, and it is the quality of this kind of faith that matters on judgment day.

Believing creeds and adhering to a certain systematic theology is not what genuine faith is about. Those things can help when they are means to the end of love. But they can hurt when they are used as ends in themselves. I believe that a person who has never heard of Jesus, but who seeks to live their life with love and compassion by the prompting of the divine light within (John 1:9) is in a much better position with God than a "believer" whose heart is filled with apathy and greed. On judgment day, I should be much more concerned with God asking my family what I was like to live with, or asking the poor in my city what I did to help them, than with God asking me to explain the doctrine of the Trinity or the correct theory of atonement. To paraphrase Wesley's words quoted earlier, God wants good hearts a lot more than God wants clear heads. We should never forget that Jesus made practical compassion—not doctrinal correctness—the fundamental criterion for judgment (Matt 25:31–46). Nor should we forget that our lives of practical compassion, or lack thereof, will one day lead us into an encounter with the Christ we either loved or rejected through how we lived. How we lived, not merely what we believed or didn't believe, will determine what happens next.[43] In the words of the Roman Catholic priest and author Ronald Rolheiser, "Given our theology of God we may not believe that a purely external, historical connection to Christianity is more important to our intimacy with God and the salvation of our souls than are gratitude, warmth, humility, willingness to reconcile, and openness of heart . . . [and] it is wise

---

past the "age of accountability" who haven't heard the gospel and accepted it are surely damned. Some maintain that the former group is "unevangelizable," while the latter is "unevangelized." See Jennings, "God's Zeal for His World," 232. While this distinction certainly makes sense, it is not at all clear that it is a morally and theologically relevant distinction in this discussion.

43. This is not "works-righteousness," because on this view one can still maintain that all of our good actions are prompted by and empowered with divine grace. We are not saved because we have been good people; we are saved by responding to the promptings of divine grace with acts of compassion.

to believe that compassion of heart . . . trump[s] all externals in terms of our connection to God."[44]

Now, I am sure that some will recoil from this last paragraph, and accuse me of drawing a false distinction between believing the right things and living a good life, and some might be inclined to point out that the apostles in the New Testament certainly seemed concerned with doctrine as much as right living (e.g., Gal 1:8–9; 1 John 4:1–6).[45] I would say you are right, to a degree. Doctrine is important, because true doctrines about God lead us to love God and others more, while false doctrines about God lead us to love God and others less. One of the main reasons I am motivated to argue against the everlasting damnation of all non-Christians is that I believe this doctrine is false, and actually keeps many people from fully loving God with all they are, because deep down, to them God is a monster they are scared of, not a Father they adore. Right doctrine is very important for right living, and for that reason doctrinal and theological concerns are an important focus. But when push comes to shove, I think one would have a very hard time trying to show that right ideas are intrinsically more valuable and desirable to God than compassionate ways of living. I could be wrong about this, of course, but I simply find it impossible to believe that for God, *being right* is more important than *being good*.

I need to confess that it has taken me a long time to get this. For years, I would stay up late at night reading and studying and worrying that I really didn't know how to articulate the precise nature of the relationship between divine providence and human freedom, how to describe exactly how Jesus's death on the cross saves people, how to conceptualize the relationships among the persons of the Trinity, and many other profound theological concerns. I tried with all my might to avoid believing anything even close to heresy, and I thought that what God really wanted was for me to be able to explain God to God! For me, trying to understand the

---

44. Rolheiser, "Christian Attitude."

45. See Carson, *Gagging of God*, 296. In philosophical terms, I am saying that a cognitive grasp of the gospel is neither necessary nor sufficient in this life for saving faith, although I do believe that in the age to come all will see Christ face to face and will know him wholly and fully (1 Cor 13:12). Those who demur would probably say that while a cognitive grasp is not sufficient (it must manifest itself in works of love), it is necessary for intellectually capable persons. One of the big problems with this is that there is hardly any agreement on what exactly constitutes the actual minimal cognitive content.

cognitive content of the gospel actually became a substitute for seeking to really live out the challenge of Jesus's good news for all people.

Jesus once told a story about three people who encountered a beaten and battered man on the side of the road (Luke 10:29–37). The first two had all the right religious beliefs, and indeed were official representatives of their biblical religion. The third man was a heretic, from the perspective of the first two men. The first two men passed by without helping. The third man went out of his way to help the stranger, and this is the man Jesus held up as the model for what God asks of us. It's a haunting and powerful story that challenges the way in which we want to make being right with God about something as easy as believing the right creed or engaging in the right religious ritual, rather than accepting the challenge of letting divine compassion fill our hearts until they overflow with action. Jesus defined real heresy as hard-hearted living, not simply wrong-minded thinking.

Inclusivism strikes me as the theological option that is most open to making room for this central insight of Jesus. On this view, what matters most is actually walking the Way of Jesus; the Way of unlimited forgiveness, unbounded compassion, restorative justice, and nonjudgmental truth-telling. People from a variety of religious perspectives, or no particular religious perspective at all, can walk on this Way of life that Jesus incarnated. We can be assured that when we walk this Way, it will lead us directly into the heart of God (whether that is our goal or not[46]). Perhaps, with this in mind, John 14:6 isn't a harsh threat at all. What if Jesus meant it as an assuring promise? When we follow "the Way, the Truth, and the Life" that he fully embodied, we can be assured that we are walking the path to God.

---

46. It is important to note that the sheep in the judgment parable in Matt 25:31–46 did not consciously or explicitly know that the works of compassion they did were for Jesus, but they later discovered to their surprise that they were.

CHAPTER 6

Are We Just Preaching for the Hell of It?

Objection #5: "Universalism undermines evangelism."

IF EVERYBODY IS GOING to be saved, then why bother with trying to spread the gospel? If there is no everlasting hell, and ultimately everyone will be reconciled to God anyway, then there is no reason or motivation for engaging in evangelism. This key practical objection is frequently raised against Christian universalism, and it deserves a thoughtful and biblically-rooted response. At the outset, we can say that this objection poses a much bigger problem for other versions of universalism than it does for the particular Christian vision of universal salvation presented in this book. For example, a pluralistic understanding of universalism (where all responses to the divine are seen as equally valid), or a Christian account of universalism that diminishes or eliminates a place for divine wrath and judgment altogether, are much more hard-pressed to find good reasons why Christians should engage in evangelism. When contemplating the significance of this objection, it is very important not to forget that I am not trying to defend just any old version of universalism, but a very particular Christian vision of universalism where the uniqueness of Christ and the reality of postmortem punishment are integral and foundational aspects.

Before going much further in responding to this objection, I should acknowledge that there will be many Christians for whom this objection carries little weight. For some, "evangelism" has become a bad word that carries connotations of religious arrogance and cultural imperialism, and because of this they would be in favor of dropping evangelism completely.

Much of the contemporary dis-ease with evangelism among Christians stems from the relatively recent history of American Protestant world missions, and its entanglement with ethnocentric assumptions and colonialist aspirations. Harold Netland, Professor of Mission and Evangelism at Trinity Evangelical Divinity School, observes, "For many in the West are drawn to pluralism in part out of a deep sense of postcolonialist guilt—and surely there is much in its treatment of non-Western peoples for which the West ought to feel profoundly guilty."[1] In the past century, the spread of the Christian gospel at times certainly became illegitimately enmeshed with spreading Western culture and economic structures.[2] This has left many Christians deeply suspicious of missions altogether. While we should certainly be quick to confess the sins and mistakes of the past, to assume that these errors somehow invalidate all forms and expressions of Christian evangelism would be overly simplistic. It would also be misleading to assume that the modern missions movement has merely been a religious justification of Western imperialism. As Dana Robert, Professor of World Missions at Boston University, points out, "Missionaries have often been the last line of defense for indigenous peoples against exploitation by commercial and political interests."[3] While the recent history of missions should caution us against too uncritically identifying the gospel of Jesus with the cultural forms in which the gospel is embedded, to conclude that the abuses of evangelism lead to doing away with evangelism altogether would be an unwarranted leap.

My own background and experience with evangelism is somewhat complex. In my early twenties, I was the sort of person who would go door-to-door in college dorms, inviting people to ministry events and sharing my faith with them. In all honesty though, I was never really comfortable doing this, and I don't think I was really very good at it, but I did it because I thought I was supposed to. In my mid-twenties, I went through some very deep struggles with my faith, and really didn't have anything solid to share with anyone, even if I had wanted to. I have now come around to believing that I do have something worth sharing with people, but I approach evangelism much differently than I did a decade ago. The problem with a lot of expressions of evangelism is that

1. Netland, *Encountering Religious Pluralism*, 33.
2. See A. Walls, "Great Commission 1910–2010."
3. Robert, "Great Commission," 29.

the evangelist becomes something of a spiritual salesperson trying to get the potential convert to sign on the dotted line. Sometimes people are treated as objects to be changed rather than as subjects to be respected. I hate feeling like a salesperson, probably because I hate it when I feel someone is trying to manipulate me. I suspect that my own unease with high-pressure, decision-oriented evangelism is what first got me to thinking that perhaps evangelism could be more than a prepackaged testimony or a four-step outline of salvation.

Why is Evangelism Important?

The Christian faith has an indelibly evangelistic impulse to it, because central to our faith is that God has done something remarkably and extravagantly wonderful for the whole world through Jesus Christ. The word "evangelism" has its roots in the Greek word *euangelion*, which literally means "good news," and is often translated as "gospel." Interestingly, in the world in which Jesus and his first followers lived, the word *euangelion* came from the realm of Roman political propaganda.[4] When a new emperor took the throne, or when he won a decisive battle that would greatly benefit the Roman Empire, this was heralded as *euangelion*. Everyone needed to know about this world-changing announcement. When this happened, messengers were sent throughout the empire to announce this good news.

Christian evangelism, then, is nothing more and nothing less than sharing the world-changing good news with the world, through word and deed, that Christ is King and his kingdom is a kingdom of love. Because announcing Christ's kingdom is most fundamentally about enabling people to experience the reign of divine love on earth as it is in heaven, it follows that genuine evangelism should never be coercive, manipulative, or disrespectful of the unique personhood of another, or the cultural and religious tradition in which they have been formed.[5] As Christian evangelists, we can witness to the Christ that has brought us to God without disparaging or dismissing the ways in which the light of Christ may already

4. See Crossan, "Roman Imperial Theology."

5. Elaine Heath, evangelism professor at Perkins School of Theology at Southern Methodist University, writes, "Real evangelism is not colonialism, nationalism, or imperialism. Evangelism rightly understood is the holistic initiation of people into the reign of God as revealed in Jesus Christ" (*Mystic Way of Evangelism*, 13).

be shining into a person's life through their own religious background that may be very different from ours.

Evangelism, at its best, must embody both a joyful confidence in the good news of Christ that has grasped us, and a humble modesty concerning our grasp of theological truth. Because God is very generous and is universally at work in the world, our interactions with people of other faiths, or no religious faith at all, should never be approached as just a chance for us to teach others about God. Those we assume are further from God than ourselves actually just have a few things to teach us about what it means to be a person of moral integrity and spiritual authenticity (Gen 20:1–18).

Evangelism is important, then, and I would hate to ever give any Christian less motivation for living and speaking in such a way as to draw others to the Christ that reigns in heaven and dwells within us. But on the view that I have been struggling to articulate, many would say that I am doing precisely just that. In presenting a view of the afterlife that ends with everyone being reconciled to God, this nullifies the real motivation here and now for sharing the gospel of Jesus with others. If everyone ends up in heaven, what is the point of evangelism?

I am going to respond to this objection in several ways, but before doing that I feel the need to admit something and then to state an objection related to that admission. We need to admit up front that the Christian exclusivists do, in fact, have the strongest reason for engaging in evangelism. If all non-Christians over the "age of accountability" are going to experience a never-ending duration of maximal pain, then evangelism is the highest priority imaginable. Any view, then, that allows for the salvation of anyone outside of explicitly accepting the gospel message in this life certainly lessens one major motivation for evangelism. But just because the Christian exclusivist has the strongest reason for evangelism, it doesn't follow that the Christian universalist then has no strong reasons for evangelism. I hope to show that the Christian universalist still has very strong reasons that are sufficient to motivate Christian evangelism. Also, we should take note that effectiveness in motivating people to engage in evangelism is not how theological truth is determined. The evangelical theologian Millard Erickson reminds us that to adopt as true whatever view makes missions the most important is to fall into a pragmatic way of viewing truth.[6] What is true, theologically, is not what practically produces the most evangelistic zeal, but rather what coheres best with God's vision as taught by Jesus and expounded upon by the inspired biblical authors who bear witness to him.

Now for my objection related to this admission. While the exclusivist position may in fact be what inspired thousands upon thousands of missionaries in the past, and still does to this day, it seems to me that this position has not and does not motivate people as much as it should if it is really believed to be true. Many exclusivists feel no personal need or duty to share Christ with non-Christians. Now, I understand that some would just point out that this is a case of lukewarm Christians not fulfilling their duty. But what if it is more than that? What if most Christians feel no need to evangelize because deep down they do not think that exclusivism is true, but are simply afraid to question it? Or what if it is because they are not convinced that they really have "good news" to share? I realize that speculating about the psychology of others is a dangerous thing, and that this is probably a simplistic generalization, but I have a suspicion there is at least some truth in it. Interestingly, I have more energy and passion for evangelism now that I am a universalist than I ever did when I was an exclusivist. I think that is because I finally feel deep in my bones that I really have genuinely good news to share.

Why Evangelism is Still Important for Christian Universalism

Hell exists

Let me share five reasons why I think evangelism is still highly important for a Christian universalist. First, according to the view of Christian universalism I have sketched out thus far, there is still such a thing as hell that can be experienced here and now, and in the life to come. There is an ultimately moral structure to the universe that God has created, and because of that we reap what we sow (Gal 6:7), and sinful actions have serious consequences that we should seek to avoid and warn others to avoid as well. We should not overlook that there is still a place within

6. Erickson, *How Shall They Be Saved?*, 255.

Christian universalism for warning people about the painful reality of hell. Just because hell isn't *forever* doesn't mean it isn't *extremely serious*. If someone lives their whole life out of sync with God's purposes, then that person has wasted their life. To stand before God and be told that your life was a waste is something certainly to be avoided, and Christian universalists should do all we can to appropriately and compellingly warn people of the consequences of rejecting God. On the view that I have been outlining, hell is not some small thing that really isn't that big of a deal. Hell is the experience of being drawn into the flames of holy love, and for the person that resists God and has lived a life of unholy rebellion against God, this will hurt . . . like hell. The Father's arms may always be open, but whether the divine embrace feels like heaven or burns like hell is up to us.

I know that some readers are thinking, "But look, if there is ultimately going to be a universal reconciliation, then there really is not as much motivation for warning people of the consequences of sin or to make any sacrificial effort to invite people into the kingdom of God." Let me respond with this thought experiment. Let's say that Kevin and Bill are good friends, and Kevin knows that Bill has been having thoughts of cheating on his wife with a co-worker. Kevin loves Bill and Bill's wife. He knows that Bill's wife is the most forgiving and compassionate person that he has ever met. She has a long track record of letting go of wrongs easily and working to reconcile with people who have hurt her in the past. So Kevin thinks to himself, "I don't need to confront Bill about this relationship with his co-worker, because even if he does have an affair, his wife will forgive him and they will be reconciled one day, I'm sure of it." I trust that you can see where I am going with this. This is stupid reasoning. Even if it is true that Bill's wife will forgive him and be reconciled to him, if Bill has an affair it will cause a huge amount of pain for both of them that will be extremely difficult to work through. You see, even if Kevin could know for sure that one day Bill and his wife would be reconciled, that still would not at all undermine his motivation to want to help his friends avoid going through a temporary time of horrendous pain and difficulty. Pain that is worth avoiding— pain that is worth warning others about—doesn't have to be everlasting in order for it to be serious enough to warrant deep concern. The Christian universalist should not refrain from speaking about the consequences of rejecting the Way of Christ just because they have an assurance that one day all will be reconciled to Christ. Some roads are still much better to take than others. The contemporary Wesleyan philosophical theologian Jerry Walls, who is a critic of universalism but still holds that it is possible for people to repent in the age to come, argues persuasively that such a belief doesn't trivialize our decisions here and now because "the more we sin and persist in our rebellion, the more complicated will be our repentance and subsequent transformation."[7] Some roads lead to harmony and fulfillment, and some lead to self-destruction and frustration (Matt 7:13–14). The Christian universalist can, and should, acknowledge this reality.

Salvation: transaction vs. transformation

The second thing that can be said of Christian evangelism is that it is about much more than making sure people are headed towards the right destiny in the age to come. In some Christian circles, "evangelism" has come to basically mean getting as many people as possible to say they believe in Jesus so that they'll be set up in the afterlife. J. I. Packer, the well-respected evangelical theologian, writes, "What is the main job of the Christian missionary witness? To win men to Christian faith? Or to do something else for them? Universalism prompts the latter view."[8] Packer seems to assume that *real* evangelism is focused solely on getting people to accept the Christian faith so that they will not go to hell in the afterlife. Salvation has come to mean simply escape from God's punitive punishments in hell. In the New Testament, however, salvation is about much more than just getting our soul into heaven when we die, and evangelism is about much more than getting our name on the right side of the divine ledger. Salvation is about getting heaven, the realm of God's saving presence, into all the different aspects of our life here and now. The early Christians did not understand their mission in life to be to simply get people to assent to certain religious beliefs so that they would have a good afterlife waiting for them. They believed that Jesus is the world's true ruler, and so their mission was to live in that truth and announce it to the world. The first Christians believed that through his resurrection and ascension, Jesus was exalted as King over all, and so the way we enable

---

7. J. Walls, *Purgatory*, 147. In responding to this objection, Walls does a nice job of also pointing out the inconsistency in claiming that opportunities for postmortem conversion trivialize this life while "deathbed repentance" does not. If repenting one minute before death doesn't trivialize this life, then why would repenting one minute after death?

8. Packer, "Problem of Universalism Today," 171.

God's kingdom to come on earth as it is in heaven is by following Jesus here and now.

Let's take a closer look at the foundational passage for Christian evangelism, the so-called "Great Commission" that Jesus gives us in Matthew 28:

> And Jesus came and said to them, "All authority in heaven and on earth has been given to me. Go therefore and make disciples of all nations, baptizing them in the name of the Father and of the Son and of the Holy Spirit, and teaching them to obey everything that I have commanded you. And remember, I am with you always, to the end of the age." (vv. 18–20)

Evangelism, as Jesus describes and commands, is not a matter of simply getting people to believe certain things that will merely ensure their eternal destiny. Evangelism is the process whereby we who are disciples (students or apprentices) of Jesus initiate others into a life of following him and teaching them to obey everything that he commands. The contemporary Christian philosopher Dallas Willard forcefully argued that much of contemporary evangelism has settled for making converts to Christianity, rather than making real disciples of Christ, people who actually seek to listen to Jesus and do what he says. He describes the lack of emphasis on discipleship in today's churches in the West as the "great omission" in our evangelistic endeavors.[9]

One of the most horrific and tragic manifestations of this omission from our gospel proclamation is the genocidal atrocities that took place in Rwanda in 1994. Rwanda had been held up as the most "Christian" country on the African continent, and was seen as one of the greatest successes of Christian missions ever, with about 90 percent of the population identifying as Christian. Yet, over a 100-day period, these fellow Christians killed 800,000 of their Rwandan brothers and sisters (20 percent of the population). As Lee Camp observes, "The Western Christianity imported into the heart of Africa had apparently failed to create communities of disciples."[10] The gospel that they had received had apparently neglected to teach them that salvation in Christ is not just about a one-time transaction that gets us into heaven, but instead it is about a lifelong process of

9. Willard, *Great Omission*. See Kallenberg, *Live to Tell*, 47–64, for more on the integral relationship between evangelism and discipleship.

10. Camp, *Mere Discipleship*, 20.

transformation into the likeness of Christ. Evangelism that leaves people's fundamental identities unchanged and their way of life undisturbed is not real evangelism.[11] Evangelism that creates converts to a belief system, and not disciples to a way of life, is a counterfeit version of genuine evangelism. Brian P. Stone, Professor of Evangelism at Boston University School of Theology, writes, "The problem is this: when the practice of evangelism becomes so preoccupied with entry that it loses sight of the journey itself, it is capable of being taken over by a logic foreign to the journey and even antagonistic to it."[12] This is certainly what happened in Rwanda, and what happens anywhere when evangelism is about anything other than an invitation to actual discipleship to Christ here and now.

I have found that when most people raise this objection to Christian universalism, what they have in mind is a kind of evangelism that is divorced from, or at least not integrally connected to, following Jesus as our teacher in life. If evangelism is about inviting people to become apprentices to Jesus's way of life, as Jesus said it should be, then the only way we can doubt the importance of evangelism is if we doubt the value of being a disciple of Jesus in the first place.

While belief in an everlasting hell may be what has motivated many evangelists and missionaries, I would argue that it is precisely this belief that has largely contributed to a transactional, decision-oriented focus towards evangelism that has made accepting the gospel the minimal entrance requirement for heaven. In contrast, Jesus said evangelism is to be about making disciples by teaching people how to live as he taught through empowerment of his Spirit. If we think that people are going to be tortured for an eternity if they do not believe the right things, then all of our focus is on getting them to say a certain prayer or accept a certain creed to escape that fate. What matters, on this view, isn't getting the whole gospel into people as deeply as possible, but rather what becomes top priority is simply getting just a part of the gospel into as many people as possible. But, when the part becomes the whole, then the whole thing gets distorted. Teaching people how to live in the Way of Christ becomes optional on this view, instead of being essential as Christ said it should be.

Evangelism is still of the utmost importance within Christian universalism because the kingdom of God has not yet come in its fullness,

11. In the case of the genocide in Rwanda, the message of Jesus did not change and touch the rival ethnic identities of the Hutus and the Tutsis.

12. Stone, *Evangelism after Christendom*, 260–61.

and the way that happens more and more is through people committing to be disciples of Christ. Each day when I pray for God's kingdom to come "on earth as it is in heaven," I am not only engaging in intercession, I am renewing my enlistment as a disciple of Christ through which God can work to make this happen. Trusting that God has the power to ultimately make all things well does not absolve us Christians of the responsibility here and now to be God's co-laborers in bringing the world into alignment with God's dream for the world (1 Cor 3:9). Knowing that God has the resurrection power to transform and renew all of creation doesn't render our work for the Lord meaningless. Instead, it infuses it with meaning and purpose, because we know that God will somehow use our grace-empowered evangelistic efforts for the eternal glory of Christ's kingdom.[13] After the longest and most thorough discussion in the New Testament of the future resurrection and God's plan and power to set all things right through Jesus Christ, the apostle Paul makes this conclusion: "Therefore, my beloved, be steadfast, immovable, always excelling in the work of the Lord, because you know that in the Lord your labor is not in vain" (1 Cor 15:58). The faith of a Christian universalist, a faith that is rooted in a strong confidence in the power of God to ultimately conquer all evil and destroy all forces of sin and death (1 Cor 15:24–27) as part of the final goal to bring all things together in Christ (Eph 1:10), is not one that encourages apathy and indifference. This kind of faith in God's future inspires profound hope in the present. Our evangelistic efforts are never wasted, but will be used by God in some way for the building up of his kingdom, regardless of the results here and now.

The apostle Paul certainly didn't see a robust hope in the purpose of God and the power of Christ to reconcile all things to himself as an impediment to evangelism and mission. He saw this vision for the future as having the power to inspire us to draw the future into the present through our obedience in spreading Christ's good news. Believing as Peter did in the restoration of all things (Acts 3:21), as Paul did in the reconciliation of all things (Col 1:20), and as John did in the renewal of all things (Rev 21:5), does not hamper motivation for evangelism at all. Just as the hope of universal salvation inspired Peter, Paul, and John, so can it inspire us to preach fearlessly, love limitlessly, and obey unconditionally.

---

13. See N. Wright, *Surprised by Hope*, 207–32.

So, the goal of the Christian life is not to wait on getting to go to God's kingdom *then* and *there*, but praying and working to get God's kingdom to come *here* and *now*. This is why in the book of Acts we see the early Christians making huge shifts and major reorientations in their way of life. They started living, for example, as if distinctions of economic class and race did not matter. They took care of people they did not know, and in a world with absolutely no social safety nets, the world around them took note and caused their community to grow exponentially. Evangelism for the first Christians was never a message about a mere transaction, where they accept Jesus and get their ticket punched for entrance into heaven. Instead, their message about Jesus was very much centered on the possibility of present transformation, both personal and social, as people are ushered into the liberating reign of God. To diminish or minimize the importance of life here and now is to misunderstand the gospel of Jesus that from the beginning was intended to be a catalyst for spiritual and social transformation.

Interestingly, "hell" is never mentioned in any of the sermons recorded in the book of Acts. This is highly significant because Acts offers us an account of the spread of the church in its earliest years (from roughly 30–60 AD). The whole book is filled with one missionary story after another, and yet not once do the apostles threaten eternal punishment to people if they do not accept their good news. They didn't see their mission as getting people to buy "celestial fire insurance."[14] They do preach a judgment in the age to come, but as we have seen, one cannot simply read into an affirmation of judgment an eternally dualistic outcome. While the preachers in Acts do not preach a doctrine of everlasting hell, one preacher named Peter (as noted above) did in fact proclaim that one day there would be a "restoration of all things." Even though Peter apparently believed that one day God would restore and reclaim all things, this didn't at all dampen his missionary zeal. In fact, Peter argues that because one day the work of Christ will be consummated in a universal restoration, we should repent here and now so our sins will be forgiven and so that we can begin to live in tune with how life in the kingdom of God will be (Acts 3:19). If the kingdom that is coming is one where there is absolutely no evil allowed to spoil the goodness of God's creation, if there is no room for prejudice, greed, lust, apathy, anger, and hate, and if the only way to be at

14. Abraham, *Logic of Evangelism*, 19.

home in this kingdom is to be rid of all these things, then we better start allowing God to change us, to make us fit to dwell where "righteousness is at home" (2 Pet 3:13).

The logic of Christian universalism isn't that because all will be reconciled to God, we should therefore not be concerned about how life is lived here and now. No, the logic of Christian universalism is that because we are all headed towards an inescapable encounter with the complete truth about ourselves and about God, we should open ourselves up to the light of God here and now so that the light can begin to dispel the darkness and we can begin to be transformed now and experience a glimpse of the fullness and richness of life with God in the age to come (Acts 3:20).

Gratitude for good news

Christian universalists have genuinely good news that God is love and light (1 John 1:5; 4:6), and that God is for every one of us (Rom 8:31); therefore, this is the third reason I believe evangelism to be crucial. This good news is inherently worthy of being announced and made known to all people. The message of Jesus was first seen as a world-changing announcement of God's unfathomable and unconquerable love, and should still be seen that way today. I think it is really impossible to genuinely receive this message without having a desire to share it, in word and/or deed. The reception of the message creates a desire to share the message. Paul said that his awareness of Christ's universal love "compelled" him to share this good news with others (2 Cor 5:14). Evangelism is simply what flows out of a heart that has been taken hold of by Christ's love. As the great Wesleyan scholar Albert Outler reminds us, "The prime motive for evangelism is gratitude."[15] We do not need the fear of divine exclusion to motivate us to be evangelists; the joy of divine inclusion is more than sufficient to light that fire within.

Blessed assurance

One of the central blessings of knowing God through Christ is that we are given a deep inward assurance that we are children of God (Rom 8:15–16). When we become aware of God's great love for us in Christ

15. Outler, *Evangelism in the Wesleyan Spirit*, 47.

and open ourselves up to this reality, then the love of God fills our hearts with an unshakeable hope (Rom 5:5). Even though I have argued that non-Christians can ultimately be saved, without hearing the gospel and embracing it a person will be without this Spirit-inspired assurance that is of inestimable worth. The fourth reason and one of the main motivations for evangelism from the perspective of Christian universalism is that we want others to have the assurance that in the midst of life's trials and tragedies, there is a good God whose redemptive power is at work in all situations (Rom 8:28), and who will ultimately make all things well (Rev 21:5).

Believing that Christ is actually the Savior of all people doesn't stop us from wanting to share this message. It certainly didn't work that way for the apostle Paul who wrote, "The saying is sure and worthy of full acceptance. For to this end we toil and struggle, because we have our hope set on the living God, who is the Savior of all people, especially of those who believe" (1 Tim 4:9–10). Paul believed that Christ is the Savior of all, yet he worked with all his energy and strength to spread the good news because believers have the special benefit of being assured of God's saving love. Paul knew this assurance and wanted others to know it too.

Gifts of the Spirit

The Holy Spirit that indwells those who are receptive to Christ not only offers the gift of inward assurance, but she also offers gifts to each person for the purpose of building up the church so that it can advance Christ's kingdom of love (Rom 12:3–8; 1 Cor 12:4–31). The fifth reason for holding to the importance of evangelism is that receiving the gospel and seeking the indwelling of the Spirit enables us to tap into the gifts for life and ministry that we have been given. In my own life, discovering my spiritual gifts of preaching and teaching has been an enormous source of joy and purpose. The Christian universalist, then, can be motivated to share the good news of Jesus with others so that they too can uncover their gifts for ministry and service in God's kingdom.

Conclusion

The objection that evangelism is undermined or rendered meaningless by the belief in the reconciliation of all things in Christ has been shown to be without much merit. As we noted earlier, this objection is more substantial when leveled against forms of universalism that, unlike the one advanced in this book, do not maintain the uniqueness of Christ and the reality of postmortem judgment. If the threat of everlasting conscious torment is needed for evangelism to have solid grounding and sufficient motivation, then Christian universalism has a problem. I have argued that while denying everlasting conscious torment does perhaps lessen the gravity of evangelistic work, it in no way robs evangelism of vital energy, clear motivation, and profound purpose. In fact, when evangelism is rooted in not just what we are saved *from*, but what we are saved *for*, there are still more than enough reasons to inspire and motivate Christian universalists to share the world-changing announcement of Jesus. Christian universalism allows us to place our evangelistic energies not just in anxiously trying to convert people to the minimal entrance requirements for heaven, but in confidently working to become the kind of faith-filled, love-driven, hope-inspired kind of disciples who can help others experience Jesus's kingdom of love here and now . . . and forever.

CHAPTER 7

Hell-Bent on Holy Living

Objection #6: "Universalism undermines holy living."

WITHOUT THE THREAT OF eternal punishment, there is often fear that moral chaos will result. In fact, some Christian universalists, such as the early church father Origen, have thought that it isn't a good idea to preach about universal salvation too openly out of fear that people will twist the message to mean that holy living is no longer important. As we begin to respond to this objection, I think it is important to acknowledge that the same objection has been raised against the very gospel of grace itself. After Paul talked triumphantly about the power of divine grace that is more than sufficient to overcome all human sin, he entertained the objection, "What then are we to say? Should we continue in sin in order that grace may abound? By no means! How can we who died to sin go on living in it?" (Rom 6:1–2). A message that says that God's grace is big enough to wash away every sin is a message that could easily be taken as license to sin as much as we want. We like to sin; God likes to forgive; what a deal! Paul responds by pointing out the absurdity or incongruence of coming to know the goodness and love of God and then living in such a way as to deny this. Trusting that God is for us and then living as if God is against us doesn't make much sense.

The Christian universalist can make a similar response to this charge. Not only does coming to know God as completely good and totally loving not undermine holy living, it actually profoundly inspires holy living by assuring us that God really is for us and that God only asks of us what is really best for us. We can trust that God has our best interest in mind when he commands us to do something. Unlike the view of God depicted in the traditional doctrine of everlasting hell, the God envisioned in Christian universalism has no dark side (1 John 1:5). God is pure and holy love through and through, and so this God can be fully trusted and deeply loved.

God isn't just looking for our obedience. If all God wanted was obedience, God could have made robots and programmed us to obey. God wants more than obedience. He longs to love us and have that love returned. This is why in the scriptures the dominant images of the God-world relation is that of a close interpersonal relationship, such as between a husband and wife, or a parent and child. The doctrine of everlasting punishment may in fact prompt obedience simply out of fear of the consequences. But fear cannot compel a response of love, which is what God is really looking for from us. The apostle John makes this clear when he writes,

> So we have known and believe the love that God has for us. God is love, and those who abide in love abide in God, and God abides in them. Love has been perfected among us in this: that we may have boldness on the day of judgment, because as he is, so are we in this world. There is no fear in love, but perfect love casts out fear; for fear has to do with punishment, and whoever fears has not reached perfection in love. We love because he first loved us. (1 John 4:16–19)

Perfect love casts out fear. God does not want us to be intimidated into obedience; God wants us to be drawn into a response of love that comes from receiving the free gift of love given to us in Christ. Tragically, the church often doesn't trust in the power of love to draw people to God, and so instead resorts to promoting a fear-based religion full of threats. The Christian universalist simply insists on the truth that love is a better way than fear.

If the charge is made against Christian universalism that it dilutes the motivation for holy living, not only can the previous defense be offered, but we can also go on the offensive and make the case that it is actually the traditional doctrine of everlasting hell that potentially undermines holy living insofar as it actually distorts what God's holiness is all about. Recall that earlier we said God's holiness is God's "otherness," that is, it is what makes God essentially different from us. According to the traditionalists, God's holiness lies in God's right to retributively punish sin forever out of being offended by human sin. However, Jesus defined God's holy perfection much differently. He didn't describe God's holiness as God's desire or need to restore his offended majesty, but rather he explicitly and clearly defined God's holiness as God's unbounded love for God's enemies (Matt 5:43–48). Remember, it was the Pharisees who defined God's holiness in terms of separation from sinners. The Pharisees (whose name means "separate ones") excluded sinners from their fellowship because they believed they were imitating the way God relates to sinners. Jesus, on the other hand, welcomed sinners into fellowship with himself because he believed he was imitating the way God relates to sinners. Jesus subversively redefined God's holiness as compassion, not separation.[1] When thinking about the holiness of God, it is crucially important that we let Jesus define divine holiness for us, since he is the pinnacle of God's revelation to us. "No one has ever seen God," the apostle John writes, but Jesus "who is close to the Father's heart has made him known" (John 1:18). God is holy, to be sure, but traditional defenders of hell rely far too much on the vision of divine holiness put forth by the Pharisees, and not enough on the way Jesus revealed the holiness of God as compassionate love.

Christian universalism, unlike the traditional view of hell, refuses to dilute Jesus's radical message that God's holiness and perfection is defined by a refusal to embrace retaliatory justice and limited forgiveness (Matt 5:38–42; 18:21–22). God's holy perfection is not a retributive drive to punish sinners. God's holy perfection is a restorative impulse to forgive sinners and, through a non-retaliatory love that absorbs sin, make reconciliation possible. Forgiving love is at the heart of who God is. Forgiveness isn't just something that God does. Forgiveness, the willingness to take on the pain caused by others and to not strike back, is at the core of God's being. The cross of Jesus is the ultimate revelation of God's self-sacrificial and nonviolent love. In Christ, we see a God who refuses to fight evil with evil, but instead overcomes evil with good and calls us to walk the path that he pioneered for us (Rom 12:14–21).

The Christian univeralist, then, will see living with forgiveness as essential to holy living. Because God is deeply forgiving and non-retaliatory, our journey of seeking to imitate God must then make forgiveness front and center for our way of life. There is no doubting the fact that the way of forgiveness is absolutely central to the Christian way of

1. See Borg, *Conflict, Holiness, and Politics*, 135–55.

life (e.g., Matt 6:7–15; Col 3:13). While I would never claim that people who hold the traditional view of hell are necessarily less forgiving than Christian universalists, I do think that Christian universalism can do a better job, theologically and psychologically, of actually justifying a way of life centered on forgiveness because its vision of God supports this way of life more than the traditional view. As Jurgen Moltmann affirms, "The universalism of hope in God's future for the whole universe opens us to love without limits."[2]

On the traditional view, God essentially asks of humanity what God is not willing to do. God asks us to not seek merely retributive punishment and to forgive indefinitely, yet God is not willing to do this himself. On the traditional view, it is easier to write people off and condemn them because it is believed deep down that this is what God in fact does with the majority of people. On the universalist view, restorative justice and reconciliation are the ultimate reality. Because the universalist believes that the world is heading towards the reconciliation of all things, we are motivated and inspired here and now to begin to make that a reality. Brian McLaren writes that Christians should live with an "ethic of anticipation" where "we seek to have our present way of life shaped by our vision of God's desired future."[3] Our vision of how God will treat people in the end profoundly shapes how we treat people now. Our doctrine of hell functions deeply in shaping the way we relate to others here and now. For this reason, among others, the doctrine of hell is in no way a peripheral issue for Christians. Our view of hell reveals what we really believe God is like, and that in turn forms how we will actually relate to others in this life, especially those who have wronged us. In the rest of this chapter, I would like for us to explore the centrality of forgiveness for the Christian way of life, and how holding to the universalist vision of the end can empower us to be people grounded in the goal of reconciliation now.

The Futility of Revenge

When we are significantly wronged, we have essentially two options: revenge or forgiveness. Revenge, though, can take two basic forms: aggressive or passive. Normally when we think of revenge we think of the more

2. Moltmann, "Final Judgment," 227.
3. McLaren, New Kind of Christianity, 200.

aggressive type where we actively and perhaps even violently seek to harm another person in return for what they did to us. But there is another type of revenge that is more pervasive, subtle, passive, and less noticeable, but nevertheless is still a destructive form of revenge. With this passive mode of revenge, instead of violently and harmfully confronting someone, we give them the cold shoulder. We make sure we tell everyone how bad they are. We ignore them. We write them off for good. We resent them.

The opposite response to revenge is the way of forgiveness. Forgiveness is often seen as a noble, but ultimately unrealistic ideal. If forgiveness is our primary way of responding to wrongdoing, people fear that evil may grow unchecked and justice will be denied. Also, revenge is often seen as the strong thing to do, while forgiveness is seen as the weak thing to do. But we need to ask some probing questions about these common assumptions. What if revenge is actually the unrealistic ideal? What if revenge is actually an insatiable desire, a drive that can never actually be satisfied? What if we can never really "get" revenge? And what if revenge is actually a very weak thing to do.?

Let's begin these reflections by looking at one of the oddest and most tragic revenge stories in the Bible, the story of Samson as it is told in Judges 15. The larger biblical context for this story is that after God sets his people free from slavery in Egypt, and leads them into the land he has promised where they can be free to follow his commands, a series of "judges" then leads the people.

With each successive judge, things get worse and worse. Samson is among the last of the judges of Israel, and, as we will see, with him things really bottom out.

> After a while, at the time of the wheat harvest, Samson went to visit his wife, bringing along a kid. He said, "I want to go into my wife's room." But her father would not allow him to go in. Her father said, "I was sure that you had rejected her; so I gave her to your companion. Is not her younger sister prettier than she? Why not take her instead?" Samson said to them, "This time, when I do mischief to the Philistines, I will be without blame." (vv. 1–3)

The story begins when Samson comes home after a long time away and tries to impress his wife by bringing her a young goat. (Maybe the flower store was closed that day?) His father-in-law, interestingly enough, assumes that Samson isn't coming back, so he gives his daughter to one of Samson's companions, a Philistine. He then tries to make up for this by giving him her younger sister. So far, the story seems like an ancient Jerry Springer show! Note carefully what Samson says in response, "When I do mischief to the Philistines, *I will be without blame*." Revenge feels intoxicating and empowering because there is this sense that we can do something wrong, but cannot be blamed because we are just getting even. So what kind of blameless "mischief" does Samson have in mind to make up for his wife being stolen from him? (Caution: Don't try this at home!)

> So Samson went and caught three hundred foxes, and took some torches; and he turned the foxes tail to tail, and put a torch between each pair of tails. When he had set fire to the torches, he let the foxes go into the standing grain of the Philistines, and burned up the shocks and the standing grain, as well as the vineyards and olive groves. Then the Philistines asked, "Who has done this?" And they said, "Samson, the son-in-law of the Timnite, because he has taken Samson's wife and given her to his companion." So the Philistines came up, and burned her and her father. Samson said to them, "If this is what you do, I swear I will not stop until I have taken revenge on you." He struck them down hip and thigh with great slaughter; and he went down and lived in the cleft of the rock of Etam. (vv. 4–8)

A family dispute leads to toasted foxes and scorched farms, and toasted foxes and scorched farms then lead to two people being burned to death. Now Samson must respond in order to make things "right," so he engages in mass murder. We've gone from family dispute to mass murder, and all in the name of "getting even." It gets even weirder:

> Then the Philistines came up and encamped in Judah, and made a raid on Lehi. The men of Judah said, "Why have you come up against us?" They said, "We have come up to bind Samson, to do to him as he did to us." Then three thousand men of Judah went down to the cleft of the rock of Etam, and they said to Samson, "Do you not know that the Philistines are rulers over us? What then have you done to us?" He replied, "As they did to me, so I have done to them." They said to him, "We have come down to bind you, so that we may give you into the hands of the Philistines." Samson answered them, "Swear to me that you yourselves will not attack me." They said to him, "No, we will only bind you and give you into their hands; we will not kill you." So they bound him with two new ropes, and brought him up from the rock. When he came to Lehi, the Philistines came shouting to meet him; and the spirit

of the LORD rushed on him, and the ropes that were on his arms became like flax that has caught fire, and his bonds melted off his hands. Then he found a fresh jawbone of a donkey, reached down and took it, and with it he killed a thousand men. And Samson said, "With the jawbone of a donkey, heaps upon heaps, with the jawbone of a donkey I have slain a thousand men." When he had finished speaking, he threw away the jawbone; and that place was called Ramath-lehi. (vv. 9–17)

Let's take stock of what has happened again: The problem starts with a guy, a girl, and a goat, which leads to 300 roasted foxes and burnt crops, which leads to two people being burned at the stake, which leads to "great slaughter," which then leads to the donkey jawbone massacre of 1000 men. I think it would be fair to say that in terms of how the "getting even" develops, there is a strong escalation of violence. What starts as an interpersonal conflict ends up as a major catastrophe with way too many foxes being burned and way too many people being killed. It is obvious to the objective reader looking in that there is an inflammatory nature to what is happening. The responses of revenge keep getting bigger and bigger. However, throughout the story each party claims to only be doing to the other what was first done to them.

Near the beginning of the story, Samson vows that he will not stop until he gets revenge. When exactly would that be? There is an inherently inflammatory nature to the revenge impulse. Revenge always irrationally escalates and wants more. Retaliation promises what it can't deliver. Revenge writes checks that it can't cash. Vengeful desire creates the illusion that a payback will nullify the offense, when in reality evil is multiplied.

Revenge, whether aggressive or passive, can feel almost intoxicating because it is fueled by a sense of righteous indignation, moral immunity, and justice. There is something very important to acknowledge here: the desire for revenge does in fact have a *core* of moral goodness to it. It is driven, in part, by the acknowledgment that something happened that shouldn't have and something needs to be done to address it. The desire for revenge is rooted in an inherent sense of justice. However, and this is a big "however," the morally good aspect of the desire for a wrong to be righted easily morphs into a very blinding and self-centered desire to simply do to others the evil that was done to us. Christopher Marshall writes,

> We feel that the most effective way to appease the hurt of the of-
> fense is to inflict equal suffering in return. But in reality the "pay-
> back" instinct manifests the most terrifying characteristic of evil,
> its pernicious power to turn those who are sinned against into
> sinners in their own right, to suck the innocent into a pattern of
> imitative behavior that brings its own guilt.[4]

The most dangerous and destructive aspect of having evil done to us is that evil has the power to suck us into its ways, to bring us down to the level of the wrong done to us. The revenge impulse pulls us in to becoming the evil that is done to us. Revenge multiplies the very thing it seeks to destroy. The desire for revenge makes us think that we are just doing what is just, when in reality the revenge impulse always escalates. The craving for revenge deludes our thinking; it tricks us into believing that striking back will actually make things balanced and whole. Revenge may seem like the way to pour water on the flames of pain and destruction, but in reality is like pouring gas on those flames.

The Way of Forgiveness

We have looked at probably the most extraordinary revenge story in the Bible. Now let's turn to looking at the most significant story where revenge is rejected.

> While he was still speaking, Judas, one of the twelve, arrived;
> with him was a large crowd with swords and clubs, from the chief
> priests and the elders of the people. Now the betrayer had given
> them a sign, saying, "The one I will kiss is the man; arrest him." At
> once he came up to Jesus and said, "Greetings, Rabbi!" and kissed
> him. Jesus said to him, "Friend, do what you are here to do." Then
> they came and laid hands on Jesus and arrested him. Suddenly,
> one of those with Jesus put his hand on his sword, drew it, and
> struck the slave of the high priest, cutting off his ear. Then Jesus
> said to him, "Put your sword back into its place; for all who take
> the sword will perish by the sword." (Matt 26:47–52)

When wronged or hurt by someone else, the strong thing may seem to be to strike back, to pull out the sword and start swinging, to write a nasty email back to that person, to spread rumors about that person, to say that one thing to that person that you know will push their angry

4. Marshall, *Beyond Retribution*, 57.

button. But it takes more strength to refrain from acting on the revenge impulse than it does to act on it. In this scene, who is really strong? The soldiers with swords and clubs may seem like the strong ones, or Peter, the one who pulls out a sword and slashes the face of a guard may seem strong, but actually the strongest person on the scene is the one who refuses to get pulled into the downward spiral of vengeance and retaliation.

Greater strength is required to refrain from acting on the revenge impulse than to act on it. More intelligence is also required to refrain from acting on the revenge impulse. Revenge is ultimately very stupid, according to Jesus, because in attempting to destroy someone else we devour ourselves. To retaliate is to ignorantly and blindly react on the same moral level as the wrongdoer. To forgive is to follow Jesus and intentionally act on a higher moral and spiritual level. Miroslav Volf writes,

> He refused to be sucked into the automatism of revenge, but sought to overcome evil by doing good—even at the cost of his life. Jesus' kind of option for nonviolence had nothing to do with the self-abnegation in which I completely place myself at the disposal of others to do with me as they please; it has much to do with the kind of self-assertion in which I refuse to be ensnared in the dumb redoubling of my enemies' violent gestures and be reshaped into their mirror image.[5]

Jesus was willing to take God's way of forgiveness and nonviolence all the way. When Jesus was being crucified he prayed, "Father forgive them, for they don't know what they are doing" (Luke 23:34). Jesus refused to participate in the cycles of betrayal, vengeance, and violence. In his death, he both judged all of humanity in its sin and saved all of humanity from its sin. His death on the cross revealed both the sinfully violent impulses of the human heart, and the shockingly gracious love of the divine heart. Jesus's unflinching refusal to give into the sinful dynamics of revenge saves us and heals us when we make Jesus's Way our way.

Jesus in the book of John says, "And just as Moses lifted up the serpent in the wilderness, so must the Son of Man be lifted up, that whoever believes in him may have eternal life" (3:14–15). Jesus is alluding to a strange story told in Numbers 21 where the Israelites complain a lot and so God sends some poisonous snakes to shake things up a bit. (Be careful not to gripe too much!) The snakes start biting them, and so God tells

---

5. Volf, *Exclusion and Embrace*, 292.

Moses to make a bronze serpent on a staff and whenever people look at this they will be healed of the snake's venom that has infected them. According to this passage in John, Jesus understood his death in which he would be lifted up on a cross as a source of healing for those who would look deeply at him. All of humanity has been infected with the venom of vengeance, and the cure is to look deeply at the person of Jesus dying on a cross forgiving his enemies, and winning a decisive victory over the power of evil. Samson may have had a bodybuilder's physique and more than his fair share of testosterone, but ultimately he was a very weak and stupid man. Jesus may have ended up on a humiliating and torturous execution stake, but in the way he did so, he showed himself to be the smartest and strongest person to ever live.

What Forgiveness is Not

Forgiveness is a notoriously difficult concept to grasp, and its precise meaning and implications are often contested. Living with forgiveness is an extremely hard thing to do, and it is often compounded by the fact that we frequently misunderstand just what forgiveness is about. In an attempt to clarify what forgiveness actually is, let's walk through several things forgiveness is not.[6]

Tolerating — When we tolerate something, we put up with it; we "let it slide." We tolerate something when we don't feel like it is such a big deal that we should make a fuss about it. Sometimes tolerating is the right thing to do when it comes to *the very small collisions of daily life* that we encounter. "Bear with one another," Paul would say to people in his churches (Eph 4:2; Col 3:13). A good deal of keeping the peace in a family, a church, or a community is learning to bear with one another, learning to tolerate the little things that may rub us the wrong way. To tolerate is to give people space to be different than what we want them to be. But let me emphasize that toleration is a good policy only for the minor non-moral annoyances that other people might cause us. Toleration is not the way to deal with moral infractions, serious conflict, or major harms.

Denying — Forgiveness is not denying the wrongness of an action. It's not about saying, "It wasn't that bad after all." Forgiveness starts with

6. The following discussion is indebted to Worthington, *Just Forgiveness*; Volf, *Exclusion and Embrace* and *Free of Charge*; Enright, *Forgiveness is a Choice*.

the acknowledgment that what was done to us is wrong and shouldn't be done again. Judgment is actually the first step in forgiveness. To be forgiving doesn't mean we turn a blind eye to wrongdoing. Jesus certainly was not in denial about the hurt and evil of the world. On the contrary, he was totally clear-sighted and very clear-spoken about what went on around him. Take, for example, what Jesus says in Matthew 18:6, "But whoever shall offend one of these little ones which believe in me, it were better for him that a millstone were hanged about his neck, and that he were drowned in the depth of the sea." Jesus names child abuse as a horrific crime that is taken very seriously by God in the same chapter that he talks about divine and human forgiveness. Whatever Jesus means by forgiveness, it can't mean being "soft" on sin or turning a blind eye to wrongdoing. Any action or way of life that harms another person should be named and dealt with. Forgiveness will impact how we deal with the wrongdoing, but it doesn't mean denying that there was wrongdoing.

Excusing — When we excuse someone, we discover reasons that get the person off the hook. Sometimes this needs to be done, because sometimes we misunderstand others' intentions, but forgiveness is different. If we hear that someone says something about us and we then discover that the person who told us what they said took it out of context and that person really didn't mean what we thought they meant, then we excuse that person, we don't forgive them. Again, a central element of forgiveness is a judgment on someone's actions.

Forgetting — The phrase "forgive and forget" (which isn't in the Bible by the way) may be one of the most misleading ideas for thinking about forgiveness. Forgiving and forgetting are two different things, although there is a certain degree of truth in the phrase. When we forgive there is a sense in which we forget, in that it may no longer dominate our consciousness like it once did, but forgiveness doesn't magically wipe the slate clean. Forgiveness does not produce amnesia. You may remember the movie *Men in Black* where some of the characters had wands they could hold up to people's faces and make them forget the alien encounter they just had. Forgiveness is not a magic wand that makes us forget the harm done to us. Someone once told me that she hadn't forgiven someone because she still remembered what they did. Of course! Forgiveness doesn't erase the past; it reshapes the future. We will always carry the past with us into the future; there is no choice in that matter. But we do have a choice as to *how* we carry the past into the future.

In some cases, forgetting is not only impossible, but we would be outright wrong to try to forget. Some things need to be remembered and proper space and boundaries put in place to prevent further harm. Proverbs 26:11 says, "Like a dog returns to its vomit, so a fool returns to their folly." That is a Bible verse I would love to see cross-stitched on a pillow! The point is that some people will keep returning to their destructive ways and we don't have to be there when they do.

Reconciling — Forgiveness is a gift offered from one person to another. Reconciliation requires that the gift be accepted. Forgiveness is unilateral. Reconciliation takes two. Even when there is repentance and forgiveness, reconciliation may not be possible or desirable. Reconciliation not only requires repentance and forgiveness, it also requires the restoration of trust as well. Forgiveness does not require the offender to repent, but reconciliation does. Forgiveness is very difficult when the offender doesn't acknowledge their wrongdoing, but it can still be done.

Denying justice — Forgiveness is not about letting people escape the consequences of their actions, especially if those actions are crimes against the state as well. For example, a person who was abused as a child may forgive someone of the abuse, but still testify against them in order to protect others from them. Forgiveness is an interpersonal action that can run parallel with state-imposed punishment. Forgiveness is not about foregoing legal justice. For example, I have read numerous stories of murder victims' families who forgive the murderer and plead against the death penalty but still think a long-term prison sentence is the appropriate action. (One of the most notable examples of this is Bud Welch who publicly forgave Timothy McVeigh for murdering his daughter and did not want the death penalty for him, but wanted him in prison for life.) The relationship between personal forgiveness and the impersonal state process of sentencing is a very important and complex issue, and while forgiveness can, and in some cases should, affect the state's response to a wrongdoing, forgiveness does not rule out state-imposed punishment.

Impersonal — Institutions, like churches or businesses, do not hurt us. Individuals within those organizations do. For this reason, forgiveness must always be personal. Sometimes people will say, "I'm mad at that church." No you're not. The "church" didn't do anything to you. A person within it did. Forgiveness must always be personal.

Easy — Forgiveness can be very hard work. A Christian psychologist named Everett Worthington makes a very helpful distinction between *decisional* and *emotional forgiveness*. Decisional forgiveness is something we have direct control over, while emotional forgiveness is something that, at best, we have indirect control over. Decisional forgiveness is choosing to forgive. It is making the commitment to forgive. Forgiveness will not happen without this intention. Emotional forgiveness is the process that follows that decision in which we become healed of negative feelings like bitterness and vengeance.

The 1999 film *The Straight Story* illustrates how long the journey of forgiveness can be. In this film, which is based on a true story, Richard Farnsworth plays the role of Alan Straight, an elderly WWII veteran living in Iowa with his mentally challenged daughter. Alan discovers that his estranged brother living in Wisconsin has had a stroke. They haven't spoken to one another in over a decade. Alan decides that he must go make peace with his brother before it is too late, but poor health prevents him from having a driver's license and he doesn't have anyone to drive him. So, he decides that he'll make the three-hundred-mile journey on his riding lawnmower. The movie is essentially a camera following this man riding his lawnmower on the side of the highway. (Sounds riveting, doesn't it?) When he sets out initially, his mower breaks down after just a few miles, and so he gets out a rifle, shoots it, and it blows it up. He then goes and buys another used John Deer mower for his journey. Along the way, he must face several meaningful encounters and challenges, but he finally makes it to the country shack where his brother lives. Alan Straight's journey on his lawnmower offers a very helpful parable of what the journey of forgiveness can be. It can be slow moving, and sometimes it can blow up and we have to start over. But Alan does the hard work of staying on the lawnmower and keeps going. Forgiveness is the hard task of persevering in the choice to stay on the lawnmower.

Weakness — Forgiveness is not weakness. Forgiveness takes guts. Forgiveness takes a big and strong heart. Forgiveness isn't for spiritual weaklings. Anyone can seek revenge. Anyone can strike back. Anyone can snap back. Anyone can hold a grudge. That's not hard at all. Forgiveness requires strength of the soul to transcend and rise above the wrong that was done.

The list of what forgiveness does not constitute is long. As we have worked through these negatively stated ideas, some ideas about what forgiveness is have already emerged, but let me offer some bite-sized ways of thinking positively about what forgiveness really is about.

1. To forgive is to justly condemn an offense while mercifully refusing to condemn the offender.

2. To forgive is to transcend what happened to you by refusing to let it control your inner life.

3. To forgive is to move from ill-will to good-will towards a person.

4. To forgive is to give someone the gift of release from the moral debt that they owe you.

5. To forgive is to set a person free from your prison of bitterness, and then to discover that you were the prisoner.

Forgiveness and Restorative Justice

Christian universalism sees forgiveness as occupying an indispensable and foundational place in the Christian vision of the moral life. It sees justice as not being fulfilled until reconciliation and restoration is ultimately made a reality. The nineteenth-century Scottish universalist George Mac-Donald questioned whether the view of the traditionalists could really affirm an ultimate justice that would right all wrongs. He writes,

> What better is the world, what better is the sinner, what better is God, what better is the truth, that the sinner should suffer— continue suffering to all eternity? Would there be less sin in the universe? . . . What setting-right would come of the sinner's suffering? . . . But I may be saved from it by learning to loathe it, to hate it, to shrink from it with an eternal avoidance. The only vengeance worth having on sin is to make the sinner himself its executioner.[7]

Punishing someone for eternity does nothing to really make things right. Let's return to the case of Hitler. How can everlasting punitive suffering really make up for the horrendous evil he perpetuated into so many lives? No amount of suffering as such can ever really make up for a wrong that is done. Retribution has a proper place in human systems of justice, but ultimately retribution is very limited in terms of establishing divine and perfect justice. To think that "getting even" is what heals life's deepest wounds is a myth. It is a powerful myth, a deeply ingrained cultural myth, and an understandable myth, but it is a myth nonetheless.[8]

7. George MacDonald, "Justice," 511–12.
8. See Wink, *Powers that Be*, 63–97.

True justice can only be achieved when the offender is brought to such an awareness of his wrongdoing that he himself seeks to rid himself of that sin and strive to do all that he can do to make up for it. Granted, in this life there are many constraints on what a person can do to seek restoration and reconciliation. But in the age to come, we can imagine that God will make it possible for all of us to participate in God's mission to heal every wound and right every wrong that we have caused. Hitler, for example, may be given a role to play in the restoration of his victims. We can imagine God enabling his victims to offer him forgiveness, and in turn God enabling Hitler to feel and see the horror of his wrongs, and then, with God's help, to repent and do all he can to make reconciliation and restoration possible. This strikes me as a much more biblically-shaped and Christ-centered view of justice than simply consigning Hitler to never-ending punishments where he never realizes and fully agrees with God's condemnation of his sin. On the traditional view of hell, Hitler gets off too easy.

I realize this is speculative, but to some degree all of our talk about the life to come is speculative, and requires the use of our imagination as much as our intellect. The religious imagination that is shaped by the traditional view of an everlasting hell is likely to see merely punitive retribution as satisfying the requirements of justice, and thus in this life is less likely to live with reconciliation as the ultimate goal and with forgiveness as the method to getting there. On the other hand, a religious imagination that is formed by a hopeful vision of the reconciliation of all things is much more likely to refuse to give up on people, to refuse to condemn people, and to seek God's help in putting away bitterness and anger in order to live with forgiveness. Far from undermining holy living, Christian universalism can give a clearer and sharper focus on what is truly distinctive about the Christian way of life, which is imitating the steadfast love and boundless forgiveness of our Lord.

CHAPTER 8

A Hell of a Lot to Think About

Additional Questions

WHILE I HAVE TRIED to offer thoughtful responses to the key questions that can be raised about Christian universalism, I know that there is much more that could be said about each of these questions. My hope, though, is that I have said enough to clear up some misunderstandings, diffuse some objections, and spur you to think more deeply about these issues. I am also aware that Christian universalism raises more questions than the main ones to which I have responded in this book. In my discussions with folks about this topic, there are a handful of other subsidiary questions that are often raised and I will respond to them very briefly.

Will the Devil be Saved?

I am not sure. My ambivalence in approaching this question does not come from a sense of hesitancy in affirming that God has the power to transform agents of evil, whether human or spiritual. Paul was bold enough to claim in Colossians 1:19–20, "For in him all the fullness of God was pleased to dwell, and through him God was pleased to reconcile to himself all things, whether on earth or in heaven, by making peace through the blood of his cross." My hesitancy and confusion comes from the fact that I am not really sure what the devil is. Some Christians think of the devil as simply a mythological construct that is useful, in varying degrees, for describing evil that seems too big to simply come from human beings. I think the devil is more than this. No doubt many of our ideas about the devil are mythological constructs (red, pitchfork, etc.), but I believe that there is such a thing as substantial powers or spiritual energies that work for evil. I think this is true partly because I trust Jesus, and Jesus perceived and worked against evil spiritual powers at work in the world.

While I think that genuine spiritual powers exist, I am not sure that they are "personal beings," in the sense that they have wills that can be changed, or if they are simply "impersonal" powers of evil that need to defeated and destroyed. I will respond this way: If the devil is a personal spiritual agent that is in need of being saved and can be saved, then I believe that ultimately the devil will be saved. If, however, the devil is really an impersonal force of pure evil, then I think God will destroy it (and all demonic powers) in the age to come. For two very different, but immensely insightful ways of approaching the question of what demonic powers are, I recommend Walter Wink's *The Powers That Be* and Gregory Boyd's *Satan and the Problem of Evil*.

Should Christian Universalism be an Essential Doctrine?

No. I think that the framers of the early ecumenical creeds, in contrast to later creedal developments, were wise to leave room for a good deal of latitude regarding the nature and duration of the punishment in the age to come. I would not want to make accepting this perspective essential for Christian identity, any more than I would want other Christians to make the annihilationist or everlasting conscious torment perspective as foundational for being a Christian. Although I think this position should be given a fair hearing, and I think that this view is the one that coheres best with other core affirmations that Christians make about God, none of the three main options are immediately obvious or abundantly clear from scripture. This should be one of the many things that Christians agree to disagree on without defining one another outside the fold.

I must say that I find a good measure of plausibility, both exegetically and theologically, in the arguments made for the annihilationist perspective. (The main defense of this position is Edward Fudge's *The Fire That Consumes*.) I have interacted very little with this perspective throughout this book, primarily because my main goal is to criticize the dominant view of an everlasting hell and to respond to objections to Christian universalism from those within that perspective. If it turns out that some people are irredeemably evil, that some are so bent on rejecting God that they lose any ability or desire to turn to God no matter what God does in this life and the next, then it seems to me that a loving God would opt to withdraw life and being from such persons. So, I think the annihilationist perspective has a better chance of being true than the everlasting conscious torment view, but my strong hope and confidence is in the power of God's holy and just love to destroy the sin that keeps sinners from God.

I have two main problems with the annihilationist view, though. First, I find that it severely compromises God's victory over evil. In the case of the people who would be annihilated, in their lives the powers of sin and death are ultimately victorious, and God's desire that all be saved goes unfulfilled. Second, I cannot see how the annihilation of wicked people really serves the cause of God's justice, which is revealed consistently through the Bible to be a restorative justice, not a merely retributive justice.

That said, I have a great deal of respect for Christians in this camp, and I also consider Christians who believe in the eternal conscious torment of non-Christians (or "the wicked" or however they want to put it) to be fellow Christians. I think it would be great if more of these folks would loosen their grip on this view to allow for discussions of other possibilities. However, church tradition has enjoyed tremendous support from this position and it is not hard to see the multiple scriptural passages that support this view, even though, as I have argued, this doctrine is often read into these pages rather than read out of them.

If Universalism is True,
Why Didn't New Testament Authors Make it Clearer?

As I mentioned above, none of the three main positions on this issue are clear and obvious, hence the discussion and debate that has been going on from the beginning. This question, then, could be asked of the defenders of any of these positions, and shouldn't be taken as a knock against universalism. But let me say a little more about what is behind the question. Sometimes in discussions with people about this issue, I have noticed deep frustration with how complex it all seems, and how much work we have to do to understand certain biblical passages and fit them together to form a coherent theology. I understand this frustration completely. Over the past decade or so I have spent a great deal of time studying the issues raised in this book. I have had lots of sleepless nights and anxious days, wondering why God hasn't made things clearer, and how we are to know what to believe in the midst of such ambiguity and uncertainty. Had the scriptures come with footnotes that clarified interpretive difficulties for us would certainly have been nice.

For my own part, though, I have come to feel much more at home in the ambiguity that we face as small and finite creatures trying to fathom the mysteries of God. Certainty is an illusion in these matters, and a potentially dangerous one at that. What I have is a deep *assurance*, rooted in the death and resurrection of Jesus and shaped by the inward testimony of the Holy Spirit, that the love of God is powerful enough to ultimately set things right and make all things well. But I am not *certain* about any of this. I could be wrong about it all, and I acknowledge that. I am convinced of the position for which I have argued, but many days I have doubts, and most days I lose sight of the brilliant and beautiful hope that I profess to believe in. It's a struggle for me. But I have come to think that if the grace of God is big enough to put the world back together, it is big enough for my doubts.

What About Old Testament Passages that Portray God as Violent?

Even though the Old Testament does not explicitly teach a doctrine of hell, the picture of God that it sometimes paints certainly looks like a God who might be okay with eternally torturing people. Even though these difficult passages can sometimes be overblown, while contrary passages that affirm the mercy and patience of God are overlooked, we shouldn't try to avoid the fact that there are many passages in the Old Testament that depict God as arbitrary, cruel, vindictive, and seemingly bloodthirsty. For a thorough list of such passages, as well as a great response to them, I would encourage reading Eric Seibert's *Disturbing Divine Behavior*. Because this topic is so important, I have preached on it from time to time. The remainder of this section is an excerpt from a sermon I preached several years ago on this issue. I don't claim to have a final word on this, but this presents the essence of how I struggle to think about this topic. We begin by looking at several key verses of scripture:

> In the beginning was the Word, and the Word was with God, and the Word was God . . . And the Word became flesh and lived among us. (John 1:1, 14)

> He is the image of the invisible God. (Col 1:15)

> Long ago God spoke to our ancestors in many and various ways by the prophets, but in these last days he has spoken to us by a Son, whom he appointed heir of all things, through whom he also created the worlds. He is the reflection of God's glory and the exact imprint of God's very being. (Heb 1:1–3)

All of these passages point to is the fact that God didn't reveal God's heart by dictating a book. God revealed God's heart by becoming a human being in the person of Jesus of Nazareth. Jesus is the Word of God, and the value and authority of the Bible comes from its ability to point us towards God's ultimate and most clear revelation in Jesus. As Christians, we should have a thoroughly Christ-centered interpretation of scripture. This means that all of our interpretations of scripture, particularly the Old Testament, should be seen through the lens of God's most complete revelation of who God really is in Jesus. It doesn't mean that the Old Testament is worthless. It simply means that in Jesus we get a fuller and more accurate picture of God than from any revelation that came before Jesus.

Let's apply this interpretative method to one of the most vexing and frustrating issues for people who take the Bible seriously for their faith: the issue of God and violence in the Old Testament. I have a book on my shelves called *Disturbing Divine Behavior* (an excellent book by Eric Seibert) and it explores all of the disturbing passages about God in the Old Testament. There are a lot of them, but out of them all, perhaps this one is the most disturbing:

> When the Lord your God brings you into the land that you are about to enter and occupy, and he clears away many nations before you—the Hittites, the Girgashites, the Amorites, the Canaanites, the Perizzites, the Hivites, and the Jebusites, seven nations mightier and more numerous than you— and when the Lord your God gives them over to you and you defeat them, then you must utterly destroy them. Make no covenant with them and show them no mercy. (Deut 7:1–2)

The theology of holy war that undergirded the Crusades and the European genocidal actions towards Native Americans is found here. This passage is used to defend the idea that sometimes it is necessary to use unrestrained violence to advance God's purposes and God's plans. How exactly do we fit that with these words from the lips of Jesus?

> You have heard that it was said, "You shall love your neighbor and hate your enemy." But I say to you, Love your enemies and pray for those who persecute you, so that you may be children of your Father in heaven; for he makes his sun rise on the evil and on the good, and sends rain on the righteous and on the unrighteous. (Matt 5:43–45)

Are we to exterminate our enemies or are we to love them? If we take a Christ-centered approach to scripture, then I think the conclusion to be drawn is that this earlier understanding of how to treat enemies does not reflect what God really wants. I think at that stage of development of God's people they had an incomplete and in some ways misguided understanding of what God is really like. While the story of the conquest reveals God's abhorrence of evil, and can still be useful for Christians as an allegory for the spiritual warfare that Christ calls us to engage, it does not reveal clearly how God deals with evil. We see how God deals with evil most clearly and most deeply on the cross of Calvary where God in Christ conquers evil by dying for God's enemies, not killing God's enemies.

The response to this approach is often: "So are we just free to pick and choose what we like?" I have often heard people say, "It's either all or nothing, you can't pick and choose." To that I say, not only *can* we pick and choose, we *must* pick and choose, and as a Christian we must pick and choose with Jesus as our guide. Jesus himself gave us a key for how to interpret Old Testament texts that depict God as violent and vengeful.

> When he came to Nazareth, where he had been brought up, he went to the synagogue on the sabbath day, as was his custom. He stood up to read, and the scroll of the prophet Isaiah was given to him. He unrolled the scroll and found the place where it was written: "The Spirit of the Lord is upon me, because he has anointed me to bring good news to the poor. He has sent me to proclaim release to the captives and recovery of sight to the blind, to let the oppressed go free, to proclaim the year of the Lord's favor." And he rolled up the scroll, gave it back to the attendant, and sat down. The eyes of all in the synagogue were fixed on him. Then he began to say to them, "Today this scripture has been fulfilled in your hearing." (Luke 4:16–21)

Here is one of the key questions: Why did everyone "fix their eyes on him" when he rolled up the scroll? The Greek word for "fix" is *ateinzo*, which means to gaze intently. The root of the word means to "stretch." So their eyes were stretched wide open and their gaze was fixed on him. Why? Let's look at the passage he is reading from Isaiah 61:

> The spirit of the Lord God is upon me, because the Lord has anointed me; he has sent me to bring good news to the oppressed, to bind up the broken-hearted, to proclaim liberty to the captives, and release to the prisoners; to proclaim the year of the Lord's favor, and the day of vengeance of our God. (vv. 1–2)

What does Jesus do when he gets to the line about God's vengeance towards outsiders? He doesn't read it in worship. He closes the scroll and sits down. This is a foundational passage of scripture for ancient Jews. They grew up memorizing texts like this and cherishing them. The text embodies their deepest hopes and shapes their vision of the future. Everyone there would have been familiar with this passage. This is why their eyes get big and they stare at him intently when he rolls up the scroll. He finishes before the passage ends. He doesn't affirm the divine vengeance that they want to see God's enemies get.

For Jesus, God's mission isn't to bring vengeance it is to bring salvation. For Jesus, God isn't about retribution, God is about restoration. God is not on a mission to damn people, but to save people. Jesus refused to endorse this Old Testament depiction of God as violent and vengeful, and so should we.[1] Our interpretation of the Bible should always keep Jesus at the center, and he should be the lens through which we read everything else. If the Christian church had held to this approach, then our past would have far fewer dark spots.

---

1. This isn't the only time that Jesus quoted selectively from the Old Testament, deliberately excluding parts of passages that attributed violence or vengeance to God. See Jesus's response to John's inquiry in Luke 7:18–23. Jesus's response draws from three passages in Isa (29:18–20; 35:4–6; 61:1–2). Each scriptural passage contains threats of vengeful condemnation and exclusion, and promises of abundant blessing and liberation. Jesus picked out only the promises of blessing and liberation to describe his mission. When Jesus read what scripture said about God's appointed agent of deliverance and salvation, he refused to accept the descriptions that portray God as violent, retaliatory, and bent on the destruction of God's enemies. He *picked* and *chose* only those parts that portray God as longing to bring healing and restoration to people.

What If I Am wrong?

I'll admit that believing in universal salvation feels sort of risky to me, as I suspect it will for anyone who has spent most of their life assuming the traditional view of hell. What if I am wrong? What are the potentially negative or destructive consequences of embracing the particular kind of Christian universalism that I have presented in this book? Is there anything about this view that could undermine something essential about the Christian faith?

Well . . .

I don't deny that judgment from a God of holy love is awaiting us all.

I don't deny the central place that the Bible should hold in the formation of our theological beliefs.

I don't deny the moral significance of human choices here and now.

I don't deny that Christ is the unique revealer of God and the only savior of humankind.

I don't deny the importance of sharing the good news of what God has done for us in Christ with the world.

I don't deny that a life of faith entails a commitment to holiness and love in our lives.

As far as I can tell, holding to Christian universalism doesn't undermine any essential aspect of Christian belief and practice. The toughest thing about universalism is that it has been a minority belief throughout Christian history. While, as I showed in the first chapter, Christian universalism has enjoyed support from some of the church's major theologians and was clearly a live option in the early church, admittedly, the vast majority of Christian thinkers do not embrace it.

This should certainly give us pause, but it shouldn't keep us from considering it with a genuinely open mind. Staying with a majority opinion can feel safer and less risky than venturing out to believe what only a small percentage of Christians believe. However, that sense of "safety in numbers" may just be illusory. While we should respect and listen to our tradition, going with dominant opinion is certainly not an infallible guide to the truth. Appeals to "what the church has always believed" often do not adequately take into account the width and depth of the stream of Christianity that has been flowing throughout the centuries. Even if accurate, however, such an appeal traps the movement of the Spirit in the past, and denies the possibility that new light might burst forth from God's

Word. Sometimes, fidelity to the light of Christ and the spirit of truth requires that we are willing to go beyond where those in our tradition are willing to go. Just as the risen Christ went ahead of his confused disciples (Mark 16:7), I believe that Christ is not trapped in the past, but rather is always out ahead of us, calling us to try to keep up with him.

I realize that there are legitimate questions to be asked and genuine concerns to be raised with the view that holds that ultimately all will be saved through Christ. I hope I have addressed them in thoughtful and helpful ways, although I am sure I have not done so in such a way as to dispel all doubt. My hopeful belief is that these remaining doubts and concerns will turn out to be similar to the question that the women disciples asked on their way to the tomb, concerning how the stone will be rolled away (Mark 16:3). They discovered, beyond their ability to imagine or conceive, that with God, all things really are possible. Christian universalism is the conviction that their discovery, that the darkness cannot overcome the light, will one day belong to us all.

BIBLIOGRAPHY

Abraham, William J. *The Logic of Evangelism*. Grand Rapids, MI: Eerdmans, 1989.

Adams, Marilyn McCord. *Horrendous Evils and the Goodness of God*. Ithaca, NY: Cornell University Press, 1999.

———. "The Problem of Hell: A Problem of Evil for Christians." In *Reasoned Faith*, edited by Eleonore Stump, 301–27. Ithaca, NY: Cornell University Press, 1993.

Alfeyev, Hilarion. *Christ the Conqueror of Hell: The Descent into Hell in Orthodox Tradition*. New York: SVS Press, 2009.

———. "The Descent of Christ into Hades in Eastern and Western Theological Traditions." No pages. Online: http://orthodoxeurope.org/page/11/1/5.aspx.

———. *The Spiritual World of Isaac the Syrian*. Collegeville, MN: Liturgical Press, 2008.

Almond, Phillip C. "Changing View of Heaven and Hell according to Changing Times." *Asia Journal of Theology* 13:1 (1987) 159–171.

Aquinas, Thomas. *Summa Theologica*. No Pages. Online: http://www.newadvent.org /summa/5094.htm.

Augustine. *Enchiridion*. Translated by Bernard M. Peebles. New York: CIMA Publishing, 1947.

Bailey, Kenneth. *The Cross and the Prodigal: Luke 15 through the Eyes of Middle Eastern Peasants*. Downers Grove, IL: IVP Academic, 2002.

Bailey, Lloyd R. "Gehenna: The Topography of Hell." *Biblical Archaeologist* (Sept. 1986) 187–91.

Bailie, Gil. *Violence Unveiled: Humanity at the Crossroads*. New York: Crossroad, 1996.

Baker, Sharon L. *Razing Hell: Rethinking Everything You've Been Taught about God's Wrath and Judgment*. Louisville, KY: Westminster John Knox Press, 2010.

Barclay, William. *A Spiritual Autobiography*. Grand Rapids, MI: Eerdmans, 1977.

Basinger, David, et al. *Predestination and Free Will: Four Views of Divine Sovereignty and Human Freedom*. Downers Grove, IL: InterVarsity Press, 1986.

Bauckham, Richard. *God Crucified: Monotheism and Christology in the New Testament*. Grand Rapids, MI: Eerdmans, 1999.

———. "The Language of Warfare in the Book of Revelation." In *Compassionate Eschatology: The Future as Friend*, edited by Tim Grimsrud and Michael Hardin, 28–41. Eugene, OR: Cascade Books, 2011.

———. "Universalism: A Historical Survey." *Themelios* 4.2 (1978) 47–54.

Bell, Richard H. "Rom 5:18–19 and Universal Salvation." *New Testament Studies* 48 (2002) 417–32.

Blocher, Henri. "Everlasting Punishment and the Problem of Evil." In *Universalism and the Doctrine of Hell*, edited by Nigel M. de S. Cameron, 283–312. Grand Rapids, MI: Baker Book House, 1992.

Bloesch, Donald G. *The Last Things: Resurrection, Judgment, Glory*. Downers Grove, IL: InterVarsity Press, 2004.

Bibliography

Bonda, Jan. *The One Purpose of God: An Answer to the Doctrine of Eternal Punishment.* Grand Rapids, MI: Eerdmans, 1998.

Borg, Marcus. *Conflict, Holiness, and Politics in the Teachings of Jesus.* New York: T & T Clark, 1998.

Boring, Eugene. "The Language of Universal Salvation in Paul." *Journal of Biblical Literature* (1986) 269–92.

Boyd, Gregory A. *Satan and the Problem of Evil: Constructing a Trinitarian Warfare Theodicy.* Downers Grove, IL: IVP Academic, 2001.

Brattston, David. "Hades, Hell and Purgatory in Ante-Nicene Christianity." *Churchman* 108:1 (1994) 69–79.

Bulgakov, Sergius. *The Bride of the Lamb.* Grand Rapids, MI: Eerdmans, 2001.

Camp, Lee C. *Mere Discipleship: Radical Christianity in a Rebellious World.* Grand Rapids, MI: Brazos Press, 2008.

Carson, D. A. *The Gagging of God: Christianity Confronts Pluralism.* Grand Rapids, MI: Zondervan, 1996.

Center for Reformed Theology and Apologetics. The Westminster Confession of Faith. No Pages. Online: http://www.reformed.org/documents/wcf_with_proofs/.

Chan, Francis, and Preston Sprinkle. *Erasing Hell: What God Said about Eternity and the Things We've Made Up.* Colorado Springs, CO: David C. Cook, 2011.

Charlesworth, James H. *The Old Testament Pseudepigrapha.* Vol. 2. Garden City, NY: Doubleday, 1985.

Clark-Soles, Jamie. *Death and the Afterlife in the New Testament.* New York: T & T Clark, 2006.

Craig, William Lane. "Can a Loving God Send People to Hell?" No pages. Online: http://www.newchristian.org.uk/helldefended.html.

———. "Talbott's Universalism Once More." *Religious Studies* 29 (1993) 497–518.

Craddock, Fred B. *Philippians. Interpretation: A Bible Commentary for Teaching and Preaching.* Atlanta: John Knox Press, 1985.

Crockett, William, et al. *Four Views on Hell.* Grand Rapids, MI: Zondervan, 1992.

Crossan, John Dominic. *God and Empire: Jesus Against Rome, Then and Now.* New York: HarperCollins, 2007.

———. "Roman Imperial Theology." In *In the Shadow of Empire: Reclaiming the Bible as a History of Faithful Resistance*, edited by Richard A. Horsley, 59–74. Louisville, KY: Westminster John Knox Press, 2008.

Crouzel, Henry. *Origen.* Translated by A. S. Worrall. Edinburgh: T & T Clark, 1989.

Daley, Brian. *The Hope of the Early Church: A Handbook of Patristic Eschatology.* New York: Cambridge University Press, 1991.

Dalton, William J. *Christ's Proclamation to the Spirits in Prison: A Study of 1 Peter 3:18–4:6.* Rome: Editrice Pontificio Istituto Biblico, 1989.

———. *Salvation and Damnation.* Butler, WI: Clergy Book Service, 1977.

Dixon, Larry. *The Other Side of the Good News: Contemporary Challenges to Jesus' Teaching on Hell.* Ross Shire, Scotland: Christian Focus, 2003.

Dunning, H. Ray. *Grace, Faith and Holiness: A Wesleyan Systematic Theology.* Kansas City, MO: Beacon Hill Press, 1988.

Edgar, William. "Exclusivism: Unjust or Just?" In *Faith Comes By Hearing: A Response to Inclusivism,* edited by Christopher W. Morgan and Robert A. Peterson, 78–97. Downers Grove, IL: IVP Academic, 2008.

Enright, Robert D. *Forgiveness Is a Choice: A Step-By-Step Process for Resolving Anger and Restoring Hope.* Washington, D. C.: American Psychological Association, 2001.

Erickson, Millard. "Is Hell Forever?" *Bibliotheca Sacra* 152:607 (1995) 259–72.

———. *How Shall They Be Saved? The Destiny of Those Who Do Not Hear of Jesus.* Grand Rapids, MI: Baker Books, 1996.

———. "Principles, Permanence, and Future Divine Judgment: A Case Study in Theological Method." *Journal of the Evangelical Theological Society* 28 (1985) 317–25.

Evans, Rachel Held. "Rob Bell, the SBC, and the Age of Accountability." No pages. Online: http://rachelheldevans.com/rob-bell-sbc-age-of-accountability.

Fretheim, Terence E. *Creation Untamed: The Bible, God, and Natural Disasters.* Grand Rapids, MI: Baker Academic, 2010.

Fudge, Edward William. *The Fire That Consumes: A Biblical and Historical Study of the Doctrine of Final Punishment.* 3rd ed. Eugene, OR: Cascade Books, 2011.

Galli, Mark. *God Wins: Heaven, Hell, and Why the Good News is Better than Love Wins.* Carol Stream, IL: Tyndale House, 2011.

Geisler, Norman. *Inerrancy.* Grand Rapids, MI: Zondervan, 1980.

Green, Joel B., and Mark D. Baker. *Recovering the Scandal of the Cross: Atonement in New Testament and Contemporary Contexts.* Downers Grove, IL: InterVarsity Press, 2000.

Grimsrud, Ted. "Biblical Apocalyptic: What is Being Revealed?" In *Compassionate Eschatology: The Future as Friend,* edited by Tim Grismrud and Michael Hardin, 3–27. Eugene, OR: Cascade Books, 2011.

Guthrie, Shirlie C., Jr. *Christian Doctrine.* Louisville, KY: Westminster John Knox Press, 1994.

Hanson, J. W. *Universalism: The Prevailing Doctrine of the Christian Church During Its First Five Hundred Years.* No pages. Online: http://www.tentmaker.org/books/Prevailing.html.

Hasker, William. *The Triumph of God over Evil.* Downers Grove, IL: InterVarsity Press, 2008.

Heath, Elaine A. *The Mystic Way of Evangelism: A Contemplative Vision for Christian Outreach.* Grand Rapids, MI: Baker Academic, 2008.

Hick, John. *Evil and the God of Love.* New York: Harper and Row, 1966.

———. *God Has Many Names.* Philadelphia: Westminster John Knox Press, 1982.

Hurtado, Larry. *Lord Jesus Christ: Devotion to Jesus in Earliest Christianity.* Grand Rapids, MI: Eerdmans, 2005.

Jenkins, Philip. *Jesus Wars: How Four Patriarchs, Three Queens, and Two Emperors Decided What Christians Would Believe for the Next 1,500 Years.* New York: HarperOne, 2010.

Jennings, J. Nelson. "God's Zeal for His World." In *Faith Comes By Hearing: A Response to Inclusivism,* edited by Christopher W. Morgan and Robert A. Peterson, 220–40. Downers Grove, IL: IVP Academic, 2008.

Johnston, Philip. *Shades of Sheol: Death and Afterlife in the Old Testament.* Downers Grove, IL: InterVarsity Academic, 2002.

Jones, Scott J. *United Methodist Doctrine: The Extreme Center.* Nashville: Abingdon Press, 2002.

Kaiser, Walter C., Jr. "Holy Pagans: Reality or Myth?" In *Faith Comes By Hearing: A Response to Inclusivism,* edited by Christopher W. Morgan and Robert A. Peterson, 123–41. Downers Grove, IL: IVP Academic, 2008.

Kallenberg, Brad J. *Live to Tell: Evangelism for a Postmodern Age.* Grand Rapids, MI: Brazos Press, 2002.

Keller, Tim. *The Reason for God: Belief in an Age of Skepticism*. New York: Dutton, 2008.

Klager, Andrew P. "Orthodox Eschatology and St. Gregory of Nyssa's *De vita Moysis*: Transfiguration, Cosmic Unity, and Compassion." In *Compassionate Eschatology: The Future as Friend*, edited by Tim Grimsrud and Michael Hardin, 230–52. Eugene, OR: Cascade Books, 2011.

Knitter, Paul. *Introducing Theologies of Religion*. Maryknoll, NY: Orbis Books, 2002.

Kronen, John, and Eric Reitan. *God's Final Victory: A Comparative Philosophical Case for Universalism*. New York: Continuum, 2011.

Lawrence, Raymond J. *Sexual Liberation: The Scandal of Christendom*. Westport, CT: Praeger Publishers, 2007.

Lewis, C. S. "Christian Apologetics." In *God in the Dock*, edited by C. S. Lewis, 89–103. Grand Rapids, MI: Eerdmans, 1972.

———. *Mere Christianity*. San Francisco: HarperSanFrancisco, 2001.

———. *The Problem of Pain*. New York: Simon and Schuster, 1996.

Long, Jeffrey, and Paul Perry. *Evidence of the Afterlife: The Science of Near-Death Experiences*. New York: HarperCollins Publishers, 2011.

Ludlow, Morwenna. *Universal Salvation: Eschatology in the Thought of Gregory of Nyssa and Karl Rahner*. New York: Oxford University Press, 2009.

———. "Universalism in the History of Christianity." In *Universal Salvation? The Current Debate*, edited by Robin A. Parry and Christopher H. Partridge, 191–218. Grand Rapids, MI: Eerdmans, 2003.

MacCulloch, J. A. *The Harrowing of Hell: A Comparative Study of an Early Christian Doctrine*. Edinburgh: T & T Clark, 1930.

MacDonald, George. "The Consuming Fire." In *Unspoken Sermons*, 24–33. Whitethorn, CA: Johannesen, 1998.

———. "Justice." In *Unspoken Sermons*, 500–540. Whitethorn, CA: Johannesen, 1998.

MacDonald, Gregory. *The Evangelical Universalist*. Eugene, OR: Cascade Books, 2006.

Maddox, Randy. *Responsible Grace: John Wesley's Practical Theology*. Nashville: Kingswood Books, 1994.

Marshall, Christopher D. *Beyond Retribution: A New Testament Vision for Justice, Crime, and Punishment*. Grand Rapids, MI: Eerdmans, 2001.

McDermott, Gerald R. *God's Rivals: Why Has God Allowed Different Religions? Insights from the Bible and the Early Church*. Downers Grove, IL: IVP Academic, 2007.

McDonald, Lee Martin. "The Integrity of the Biblical Canon in Light of its Historical Development." *Bulletin for Biblical Research* 6 (1996) 95–132.

McGrath, Alister. "A Particularist View: A Post-Enlightenment View." In *Four Views on Salvation in a Pluralistic World*, edited by Denis L. Okholm and Timothy R. Phillips, 149–80. Grand Rapids, MI: Zondervan, 1995.

McLaren, Brian D. "On Atheism." No pages. Online: http://newsweek.washingtonpost.com/onfaith/panelists/brian_d_mclaren/2006/12/on_atheism.html.

———. *A New Kind of Christianity: Ten Questions that are Transforming the Faith*. New York: HarperOne, 2010.

Miles, Todd. *A God of Many Understandings? The Gospel and a Theology of Religions*. Nashville: B & H Academic, 2010.

Milikowsky, Chaim. "Which Gehenna? Retribution and Eschatology in the Synoptic Gospels and in Early Jewish Texts." *New Testament Studies* 34 (1988) 238–49.

Moberly, Walter. *The Ethics of Punishment*. New York: Anchor Books, 1968.

Mohler, Albert. "Modern Theology: The Disappearance of Hell." In *Hell Under Fire: Modern Scholarship Reinvents Eternal Punishment*, edited by Christopher W. Morgan and Robert A. Peterson, 15–41. Grand Rapids, MI: Zondervan, 2004.

———. "The Salvation of the Little Ones: Do Infants Who Die Go to Heaven?" No pages. Online: http://www.albertmohler.com/2009/07/16/the-salvation-of-the-little-ones-do-infants-who-die-go-to-heaven/.

———. "In the Shadow of Death: The Little Ones are Safe with Jesus." No pages. Online: http://www.albertmohler.com/2005/01/05/in-the-shadow-of-death-the-little-ones-are-safe-with-jesus/.

Moltmann, Jurgen. "The Final Judgment: The Sunrise of Christ's Liberating Justice." In *Compassionate Eschatology: The Future as Friend*, edited by Tim Grimsrud and Michael Hardin, 218–29. Eugene, OR: Cascade Books, 2011.

———. "The Logic of Hell." In *God Will Be All in All: The Eschatology of Jurgen Moltmann*, edited by Richard Bauckham, 44–47. Minneapolis: Fortress Press, 2001.

Moody, Dale. *The Word of Truth: A Summary of Christian Doctrine Based on Biblical Revelation*. Grand Rapids, MI: Eerdmans, 1981.

Morgan, Christopher W. "Inclusivisms and Exclusivisms." In *Faith Comes By Hearing: A Response to Inclusivism*, edited by Christopher W. Morgan and Robert A. Peterson, 17–39. Downers Grove, IL: IVP Academic, 2008.

Morgan, Christopher W., and Robert Peterson. *Faith Comes By Hearing: A Response to Inclusivism*. Downers Grove, IL: IVP Academic, 2008.

———. *Hell Under Fire: Modern Scholarship Reinvents Eternal Punishment*. Grand Rapids, MI: Zondervan, 2004.

Netland, Harold. *Encountering Religious Pluralism: The Challenge to Christian Faith and Mission*. Downers Grove, IL: InterVarsity Press 2001.

Newbigin, Lesslie. *The Gospel in a Pluralist Society*. Grand Rapids, MI: Eerdmans, 1989.

Olsen, Roger E. *The Mosaic of Christian Belief: Twenty Centuries of Unity and Diversity*. Downers Grove, IL: IVP Academic, 2002.

Outler, Albert. *Evangelism in the Wesleyan Spirit*. Nashville: Tidings, 1971.

Packer, J. I. *God's Words: Studies of Key Biblical Themes*. Downers Grove, IL: InterVarsity Press, 1981.

———. "The Problem of Universalism Today." In *Celebrating the Saving Work of God*, edited by J. I. Packer, 169–78. Carlisle: Paternoster, 1998.

———. "Universalism: Will Everyone Ultimately Be Saved?" In *Hell Under Fire: Modern Scholarship Reinvents Eternal Punishment*, edited by Christopher W. Morgan and Robert A. Peterson, 169–94. Grand Rapids, MI: Zondervan, 2004.

Pannenberg, Wolfhart. *The Apostles' Creed in Light of Today's Questions*. Eugene, OR: Wipf and Stock Publishers, 2000.

Parry, Robin. "Between Calvinism and Arminianism: The Evangelical Universalism of Elhanan Winchester (1751–1797)." In *"All Shall Be Well": Explorations in Universal Salvation and Christian Theology from Origen to Moltmann*, edited by Robin Parry, 141–70. Eugene, OR: Cascade Books, 2011.

Pope Paul VI. *Lumen Gentium*. No pages. Online: http://www.vatican.va/archive/hist_councils/ii_vatican_council/documents/vat-ii_const_19641121_lumen-gentium_en.html.

Peterson, Robert A. *Hell on Trial: The Case for Eternal Punishment*. Phillipsburg, NJ: Presbyterian and Reformed, 1995.

Pinnock, Clark H. *Flame of Love: A Theology of the Holy Spirit.* Downers Grove, IL: InterVarsity Press, 1996.

———. *A Wideness in God's Mercy: The Finality of Jesus Christ in a World of Religions.* Grand Rapids, MI: Zondervan, 1992.

Piper, John. *Jesus: The Only Way to God.* Grand Rapids, MI: Baker Books, 2010.

Pitstick, Alyssa Lyra. *Light in Darkness: Hans Urs von Balthasar and the Catholic Doctrine of Christ's Descent into Hell.* Grand Rapids, MI: Eerdmans, 2007.

Polkinghorne, John. *The God of Hope and the End of the World.* New Haven: Yale University Press, 2002.

Powys, David. *'Hell': a Hard Look at a Hard Question: The Fate of the Unrighteous in New Testament Thought.* Eugene, OR: Wipf and Stock Publishers, 2007.

Prothero, Stephen. *God is Not One: The Eight Rival Religions that Run the World—and Why Their Differences Matter.* New York: HarperOne, 2010.

Ramelli, Ilaria, and David Konstan. *Terms for Eternity: Aiônios and Aïdios in Classical and Christian Texts.* Piscataway, NJ: Gorgias Press, 2007.

Reitan, Eric. "Human Freedom and the Impossibility of Eternal Damnation." In *Universal Salvation? The Current Debate,* edited by Robin A. Parry and Christopher H. Partridge, 125–44. Grand Rapids, MI: Eerdmans, 2003.

Riley, Gregory. *The River of God: A New History of Christian Origins.* San Francisco: HarperCollins, 2001.

Robert, Dana L. "The Great Commission in an Age of Globalization." In *Considering the Great Commission: Evangelism and Mission in the Wesleyan Spirit,* edited by W. Stephen Gunter and Elaine Robinson, 23–40. Nashville: Abingdon Press, 2005.

Rolheiser, Ronald. "A Christian Attitude Regarding the Salvation of Non-Christians." No pages. Online: http://www.ronrolheiser.com/columnarchive/?id=791.

———. "Purgatory Revisited." No pages. Online: http://www.ronrolheiser.com /columnarchive/?id=196.

Rossing, Barbara. *The Rapture Exposed: The Message of Hope in the Book of Revelation.* New York: Basic Books, 2005.

Sachs, John. "Apocatastasis in Patristic Theology." *Theological Studies* 54 (1993) 617–40.

———. "Current Eschatology: Universal Salvation and the Problem of Hell." *Theological Studies* 52 (1991) 227–54.

Sanders, John. "A Freewill Theist's Response to Talbott's Universalism." In *Universal Salvation? The Current Debate,* edited by Robin A. Parry and Christopher H. Partridge, 169–90. Grand Rapids, MI: Eerdmans, 2003.

———. "Hell Yes! Hell No! Evangelical Debates on Eternal Punishment." In *Hell and its Afterlife: Historical and Contemporary Perspectives,* edited by Isabel Moreira and Margaret Toscano, 137–52. Burlington, VT: Ashgate Publishing, 2010.

———. *No Other Name: An Investigation into the Destiny of the Unevangelized.* Grand Rapids, MI: Eerdmans, 1992.

———. *What About Those Who Have Never Heard? Three Views on the Destiny of the Unevangelized.* Grand Rapids, MI: IVP Academic, 1995.

Scaer, David. "He Did Descend To Hell: In Defense of the Apostles' Creed." *Journal of the Evangelical Theological Society* 35:1 (1992) 91–99.

Schaff, Philip, and Henry Wace. *A Select Library of Nicene and Post-Nicene Fathers of the Christian Church.* Vol. 5. Grand Rapids, MI: Eerdmans, 1988.

Schuller, Robert. Interview with Billy Graham, "Hour of Power" radio show, May 31, 1997. No pages. Online: http://apprising.org/2006/07/27/evangelical-inclusivism-is-older-than-you-think/.

Seibert, Eric A. *Disturbing Divine Behavior: Troubling Old Testament Images of God.* Minneapolis: Fortress Press, 2009.

Smith, Christian. *The Bible Made Impossible: Why Biblicism Is Not a Truly Evangelical Reading of Scripture.* Grand Rapids, MI: Brazos Press, 2011.

Southern Baptist Convention. *Baptist Faith and Message.* No pages. Online: http://www.sbc.net/bfm/bfm2000.asp.

Sparks, Kenton. *God's Word in Human Words: An Evangelical Appropriation of Critical Biblical Scholarship.* Grand Rapids, MI: Baker Academic, 2008.

Stone, Brian P. *Evangelism after Christendom: The Theology and Practice of Christian Witness.* Grand Rapids, MI: Brazos Press, 2007.

Stott, John R. W., and David Lawrence Edwards. *Evangelical Essentials: A Liberal-Evangelical Dialogue.* Downers Grove, IL: InterVarsity Press, 1988.

Talbott, Thomas. *The Inescapable Love of God.* Salem, OR: Universal Publishers, 1999.

———. "The Just Mercy of God: Universal Salvation in George MacDonald (1824–1905)." In *"All Shall Be Well": Explorations in Universal Salvation and Christian Theology from Origen to Moltmann,* edited by Gregory MacDonald, 219–48. Eugene, OR: Cascade Books, 2011.

———. "Towards a Better Understanding of Universalism." In *Universal Salvation? The Current Debate,* edited by Robin A. Parry and Christopher H. Partridge, 3–14. Grand Rapids, MI: Eerdmans, 2003.

Taylor, LaTonya. "The Church of O." *Christianity Today* 46:4 (2002). No Pages. Online: http://www.christianitytoday.com/ct/2002/april1/1.38.html.

Tiessan, Terrance L. *Who Can Be Saved? Reassessing Salvation in Christ and World Religions.* Downers Grove, IL: InterVarsity Press, 2004.

Travis, Stephen H. *Christ and the Judgement of God: The Limits of Divine Retribution in New Testament Thought.* Peabody, MS: Hendrickson Publishers, 2008.

Truesdale, Al. "Holy Love vs. Eternal Hell: The Wesleyan Options." *Wesleyan Theological Society* 36:1 (2001) 103–12.

Trumbower, Jeffrey. "Early Visions of Hell as a Place of Education and Conversion." In *Hell and its Afterlife: Historical and Contemporary Perspectives,* edited by Isabel Moreira and Margaret Toscano, 29–38. Burlington, VT: Ashgate Publishing, 2010.

———. *Rescue for the Dead: The Posthumous Salvation of Non-Christians in Early Christianity.* New York: Oxford University Press, 2001.

Volf, Miroslav. *The End of Memory: Remembering Rightly in a Violent World.* Grand Rapids, MI: Eerdmans, 2006.

———. *Exclusion and Embrace: A Theological Exploration of Identity, Otherness, and Reconciliation.* Nashville: Abingdon Press, 1996.

———. *Free of Charge: Giving and Forgiving in a Culture Stripped of Grace.* Grand Rapids, MI: Zondervan, 2005.

Von Balthasar, Hans Urs. *Dare We Hope "That All Men Be Saved"?* San Francisco: Ignatius Press, 1988.

———. *Prayer.* New York: Paulist, 1961.

Walker, D. P. *The Decline of Hell: Seventeenth Century Discussions of Eternal Torment.* Chicago: University of Chicago Press, 1964.

Walls, Andrew. "The Great Commission 1910–2010." In *Considering the Great Commission: Evangelism and Mission in the Wesleyan Spirit*, edited by W. Stephen Gunter and Elaine Robinson, 7–22. Nashville: Abingdon Press, 2005.

Walls, Jerry. *Hell: The Logic of Damnation*. Notre Dame, IN: University of Notre Dame Press, 1992.

———. "A Philosophical Critique of Talbott's Universalism." In *Universal Salvation? The Current Debate*, edited by Robin A. Parry and Christopher H. Partridge, 105–24. Grand Rapids, MI: Eerdmans, 2003.

———. *Purgatory: The Logic of Total Transformation*. New York: Oxford University Press, 2011.

Wesley, John. *John Wesley's Sermons*. No Pages. Online: http://gbgm-umc.org/umhistory/wesley/sermons/.

———. "The Imperfection of Human Knowledge." *John Wesley's Sermons*. No Pages. Online: http://www.umcmission.org/Find-Resources/Global-Worship-and-Spiritual-Growth/John-Wesley-Sermons/Sermon-69-The-Imperfection-of-Human-Knowledge.

———. "On Faith." *John Wesley's Sermons*. No Pages. Online: http://www.umcmission.org/Find-Resources/Global-Worship-and-Spiritual-Growth/John-Wesley-Sermons/Sermon-106-On-Faith.

———. "On Living Without God." *John Wesley's Sermons*. No Pages. Online: http://www.umcmission.org/Find-Resources/Global-Worship-and-Spiritual-Growth/John-Wesley-Sermons/Sermon-125-On-Living-Without-God.

Willard, Dallas. "Apologetics in Action." No pages. Online: http://www.dwillard.org/articles/artview.asp?artID=14&quot.

———. *The Great Omission: Reclaiming Jesus' Essentials Teachings on Discipleship*. San Francisco: HarperOne, 2006.

Willimon, William. *Who Will Be Saved?* Nashville: Abingdon Press, 2008.

Wink, Walter. *The Powers that Be: A Theology for a New Millennium*. New York: Doubleday, 1998.

Worthington, Everett L. *A Just Forgiveness: Responsible Healing without Excusing Injustice*. Downers Grove, IL: IVP Academic, 2009.

Wray, T. J. *What the Bible Really Tells Us: The Essential Guide to Biblical Literacy*. Lanham, MD: Rowman and Littlefield, 2011.

Wright, Christopher. *The Uniqueness of Jesus*. London: Monarch Books, 1997.

Wright, N. T. *Evil and the Justice of God*. Downers Grove, IL: InterVarsity Press, 2006.

———. *Jesus and the Victory of God*. Christian Origins and the Question of God 2. London: SPCK, 1996.

———. *Mark for Everyone*. Louisville, KY: Westminster John Knox Press, 2004.

———. *Surprised by Hope: Rethinking Heaven, the Resurrection, and the Mission of the Church*. San Francisco: HarperOne, 2008.

———. "Towards a Biblical View of Universalism." *Themelios* 4:2 (1977) 54–58.

Yandell, Keith, and Harold Netland. *Buddhism: A Christian Exploration and Appraisal*. Grand Rapids, MI: IVP Academic, 2009.

Zehr, Howard. *Changing Lenses: A New Focus for Crime and Justice*. Scottdale, PA: Herald Press, 1995.

Zuckerman, Phil. *Faith No More: Why People Reject Religion*. New York: Oxford University Press, 2012.